An Introduction to the Foundation Phase

An Introduction to the Foundation Phase

Early Years Curriculum in Wales

Amanda Thomas and Alyson Lewis

Online resources to accompany this book are available at:
www.bloomsbury.com/an-introduction-to-the-foundation-phase-9781474264273.
Please type the URL into your web browser and follow the instructions to access the
Companion Website. If you experience any problems, please contact Bloomsbury at:
academicwebsite@bloomsbury.com.

Bloomsbury Academic
An imprint of Bloomsbury Publishing Plc

B L O O M S B U R Y

LONDON · OXFORD · NEW YORK · NEW DELHI · SYDNEY

Bloomsbury Academic

An imprint of Bloomsbury Publishing Plc

50 Bedford Square	1385 Broadway
London	New York
WC1B 3DP	NY 10018
UK	USA

www.bloomsbury.com

BLOOMSBURY and the Diana logo are trademarks of Bloomsbury Publishing Plc

First published 2016

© Amanda Thomas and Alyson Lewis, 2016

Amanda Thomas and Alyson Lewis have asserted their right under the Copyright, Designs and Patents Act, 1988, to be identified as Authors of this work.

British Library Cataloguing-in-Publication Data

A catalogue record for this book is available from the British Library.

ISBN: HB: 978-1-4742-6428-0
PB: 978-1-4742-6427-3
ePDF: 978-1-4742-6430-3
ePub: 978-1-4742-6429-7

Library of Congress Cataloging-in-Publication Data

Names: Thomas, Amanda (English teacher), author. | Lewis, Alyson, author.
Title: An introduction to the foundation phase : early years curriculum in Wales / Amanda Thomas and Alyson Lewis.
Description: London ; New York : Bloomsbury Academic, 2016.
Identifiers: LCCN 2016005927| ISBN 9781474264280 (hardback) | ISBN 9781474264280 (pb) | ISBN 9781474264303 (ePDF) | ISBN 9781474264297 (ePub)
Subjects: LCSH: Early childhood education–Curricula–Wales. | BISAC: EDUCATION / Curricula. | EDUCATION / Preschool & Kindergarten. | EDUCATION / Educational Policy & Reform / General.
Classification: LCC LB1139.3.G7 T56 2016 | DDC 372.2109429–dc23 LC record available at https://lccn.loc.gov/2016005927

Cover design by Catherine Wood
Cover images (clockwise) © 1&2: Photofusion/UIG via Getty Images / 3: Peter Cade/Getty Images / 4: Courtesy of Ysgol Pen-y-Garth / 5&6: Photofusion/UIG via Getty Images

Typeset by Fakenham Prepress Solutions, Fakenham, Norfolk NR21 8NN
Printed and bound in India

Contents

Acknowledgements

We would like to thank family, friends, colleagues and students who have supported and encouraged us in writing this book. Useful feedback has helped to improve and shape the final publication. We would also like to thank the publishers for their help and guidance.

List of Illustrations

Introduction

Since **devolution** in 1999, the Welsh Government has finally been able to decide and implement its own educational policies and initiatives. This book examines one significant flagship policy change within education in Wales for its youngest learners, called the Foundation Phase. Before 2008, Key Stage 1 of the National **Curriculum** was in place for 5- to 7-year-olds but it is now abolished and has been replaced with a framework for 3- to 7-year-olds known as the Foundation Phase. The new curriculum has seven Areas of Learning which should be integrated. This is moving away from formal traditional methods of teaching young children with opportunities for **practitioners** to (a) reflect on practice, (b) become playful partners, (c) co-construct knowledge, (d) empower young children and finally, (e) become creative thinkers. The Welsh Government feels 'it is important that children are not introduced to formal methods of learning too soon as this can have a detrimental effect on their future learning and development' (WAG, 2008d, p. 8). To invest in this curriculum change it was recorded in 2014–15 that the total cost of the Foundation Phase was 'just under one hundred million. This is the equivalent of an additional £1,000 per pupil per year in the Foundation Phase' (Taylor et al., 2015, p. 100).

Policies, initiatives and statutory requirements unique to Wales

The following table shows policy initiatives that have been developed over the last decade for children and young people in Wales. This highlights that Wales follows a unique policy agenda in education and childcare, *different* to that of England, Scotland and Northern Ireland.

Name of policy/initiative	Overview of initiative
Flying Start	Launched in 2006/07 Free childcare for targeted groups in the most disadvantaged areas Developing multi-agency approaches between sectors Developing parenting programmes Services delivered through integrated children's centres £55 million been allocated over the next three years 2012–15
Play policy & Play policy Implementation plan	Policy published in 2002, implemented in 2006 Raising the status and value and play Focus on play provision and risk-taking play across all sectors
Building a Brighter Future: Early Years & Childcare Plan	Introduced in 2013 Sets out a ten-year plan for childcare and provision Focus on joined up services, cooordinated approaches
Skills Framework	Introduced in 2008 *Non-statutory* document focusing on developing skills in ICT, thinking, numeracy and communication
Literacy and Numeracy Framework	Introduced in 2013 Aimed at learners aged 5 to 14 Supersedes the numeracy and communication component of the non-statutory Skills Framework (above) Statutory element delivered across all Areas of Learning/subjects
Literacy and Numeracy tests	Introduced in 2014 Aimed at learners aged 7 to 14 Introduced to raises standards

Further information on each initiative can be found using the links.

Welsh Government (2012), *Flying Start*: http://wales.gov.uk/topics/children youngpeople/parenting/help/flyingstart/?lang=en (accessed 18 December 2012).

Welsh Government (2012), *Play Policy Wales*: http://wales.gov.uk/docrepos/40382/ 40382313/childrenyoungpeople/403821/623995/play-policy-e.pdf;jsessionid=20AF AA3CCE87EE54F194AA736DB573BB?lang=en (accessed 24 November 2012).

Welsh Government information on the Skills Framework 3 to 19: http://learning.gov. wales/resources/browse-all/skills-development/?status=open&lang=en (accessed 24 August 2015).

Welsh Government information on the Literacy Numeracy Framework: http:// learning.gov.wales/resources/collections/lnf?lang=en (accessed 24 August 2015).

Welsh Government information on Literacy and Numeracy tests: http://learning.

gov.wales/resources/collections/national-reading-and-numeracy-tests?lang=en (accessed 24 August 2015).

In addition to the above, you can use the link below to access two additional resources which provide information about (a) 'useful website links' and (b) 'useful publications' linked to the Foundation Phase: www.bloomsbury.com/an-introduction-to-the-foundation-phase-9781474264273.

Why was this book needed?

There are an overwhelming number of texts available to those studying Early Years education at various levels that mainly refer to the Early Years Foundation Stage (EYFS) which is the curriculum framework for 0– to 5-year-olds in England. This can often be frustrating for students, practitioners and lecturers in Wales when local policies, practices and initiatives almost seem disregarded in texts. In addition, there is the added frustration that childcare qualification specifications for Welsh students mainly acknowledge practices and/or policies in the EYFS and this can often confuse students. What is more concerning is that the *specifications* seem removed from students' practice in Wales because it has been written for and applies to practices in another country (i.e. England). Therefore the authors, having delivered courses at Diploma, NVQ and Degree level, feel that this book is timely and significant.

Prior to this book, the only information provided on the Foundation Phase consisted of (the blue and white) Welsh Government documentation. Also, there is one text available in Welsh entitled *Y Cyfnod Sylfaen 3–7 oed* and there are single chapters within books that refer to the Welsh education system. But the authors felt strongly that students studying in Wales and potentially gaining a job in Wales, should have a comprehensive understanding of the policies and practices such as the Foundation Phase which could be found in one book. This book should clarify for students the differences in Welsh education policy to the rest of the UK and beyond. To summarize, apart from this book, the texts that are available on a range of Early Years topics, such as observation, **assessment**, planning and play, *all* refer to the EYFS and as authors we feel this is unacceptable and potentially disadvantages those studying in Wales.

What this book offers

This book gives the reader an opportunity to reflect on a play-based approach to learning, a child's readiness to learn and the importance of collaboration between various stakeholders. It does not advocate an ideal Foundation Phase setting and classroom because the ethos of every setting is different.

The book gives current insights and perceptions of the Foundation Phase through interviews with stakeholders. These opinions do not always reflect the opinions of the authors.

A brief summary of Welsh policies that are unique to Wales for Welsh students is also included. These policies have not been discussed at length as this was not the main focus of the book. Additionally, this book does not focus upon other UK Early Years curricula and policy in detail. However, an overview of UK policy can be accessed using the following link: www.bloomsbury.com/an-introduction-to-the-foundation-phase-9781474264273.

This book discusses the concerns of imposing testing within the Foundation Phase. The authors understand that standards need to be raised and agree that all children should be provided with positive learning experiences to achieve this. Arguably, testing may not be an appropriate way to assess young children. **Paradoxically**, how does the rationale of testing young children integrate within a holistic play-based curriculum approach?

The information listed below highlights some of the stakeholder responses arising from interviews about the Foundation Phase and are discussed in more detail in Part III. They have been selected to illustrate some of the concerns and comments surrounding this unique Welsh educational framework. Also, they can be used as a starting point for discussing and reflecting upon the Foundation Phase.

Comments	Concerns
• In principle I was very enthusiastic about it … • It doesn't put a limit on what children can learn … • There is a place for worksheets in Nursery … • We should have called it experiential learning not 'play' …	• The Welsh Government really are living in cloud cuckoo land and they really don't know what goes on in Primary Schools … • I've never seen them ask the children what they want to learn about … • None of the staff I work with have had the core training … • Children are only allowed to play in the afternoon … • Tests could potentially dilute a play-based approach …

How is the book organized?

The book is organized into three parts and includes activities, case studies, reflective tasks, thought-provoking questions and further reading linked to the focus of the chapter. Part I allows the reader to make sense of theory in policy; Part II provides the reader with an opportunity to make sense of theory into practice; and finally, Part III allows the reader to explore the challenges and complexities of policy and practice. A glossary of key terms is included at the end of the book to explain any unfamiliar words.

Part I provides a historical perspective to the Foundation Phase curriculum in Wales. It discusses how past and present **pioneers** have influenced the curriculum, the importance of outdoor learning and international perspectives on play. Characteristics of effective classroom practice conclude this section with a critical discussion of social and emotional aspects of learning which the Welsh Government has declared to be at the heart of the Foundation Phase.

Chapter 1 introduces the Foundation Phase and its principles and provides some brief historical **context**. It discusses why it was introduced and explores some of the challenges of implementing a radical curriculum change. The chapter draws upon evidence of what practice was like for children before it was introduced and discusses evidence from various sources about what is currently happening in settings. Key findings from a three-year evaluation of the Foundation Phase are explored and the twelve pedagogical elements are included in this chapter. The chapter considers what is needed to make a Foundation Phase setting a success.

Chapter 2 examines and explores the influential thinkers both past and present and how their theories have influenced current Early Childhood education. It links their theories to the principles of the Foundation Phase curriculum, including a play-based approach to learning; the importance of observation; the value of using the outdoors; and planning for individual learning needs. It presents the reader with opportunities to explore case studies, consider their own practice through thought-provoking questions and provides suggestions for further reading.

Chapter 3 explores the concept of play in different international curricula with a specific focus on its role and status. Specific countries are selected which relate to elements of the Foundation Phase, for example the New Zealand Early Years curriculum is mentioned because of its bilingual nature. Childhood constructs are introduced and a discussion of the role of the adult is included. A comparative discussion takes place throughout the chapter which helps to identify the various complex ways that play is understood. Learning in the outdoors is explored in depth and the chapter considers the challenges and barriers to outdoor play.

Chapter 4 considers a range of characteristics that contribute to effective classroom practice in the Early Years. The Social and Emotional Aspects of Learning (SEAL) programme is discussed at length and some of its historical and political contexts are explored. Pupil voice, participation and the rights of the child are discussed and ways of consulting with young children are mentioned. Many articles of the UNCRC are explored and a child's right to play and experience the outdoors is discussed. Also, providing opportunities for children to think in context is explored. Working in partnership and children's rights is a central theme of this chapter.

Part II explores how to make sense of theory into practice, including observation and assessment in the Foundation Phase and planning a **child-centred**, play-based curriculum. The common theme throughout this part of the book is the importance of putting the child at the centre of the curriculum.

Chapter 5 considers not only the role of observation in the Foundation Phase but also in national and international curricula. It discusses the different methods of observation and provides reflective tasks to engage the reader. Best practice is discussed from the role of the adult to the different ways of recording **observations** and how to manage confidentiality. The chapter concludes with how to analyse observations, ethical considerations and how observational findings can support child development.

Chapter 6 considers the role of assessment in the Foundation Phase. It discusses both formative and **summative assessment** methods and approaches. Links are made between assessment, planning and **pedagogy**. Assessment in the Foundation Phase is discussed in depth from the on-entry baseline assessment to ongoing **formative assessment** throughout the Foundation Phase to the summative assessment carried out in Year 2. It discusses the all-Wales reading and maths tests in Year 2 of the Foundation Phase and the impact of the introduction of the Literacy and Numeracy framework. **Assessment for learning** is evaluated, with different methods considered including how success is measured. The chapter concludes by focusing on the importance of feedback and how children's attainments are reported to various stakeholders.

Chapter 7 explores how to plan for effective and purposeful play in the Foundation Phase. It considers the importance of a play-based approach, alongside barriers to such provision. It examines how practitioners need to plan across all seven areas of learning, whilst keeping Personal and Social Development and Well-Being at the centre of the curriculum. The Foundation Phase model of delivery is discussed along with the different types of provision required. Classroom organization and the **learning environment** are analysed as well as the role of the adult. Different types of and stages of play are discussed, including the importance of play as a vehicle for learning. Barriers to a play-based approach are considered, including the impact of the Literacy and Numeracy tests in Year 2 on a play-based pedagogy.

Chapter 8 reinforces previous points made throughout the book that in order to implement radical curriculum change practitioners need to be equipped with the necessary skills to reflect on and within practice. Therefore, the chapter explains the importance and benefits of reflection and how this might relate to implementing the Foundation Phase. The skills and characteristics of a reflective practitioner are discussed but also explores the challenges of how this may work out in practice. Many students and professionals are now required to write reflectively and this chapter discusses what this involves. Various reflective cycles/models are included and discussed which could be used to help instigate change in Early Years practice.

Part III includes stakeholders' perspectives on the Foundation Phase and critically discusses practice and pedagogy and curriculum change. It explores the rationale of testing and explains alternative forms of assessment. Also, this part of the book examines the future of Early Years education in Wales. You can find additional information such as prompts for the thought-provoking questions linked to the chapters by accessing the following link: www.bloomsbury.com/an-introduction-to-the-foundation-phase-9781474264273.

Chapter 9 discusses initial and current perceptions of the implementation of the Foundation Phase. These perceptions were gathered from stakeholder interviews that were conducted by the authors and key findings from the three-year evaluation. It considers challenges and successes in implementing a play-based pedagogy. One of the many challenges discussed is the **transition** from Foundation Phase to Key Stage 2. Two reports commissioned by the Welsh Government strongly recommend that transition strategies are developed in order to ensure children cope with this change. This is significant when the chapter highlights that some Key Stage 2 practitioners do not understand or appreciate a Foundation Phase pedagogy.

Chapter 10 discusses the challenges and implications of delivering a child-centred pedagogy. Perceptions from a variety of stakeholders about providing and understanding what constitutes rich learning experiences are discussed. The chapter argues that play should be at the forefront of a child-centred curriculum. However, play is often largely misunderstood and the chapter explores reasons for this. Two models of curriculum delivery are explained to help understand the change from a more formal, traditional pedagogy to a more shared, co-constructed playful pedagogy. Concepts of **empowerment**, ownership and **agency** are drawn upon to demonstrate the principles of the Foundation Phase. Broad and narrow understandings of leadership and management are included to emphasize the difficulties of delivering effective practice and pedagogy.

Chapter 11 explores perceptions of imposing tests on young children. Also, the rationale for testing in a supposedly play-based curriculum that advocates a **co-construction** model of delivery is discussed. Testing is part of the Welsh Government's agenda to raise standards and this chapter questions to what extent exposing children as young as six to exam-like conditions is appropriate. However, arguments in favour of testing are also considered as there seems to be an emphasis on accountability within the Foundation Phase. There are many different types of assessment, and testing represents a product-type summative assessment. Alternative forms of assessment from New Zealand and Italy are discussed to argue that there are more child-centred methods of assessment available.

Chapter 12 discusses ways forward in relation to Early Years curriculum, pedagogy and assessment in Wales. The chapter refers to the twelve pedagogical elements underpinning the Foundation Phase as identified in the three-year evaluation. These elements can be reflected upon by practitioners to support effective curriculum change and help to transform pedagogy. Statutory assessment requirements are described. These highlight that in the twenty-first century the Welsh Government still supports and advocate a product-type assessment rather than a process-oriented approach. The New Deal put forward by the Welsh Government in advancing continuing professional development (for all stakeholders) appears to be rather vague. The 129 current recommendations from various reports have been scrutinized.

Part I

Making Sense of Theory and Policy

1

Understanding the Foundation Phase

Chapter aims

To explain the principles of the Foundation Phase.
To briefly explore curriculum change in Wales.
To describe how the Foundation Phase is progressing.

What is the Foundation Phase?

The Foundation Phase is the statutory curriculum framework for children in Wales aged between 3 and 7 years; this is not the same as the Early Years Foundation Stage (EYFS) in England, which is for children aged between 0 and 5 years. The Foundation Phase replaces the Desirable **Outcomes** for Children's Learning before Compulsory School Age (for 3- to 5-year-olds) and the Key Stage One National Curriculum (for 5- to 7-year-olds). This new Welsh curriculum was piloted in 2004 and then introduced in 2008 in Nursery (3- to 4-year-olds) with a roll out programme each year and was then fully introduced in Year 2 (6- to 7-year-olds) in September 2011. To summarize (a more detailed discussion takes place throughout the entire book), the Foundation Phase offers children more opportunities to engage in practical, real-life, problem-solving tasks with an emphasis on developing children's creativity and imagination. More open-ended questions are posed to children and learning is (or should be) more purposeful. Children are given plenty of time to develop skills across seven Areas of Learning (AoL), as listed below:

1 Personal and Social Development, Well-being and Cultural Diversity
2 Language, Literacy and Communication Skills
3 Mathematical Development
4 Welsh Language Development
5 Knowledge and Understanding of the World

   6 **Physical Development**
   7 Creative Development

There is a strong focus on learning in the outdoors and developing free-flow access between the indoor and outdoor environment. A balance of child-led and adult-directed tasks should be delivered on a daily basis and experiential, **active learning** with shared collaborative partnerships between children and adults should be developed (WG, 2012b). Another feature of the Foundation Phase was improved adult–child ratios. The three-year Welsh Government evaluation conducted by Cardiff University reports '1:8 for three to five year olds and 1:15 for five to seven year olds' (Taylor et al., 2015, p. 29).

The Foundation Phase is often commonly referred to as a play-based curriculum with more focus on individual needs rather than a 'one size fits all' approach. Some would argue that it is a move away from sedentary practice to more active learning, which is better for young children. Howard, Miles and Gealy (2009) state that 'play is the central feature of the Foundation Phase framework' (p. 104). A three-year evaluation recently conducted by Cardiff University for the Welsh Government report that the Foundation Phase is:

> … a radical departure from the more formal, competency-based approach associated with the previous Key Stage one National Curriculum, it was designed to provide a developmental, experiential, play-based approach to teaching and learning.
>
> (Taylor et al., 2015, p. 1)

The three-year evaluation helpfully identifies twelve pedagogical elements which include (1) child-choice/participation, (2) exploration, (3) first-hand, (4) practical, (5) stage not age, (6) balance of continuous/enhanced/focused activities, (7) open questioning, (8) reflection, (9) physical activity, (10) outdoor learning, (11) observation of children, and lastly, (12) learning zones. The final report provides a brief description of the elements and they can be found on pages 22 and 23 (Taylor et al., 2015).

What lies at the heart of the Foundation Phase?

This may seem like a straightforward question but the responses would vary if it was answered, for example, by a classroom practitioner, a politician, a Local Authority advisor or a head teacher. The framework briefly states what is central to the curriculum, and the points below could be considered as the underpinning principles of the Foundation Phase. However, it could be argued that they are not new principles at all but aspects of Early Years practice that are being re-emphasized.

- **Holistic development**
- First-hand experiential activities
- Building on previous learning experiences
- Positive partnership with parents/carers
- Progressive framework to meet diverse needs
- Focusing on stage of learning rather than age related outcomes
- Greater use of the outdoors
- Developing self-image and self-worth
- Promoting equality and celebrating diversity

(WAG, 2008b, p. 4)

The framework consists of seven Areas of Learning and the documentation clearly states that 'personal and social development, well-being and cultural diversity is at the heart of the Foundation Phase and should be developed across the curriculum' (WAG, 2008b, p. 14). However, stakeholders, practitioners and students need to understand that for this to happen, a socio-cultural view of the child is required as according to Aasen and Waters (2006, p. 124) this view 'places social interaction at the core of development and the child is viewed as an active meaning-maker'. Practitioners need to ensure that children are valued as individuals, viewed with rights, respected for their ideas, and provided with plenty of opportunities to develop their personal and social development (Aasen and Waters, 2006).

Why was the Foundation Phase needed?

According to Aasen and Waters:

> … the changes may be summarised as resulting from concerns about the inappropriate nature of Early Years education provision in some settings, and the formal nature of some children's experiences at the cost of their natural curiosity, creative expression, confidence and love of learning.
>
> (Aasen and Waters, 2006, p. 123)

The above quote reinforces the point that implementing the Foundation Phase principles would help to move away from formal teaching approaches with very young children. Those who have worked with young children know how they love to explore, touch, smell, taste, see, hear and ask questions. The evidence that supports making *radical* changes to the curriculum is quite scant. However, in April 2000, Margaret Hanney played a pivotal role in reporting on Early Years education in Wales and produced a detailed report that was published in 2000. Hanney (2000) discusses types of provision for three-year-olds, models from other countries, implications for expanding childcare and education and ways forward for young children in Wales. Wincott (2006, p. 286) reminds us that 'the adviser was to write a report suggesting possible avenues for policy development based on the results of the consultation and evidence from the best international research'.

In the report, provision for three-year-olds was best described as having a balance of adult-led and child-led tasks, a curriculum centred on the child, highly trained educators, a high ratio of staff and a stimulating environment. It was also reported that there were differences between urban and rural provision and there was a priority to achieve equity. The report also stated that nursery education (for 3- and 4-year-olds) has traditionally developed in an ad hoc way across Local Authorities and this had created differences in provision due to the absence of a national policy (Hanney, 2000). Furthermore, the report highlighted the importance of holistic development, a child's right to be educated and a need for adults who are appropriately trained to recognize that every child is unique, naturally inquisitive and loves to explore. Early on in the report, Hanney (2000) critically states that a curriculum for young children under the age of eight needs to start with the child and not with what is stated as outcomes in the documentation (such as the Desirable Outcomes or National Curriculum). For example, with regard to literacy, Hanney (2000) reports that before children are expected to acquire (pre-determined goals in) reading and writing skills it is crucial that they have opportunities to ask questions, express themselves, talk at length, engage in role-play and are able to comfortably communicate verbally and this should be a prerequisite to reading and writing fluently. Some international practice, such as Italian and Nordic approaches, has formal teaching of literacy beginning at seven years of age, when it is believed that children have acquired the necessary skills to cope and be at ease with this challenging task.

Areas for improvement in the Early Years

The Hanney report published in 2000 identified some strengths (for example, one of them being good ratios in the non-maintained sector) of Early Years provision by counties, but many of the strengths were only present in one or two of the counties. Very few strengths were evident in the majority of counties. Also, areas for improvement within Early Years practice were reported on and the authors would like you to consider (if it is relevant to your role) from the table below whether some of these areas for improvement that were documented in 2000 are currently present. In other words, do the areas for improvement still exist?

Areas for improvement highlighted in the Hanney report 2000
Insufficient practitioners trained to work in Early Years and a lack of them
Uneven standards of provision for Early Years
Lack of child development focus on training courses
No continuity in provision from 0 to 6 as in other countries

The Hanney (2000) report included a review of research from other countries and mentions the High/Scope approach (originating in the USA), which focuses on child-initiated learning, children as social actors and agents of change, and found that at the age of fifteen those children who had attended a very formal curriculum displayed more anti-social behaviour and were less engaged with education. Hence the focus on child-initiated learning and less formal instruction and/or direction in the Foundation Phase. Hanney (2000, p. 16) argues in her report that 'where children start compulsory school age at six or seven there is a firm belief that if formal activities are introduced too soon, some children who are not ready for this will begin to experience failure'.

The Start Right report (written by Christopher Ball in 1994 evaluating Early Years provision) states that the UK is not in line with developments in other parts of the world and this is a concern. The report reflects on four countries (namely, Italy, New Zealand, Spain and Sweden) that have dealt with change in curricula provision. It briefly mentions Denmark because they have what is known as an integrated system of Early Years provision where 50 per cent of publicly funded money is allocated to their youngest children. In all countries there appears to be a variety of different types of provision, with New Zealand presenting the most varied. It was reported that the UK had better ratios for under-threes, yet between the ages of three and six the UK has the poorest. Practitioners in other countries tended to be qualified teachers (or often referred to as pedagogues) with at least three years training at higher education level. In addition, partnership with parents was a strong feature of Early Years provision abroad where they are fully encouraged to participate in the provision (for example with making decisions). All countries had some form of national guidelines and/or framework in place with a focus on active, **experiential learning**, but Denmark and Sweden had more focus on using the outdoor environment for learning. However, the points made in the following quote should be borne in mind when considering the practices of international curricula:

> [T]he everyday language, ethics, routines, rituals, practices, expectations, ideas, documents and **invocations** of quality in early childhood services are formed through and motivated by very particular understandings of children and how best to educate them.
>
> (MacNaughton, 2005, p. 1)

Hanney (2000) reported that it was only Wales that had a specific focus on literacy and numeracy so early on in the educational provision. The other countries had far greater focus on self-expression and individuality and utilized different teaching strategies. Hanney observed that many Local Authorities were trialling new initiatives and strengthening **interdisciplinary** working relationships, and argues that:

> [F]or 3–5 year olds it is essential that the curriculum fosters enjoyment of learning, motivates children to approach new learning experiences eagerly and promotes the disposition to learn … [A]s the 21st century unfolds … they will need to be adaptable, imaginative, articulate and confident in their own **problem solving** abilities in an age which is increasingly technological and challenging.
>
> (2000, p. 43)

Soon after the Hanney report was published, the Learning Country document was available in 2001, setting out the agenda for education and lifelong learning in Wales up to 2010, and Jane Davidson (Minster for Education and Lifelong Learning at the time) highlighted that there may be a need to integrate the Desirable Outcomes for Children's Learning and provide a more holistic curriculum for 3- to 7-year-olds. The former minister commented in an interview for this book that 'what I was seeing was a huge variation in practice … I saw extraordinary good practice, I saw some very ordinary practice and in a couple of cases I saw appalling practice and I sent ESTYN in the next day' (2012). She also pointed out that 'the most important feature (for me) of good Early Years education is that children come through hungry for more'. This was also the clear message for all learners in Wales in the Learning Country document and, soon after, a consultation document was published about the Foundation Phase in 2003. The following aims were drafted and included in the consultation in 2003:

> – raise children's standards of achievement;
> – enhance their positive attitudes to learning;
> – address their developing needs;
> – enable them to benefit from educational opportunities later in their lives; and
> – help them become active citizens within their communities
>
> (WAG, 2003, p. 6).

It could be argued that the aims are overambitious and the Foundation Phase alone might not achieve them. On the other hand, one could argue that the aims are realistic and achievable. One of the key findings from the recent three-year evaluation of the Foundation Phase that relates to raising standards of achievement reports:

> [T]he Foundation Phase is associated with improved attainment for pupils eligible for free school meals but the evaluation has found no evidence to suggest it has made any

observable impact so far on reducing inequalities (i.e. of groups of pupils based on their gender, ethnicity, or free school meal eligibility).

(Taylor et al., 2015, p. 3)

It may be a very long time before there is evidence to show that the Foundation Phase impacts upon reducing inequalities.

What was it like for children before the Foundation Phase was introduced?

The following quotes are taken from the 2003 consultation document and two past education ministers interviewed for this book, indicating what 'school' was like for some children in Wales before the introduction of the Foundation Phase:

[T]eachers introduce formal learning too soon, before some pupils are ready, children are given too many tasks to do while sitting at tables rather than learning through well-structured play, practical activity and investigation. Some sessions are too long for young children to maintain their concentration and classrooms do not provide enough opportunities for practical activities and well supported play.

(WAG, 2003, p. 5)

[C]hildren spend too much time doing tasks while sitting at tables rather than learning through well-designed opportunities for play … The emphasis on sedentary non-interactive desk based work does not contribute well to developing independence and decision-making.

(WAG, 2003, p. 5)

[T]oo often, children are introduced to the formal skills of reading and writing before they are ready, with heavy formality and with the risk that some will lose both confidence and a love of learning.

(WAG, 2003, p. 5)

They [meaning children] were completely ill prepared to come into school on day one and be sat behind a desk. We were turning off learners in their droves … people's perceptions of what they were doing in their schools and the actuality of what they were doing were two different things.

(Past Minister, 2012a).

We wanted to learn from best practice in the world, it is about getting young people to engage with learning. To introduce learning at a pace that suits them, through a variety of different tasks and experiences.

(Past Minister, 2012b)

Reflective task   ?

If you are working within a Foundation Phase setting you may like to consider whether some of the statements above apply to your current practice and whether since 2008 (when the Foundation Phase became statutory in nursery) anything has changed. You may like to consider whether your practice is 'extraordinary' or 'ordinary'. List the characteristics in a table and use as part of an action plan.

Before the Foundation Phase

The Foundation Phase replaced two very different curriculum types, namely the Desirable Outcomes for Children's Learning before Compulsory School Age (for 3- to 5-year-olds) and the National Curriculum Key Stage One (for 5- to 7-year-olds). Both curriculum types were different in content, focus and delivery. One could argue that there was a much stronger emphasis on 'play' in the Desirable Outcomes (curriculum) than in the National Curriculum. In England, the National Curriculum Key Stage One still remains for 5- to 7-year-olds.

The Desirable Outcomes was introduced in 1996 for children aged three to five years and was then republished in 2000 following a review of the National Curriculum in Wales (Wyn Siencyn and Thomas, 2007; ACCAC, 2000). The document consisted of six areas of learning with a focus on experiential, active-learning experiences. The National Curriculum was introduced as a result of the Education Reform Act 1988, and Key Stage 1 was aimed at 5- to 7-year-olds and Key Stage 2 at 7- to 11-year-olds, and this occurred simultaneously in England and Wales. However, Wales included a Welsh language element to represent the socio-cultural, bilingual aspect of the country. Gerver (2010) reminds us that the main purpose of the National Curriculum was to create standardization and introduce parity in the education service as there tended to be inconsistencies across schools in provision for children. He states that 'the desire was to create an approach which ensured that every child, no matter where they lived, would receive an equitable experience, an entitlement to learning' (2010, p. 37). This in theory sounds like an appropriate solution but the National Curriculum can be criticized for not meeting the needs of children in the twenty-first century and for being highly prescriptive and too detailed – in other words, a knowledge-based system paying little attention to skills, the individual learner and holistic development. Richard Gerver argues in *Creating Tomorrow's Schools Today* that:

> … one of the key issues of a curriculum that is defined by its content, by facts, is that it fires a debate around what facts should be taught and when. As a result we end up

with fierce and often emotive arguments about who and what children should learn about and what is important for them to remember.

(Gerver, 2010, pp. 47–8)

It should be highlighted that the question of educating young children is fundamentally a philosophical debate which involves meeting the needs of children in the relevant century, and one that will always need to be discussed, changed and adapted.

Establishing a curriculum relevant for the twenty-first century

The Government of Wales Act 1999 provided Wales with the power to take control of services, education being one of them, and devolved power meant that Wales would have more **autonomy** in relation to services provided to young children and people. Therefore it is important to note early on in this book that the provision of education for children and young people in Wales is different from England and other UK countries, where policymakers and holders (i.e. educators) are working within very specific social, economic and political contexts (MacNaughton, 2003). In establishing a curriculum relevant for the twenty-first century, the Welsh Government (in 2008) reviewed and revised the subjects within the National Curriculum. They introduced the skills framework as a non-statutory document to support practitioners in developing skills in areas of ICT (Information, Communications Technology), Thinking, Communicating and Number for learners aged between three and nineteen and the Welsh Government (2012a) claims these are 'skills that are fundamental for learners to become successful individuals'. However, it could be questioned why the document is non-statutory if these skills are so fundamental to this age group. The reader may like to consider the extent to which *all* practitioners in Wales understand and implement the skills framework? More recently, the Communication and Number component of the skills framework has been replaced with a National Literacy and Numeracy Framework (LNF) for 5- to 14-year-olds. It seems that Literacy and Numeracy skills are the main priority for a curriculum in the twenty-first century, but one could argue that this is no different from priorities in other centuries.

The introduction of a National Literacy and Numeracy Framework in Wales

In September 2012, a National Literacy and Numeracy Framework (LNF) was introduced for learners aged between five and fourteen. In May 2013, learners aged between seven and fourteen years were required to take a literacy and numeracy test in what the Education Minister, Leighton Andrews, described as a means of standardizing and improving performance (Welsh Government, 2012c). The authors cannot see how testing and having to follow a prescribed framework such as the LNF dovetails with the Foundation Phase and its principles. When a former minister was asked whether testing would raise a challenge in a play-based curriculum, they responded:

> Well maybe I'm not certain about this, if you look at some of the best LEA's and primaries, as I understand it they are managing to integrate Literacy and Numeracy within the play-based curriculum so if that's done well then there shouldn't be any relaxation of standards or challenges. I am assured it's being successfully practiced in different primary schools around Wales.
>
> (Past Minister, 2012b)

Conversely, Margaret Hanney in her report in 2000, argues that:

> … the starting point in education is what the child can do, this is fundamental to Early Years education – starting with what we observe children can do and helping them to develop on this. This is significantly different from early testing which identifies what children cannot do and introduces an element of failure.
>
> (Hanney, 2000, p. 16)

Testing appears to focus on negative outcomes as opposed to positive ones and it is not an appropriate form of assessment for young learners. This finding was reported by stakeholders in the three-year Welsh Government evaluation of the Foundation Phase:

> [T]he majority of Foundation Phase leaders, head teacher and local authority stakeholders did not agree with the introduction of the Literacy and Numeracy tests, because they felt that their formality was not an appropriate form of assessment following a play-based experiential pedagogy.
>
> (Rhys et al., 2015, p. 2)

Also, recommendation four of the final report of the three-year evaluation states that guidance is needed about dovetailing the LNF and the Foundation Phase (Taylor et al., 2015).

Changing trajectories: Implementing the Foundation Phase principles

All adults working with young children may like to consider Mary Fawcett's view that 'we all have our own preconceptions, particular mindsets and prejudices stemming from our own cultural experiences, professional training, and the demands of the frameworks in which we work' (Fawcett, 2009, p. 15). Therefore, implementing the Foundation Phase alongside the LNF could be very challenging. Arguably, the more embedded a curriculum approach or pathway (in this case the Desirable Outcomes for Children's Learning and the National Curriculum), the more time and effort is needed to change it. Shanker and Downer (2012) refer to this as a changing trajectory (i.e. adopting or implementing a different educational journey, pathway or approach) and this is explained by Wincott (2006, p. 288):

> [T]he Welsh approach holds out the prospect of changing the character and culture of the first years of primary schooling, importing the less formal and child-centred approach characteristic of Early Years education into compulsory education. As a result Wales may be brought more into line with standard practices in many other European countries, where compulsory schooling begins at 6 or 7 years and a more 'pedagogical' Early Years philosophy pervades provision for younger children.

The tradition in Wales has been developmental, which means focusing on a child who biologically follows a series of set predetermined outcomes (Neaum, 2010). When practitioners take a developmental view of the child they see them as reaching goals and predetermined stages, measuring them against targets; the emphasis is on 'becoming' (future status) rather than taking an alternative vision where they view them as an individual who is a creative and competent 'being' (Aasen and Waters, 2006). Gerver (2010) strongly argues that 'our current system assumes that all children should be the same, reach the same learning states at the same age, be able to do the same things at the same time in the same way, know the same "stuff" and share the same interests' (p. 65). The Foundation Phase is an opportunity to move away from this tradition and an opportunity for practitioners working within Foundation Phase settings to reflect on and to some extent rethink their practice, take a different view of the child (namely socio-cultural), act differently and (more importantly) in the best interests of the child (Aasen and Waters, 2006).

However, according to the Welsh Government website, 'for each area of learning, the educational programme sets out what children should be taught and the outcomes set out expected standards of children's performance' (Welsh Government, 2012b). Terms such as 'outcomes set out', 'expected standards' and 'performance' arguably do not imply a socio-cultural approach to early childhood education. Interestingly, similar terms were used by a politician in their response to the rationale behind testing when interviewed for this book: 'Ultimately I think it is to raise standards but I think what the specific tests should do is give teachers themselves a better understanding of performance.' Margaret Fawcett makes an extremely valid point in her book with regards to documentation and discourse and suggests that 'one needs to read between the lines, but generally the official language used will reveal the underpinning **philosophy** and objectives' (Fawcett, 2009, p. 15). The authors feel that when you try to read between the lines (which can be very subjective) there appear to be different messages about the underpinning philosophy in the Foundation Phase documentation and, for example, documentation around literacy and numeracy testing. As suggested by MacNaughton (2003, p. 1), 'not all mandated curriculum explicitly labels its underpinning perspectives on the child as a learner'. The authors see this as a barrier in implementing the Foundation Phase; practitioners would benefit from explicit messages about their role and pedagogical approaches. Aasen and Waters (2006) continue to highlight that a theoretical shift, for example, from the behaviourist model to a constructivist model needs to take place and unless the changes are explained clearly and shared then there is every chance that lifelong learning opportunities could be missed. A shift that needs to take place is for children to become agents of change and practitioners to become facilitators of children's learning. Arguably, these are shifts that could pose challenges in practice and could take months or years to achieve.

Supporting curriculum change

The Foundation Phase framework contains the statutory curriculum for 3- to 7-year-olds, which sets out the skills and range for each of the seven Areas of Learning, but alongside the framework there are an additional *nine* guidance documents that are supposed to support the delivery of the Foundation Phase; for example, documents about play and active learning, observing children, and outdoor learning to name but a few. Although the documents were produced to be supportive and helpful, there may just be too many of them. There are multiple documents and policy initiatives that are in place that practitioners have to (a) be aware of, (b) understand, (c) implement and/or enact, and (d) weave together. It could be argued that:

> [E]ducation is littered with examples of innovations that have either failed or only been partially implemented because teachers weren't convinced the change was necessary and would result in real improvement. The result has been that they merely modify their practice at the edges and then abandon the change after a while because it didn't work for them.
>
> (Weeden et al., 2002, p. 127)

According to Weeden, Winter and Broadfoot (2002), if this is the case, teachers might make slight changes to their practice such as remove tables and allow children more access to floor space with construction type materials, and use the outdoors more. They (meaning the practitioners) might then become so frustrated with construction mess and chaos that they revert back to old practices (i.e. more formal). There is every possibility that practitioners could revert back to practice that suits *their* needs rather than the needs of the children. Or there is every chance that practitioners might abandon or rethink their Foundation Phase practice to meet Government needs regarding testing. Practitioners may be in complete disarray. One of the key findings from the three-year Welsh Government evaluation states that:

> ... the recent introduction of the Year 2 reading and numeracy tests has led around a fifth of practitioners and stakeholders to believe that the Foundation Phase is being 'phased out' (at least in Years 1 and 2), and has created considerable uncertainty and tension regarding the preferred balance between 'formal' and 'informal' teaching.
>
> (Waldron et al., 2015, p. 2)

Changing classroom practice – a straightforward procedure?

When teachers are considering improving and changing practice (in this case from Desirable Outcomes and National Curriculum to the Foundation Phase), it involves far more than just trying out a few new strategies and adding them to existing daily practice – it is about rethinking pedagogy (Bennett et al., 1992; Black et al., 2003). Similarly, Fullan (1991) argues that genuine change will only occur when the beliefs and pedagogical principles change. For example, the change from viewing children as passive recipients (a behaviourist approach) to viewing them as co-constructors of knowledge (a constructivist approach) (O'Donoghue and Clarke, 2010) is required. According to Siraj (2014), 'for the implementation of the Foundation Phase to be effective in Wales, it requires a fundamental change in culture ... which will take time to embed' (p. 3).

Figure 1.1 (on p. 24) presents Guskey's (2002) four-stage **linear** model of teacher change, and an example is provided of how it might apply to curriculum changes in the Early Years.

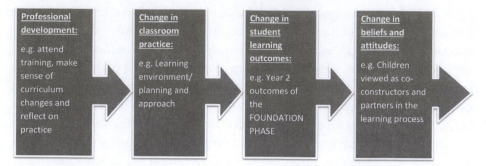

Figure 1.1 Curriculum Change

Reflective task

Considering your role, what example would you give for each stage of the model above? Compare examples in your Foundation Phase team. Are there any similarities and differences?

Change is a common characteristic of professional development but as Guskey (2002) points out, it is one that is most neglected. One of the reasons for this, he suggests, is that learning to do something new or adopting different practices requires skill, enthusiasm and effort and this can sometimes be very difficult and time consuming. Another reason why change is often the most challenging aspect of professional development is due to the social complexity (of immediate staff, wider community and political and government impact) of educational settings (Fullan, 1997). According to Smeets and Ponte (2009), the most essential prerequisite for changing practice is the quality of relationships between staff in schools, and an effective school would be one where staff learn from each other (Earley and Bubb, 2004). It can be said that some schools have a Professional Learning Community (PLC) when both children and staff are motivated and inspired to learn and become involved in self-directed inquiry (Earley and Bubb, 2004). The PLC can be extended to networked learning communities where practitioners engage in collaboration on both a national and international level (Smeets and Ponte, 2009). Therefore, the challenge for the twenty-first century is for schools to stop working in isolation and start working in collaboration and partnership (Durrant and Holden, 2006).

Currently, the Welsh Assembly Government has focused its efforts on providing Networks of Professional Practice where (families of) schools get the opportunity to share good practice, and claim that 'sharing effective practice is essential if children and young people across Wales are to benefit from the excellent work being undertaken in individual classrooms' (DCELLS, 2008, p. 16). However, the document does not clearly state how this can be successfully implemented in practice. *The Case for Change* document that was published in 2010 about schools in England states that when good practice is shared between and within schools, improvements are made (DfE, 2010). It states further that when there is a strong culture of professional development in schools, standards are raised. The *Case for Change* report states that 'South Korea encourages teachers to open up their classroom fully once or twice a month as a matter of routine so that any other teacher can come to observe their lessons' (DfE, 2010, p. 10). However, the report strongly states that professional development (particularly in England) appears to involve teachers attending short courses, sometimes not by choice, and engaging rather passively, which does not have any real impact on their practice.

Practitioners and senior stakeholders need to remember that for changes to be effective in practice, it takes time. According to Fullan (1997), it could take two to three years. It would appear that the Welsh Government's approach to change significantly contrasts with Fullan's time scale. This is evident with the introduction of testing and the Literacy and Numeracy Framework (LNF) in the Foundation Phase (i.e. the LNF was introduced within the academic year 2012–13, but the Foundation Phase had only being rolled out across all year groups since September 2011). This meant that practitioners in Year 2 only had *one* academic year to implement a new curriculum framework before the LNF was introduced. To summarize, there are far too many radical changes that practitioners are dealing with in practice which seem unrealistic.

Support and encouragement from colleagues is needed and practitioners need to be able to try out new ideas, discuss how they worked in practice and collaborate with other staff. There is clearly a new professionalism developing where a shift is taking place from outsiders instigating change to staff inside and across schools guiding, shaping and fuelling improvement (Harris and Muijs, 2005; Durrant and Holden, 2006). Therefore, change needs to be understood as a process rather than as one single event (Weeden et al., 2002; Durrant and Holden, 2006).

How is the Foundation Phase progressing?

In 2004, the Foundation Phase was piloted across forty-one settings and as a result a report was commissioned and written by Siraj-Blatchford et al. (2006) for the Welsh Assembly Government entitled *The Monitoring and Evaluation of the Effective Implementation of the Foundation Phase* (MEEIFP report). The report stated that the Foundation Phase was welcomed by almost all practitioners and that the seven areas of learning would offer children a broad, balanced and varied experience.

It also reported that 'play' is being misinterpreted and needs further explanation and that the focus on outdoor play is somewhat difficult to implement and further training is required. The additional guidance produced is not very specific and there is enormous variation between terms, for example free-play, active learning and structured play. Practitioners from the pilot settings felt that they had more autonomy with planning and it was more flexible. The report concluded with eleven recommendations (Siraj-Blatchford et al., 2006).

In 2010, Estyn reported on training within the Foundation Phase and its impact on learning and teaching. The main findings of the report are that training has been well organized and that the outdoors is being utilized more as a result of training. It also reports that the standards in personal and social development, well-being and cultural diversity (one of the seven areas of learning) are high and that children are showing more independence, with more access to resources. There have also been improvements in children's ability to problem-solve (Estyn, 2010a).

In 2011, Estyn produced a further report entitled *Literacy and the Foundation Phase*, the main findings of which noted that children's well-being was enhanced, for example their motivation to learn. The outdoor learning space was also developing well, but it does report that the variety of children's written work is often limited (Estyn, 2011).

Ann Keane, chief inspector for Estyn (the inspectorate body in Wales for education providers, the equivalent of Ofsted in England) stated in the 2010–11 annual report that children are making progress in literacy and numeracy and are becoming more independent and thinking for themselves. However, 'in nearly a quarter of schools inspected, pupils' written work is full of simple spelling and punctuation mistakes and they do not write enough at length' (Estyn, 2010b, p. 4). She adds that a carousel approach is implemented in the Foundation Phase and best practice shows a clear purpose to the activities. 'However, where activities are poorly planned, children may look busy but they make little progress. They are repeating activities without extending their knowledge and understanding' (Estyn, 2010b, p. 6).

The 2011–12 annual report stated that only a minority of children are making spelling, punctuation and letter formation errors but that literacy is still an area of concern. Ann Keane also commented on planning within the Foundation Phase, stating that 'planning is generally appropriate but in a minority of schools six and seven-year-olds do not have enhanced and **continuous provision**' (Estyn, 2013, p. 4). This indicates that the Foundation Phase may be more challenging for some Year 2 practitioners to implement because of the traditional National Curriculum trajectory; challenging in the sense that staff may find it difficult to adopt a more play-based pedagogy where children are being encouraged to have more equal, co-constructive relationships in the classroom with adults. It is important for all practitioners (nursery through to Year 2) to note that 'the Foundation Phase proposals in Wales require a way of thinking, acting and being within the Early Years classroom that is substantially different from the requirements of previous statutory curricula' (Aasen and Waters, 2006, p. 128). Arguably, this could be very challenging and some of the reasons for this could be linked to the variety of training, lack of reflective practitioners, lack of guidance, lack of resources and multiple interpretations of key terms in government documentation. However, we should be reassured because the report also states that 'by now, most teachers have a good understanding of the Foundation Phase approach and provide a good balance between adult-directed and child-initiated activities' (Estyn 2012b, p. 4). The report also highlights that there are still some schools that are providing limited opportunities for children to learn outdoors and this needs addressing.

Between September 2013 and March 2014 the Welsh Government commissioned an independent stocktake of the implementation of the Foundation Phase, chaired by Professor Iram Siraj. One of the findings was that:

> … the implementation of the Foundation Phase is variable within and between maintained schools and funded non-maintained settings, however there appears to be a general move in the right direction with this very complex change and process.
>
> (Siraj, 2014, p. 3)

The stocktake report produced twenty-three recommendations. One of the recommendations was to consider having one inspection framework which combines Estyn (education providers) and CSSIW (Care and Social Services Inspectorate Wales for non-education providers). This would be similar to England where Ofsted inspect both education and care (non-education) providers.

In 2015, the final report of the three-year Welsh Government evaluation of the Foundation Phase was published, setting out twenty-nine recommendations. One of the key findings was that 'according to national administrative data the recommended adult:child ratios are, on average, being met for Years 1 and 2 but not in Reception and Nursery classes' (Taylor et al. (2015), p. 2). The report concludes that:

> … the introduction of the Foundation Phase has led to overall improvements in children's educational achievement, wellbeing and involvement. Furthermore, these improvements have the potential to lead to even greater educational success as the children grow up.
>
> (Taylor et al., 2015, p. 108)

Also, Taylor et al. (2015) suggest that the Welsh Government should continue to support and build upon the Foundation Phase pedagogy.

What makes a Foundation Phase setting a success?

Despite some of the minority school issues, findings from Estyn (2013) suggest that the Foundation Phase could be a success. Estyn (2013) claim that the best Foundation Phase settings apply the principles of the Foundation Phase whilst retaining a strong focus on developing and improving literacy and numeracy. However, the principles are not explicitly listed by Estyn or by the Welsh Government in Foundation Phase documentation and can often be ambiguous. The twelve pedagogical elements previously mentioned from the three-year evaluation would be useful for practitioners to draw upon.

Estyn (2013) suggest that successful Foundation Phase settings get the balance right between child-led and adult-directed input. In addition, there are fewer schools poorly planning activities for children. Strong leadership is critical to the effective implementation of the Foundation Phase, where leaders need to be knowledgeable and engage in whole-school collaborations (Estyn, 2013). Waldron, Rhys and Taylor (2015) state that 'many schools think that **funding,** the clarity **of guidance, assessment procedures and transitions into Key Stage 2** need to be improved in the future, along with practitioner understanding of key Foundation Phase principles' (p. 1; bold in original).

Conclusion

The introduction of the Foundation Phase is seen (by some, not all) as a move away from formal learning (more sedentary practice), particularly for 5- to 7-year-olds. The underpinning philosophy of the new curriculum is to provide more active learning experiences which are not only better for younger children but more suited to their drive for exploration and discovery. However, allowing children to actively explore, engage and ask questions is not always what is convenient and necessary for staff, and some practitioners might be reluctant to change. Practitioners may, at a surface level, change their practice and/or learning environment, but at a deeper level may not change their ideology.

Implementing curriculum change can be challenging, and achieving a balance of child-led learning and adult-directed tasks may involve a more equal distribution of power and control. If you are a practitioner then it is up to you to improve the provision (however small) for the children you work with. Practitioners need to be somewhat reflective in their work if successful implementation of the Foundation Phase is going to take place. Children should not be required to do something that they are not emotionally, physically or cognitively able to do.

Chapter summary

- Many changes have taken place in education over the past twenty years or so and changes to the Early Years curriculum have occurred because it is reported that children are being educated inappropriately and being introduced to formal learning too soon.
- The Foundation Phase in Wales is a new play-based curriculum framework for children aged between three and seven years, which was introduced in 2008. It focuses on more opportunities to engage in experiential, purposeful learning which is suitably matched to stage rather than age-related outcomes.
- Implementing the Foundation Phase or curriculum change of any kind is very complex, and changing pedagogy and practice may be a long process. An additional challenge that some practitioners now face is implementing a National Literacy and Numeracy Framework (LNF) and administering tests to young children in Year 2 (6- to 7-year-olds).
- Reports by Estyn (i.e. the Welsh inspectorate for education providers) claim that children in Foundation Phase settings are making progress in personal and social development and well-being (one of seven areas of learning) but writing needs to be improved. They also claim that strong leadership is critical to successfully implementing the Foundation Phase.
- Findings from a recent three-year Welsh Government evaluation of the Foundation Phase positively reports that a Foundation Phase pedagogy which consists of twelve elements has many benefits.

Access the following link online to take part in a short quiz about this chapter:

www.bloomsbury.com/an-introduction-to-the-foundation-phase-9781474264273

Thought-provoking questions

- What changes have you made (for example in the learning environment) since the introduction of the Foundation Phase in 2008?
- Have your views towards the children you work with changed since 2008? Do you find them competent and capable or vulnerable and needy?
- What creative and innovative ways can you implement a play-based curriculum for 6- to 7-year-olds in light of testing young children in Year 2?
- How would you rate the leadership and understanding of the Foundation Phase in your setting?

Further reading and information

Clark, M. and T. Waller (2007) *Early Childhood Education and Care: Policy and Practice*. London: Sage.

Cockburn, A. and Handscomb (2012) *Teaching Children 3–11*, 3rd edn, London: Sage.

Estyn website – Welsh Inspectorate for Wales: www.estyn.gov.uk

Papatheodorou, T. and J. Moyles (2012) *Cross-Cultural Perspectives on Early Childhood*. London: Sage.

Welsh Government website information on the Foundation Phase: http://wales.gov.uk/topics/educationandskills/earlyyearshome/foundation_phase/eval/?lang=en.

WISERD – information on the three-year evaluation project on the Foundation Phase: http://www.wiserd.ac.uk/news/wiserd-news/evaluating-the-foundation-phase/.

2

Influential Thinkers in Early Childhood Education, Past and Present

Chapter aims

To examine and explore the theories of past thinkers in early childhood education.

To explore the theories of current thinkers in early childhood education.

To link these theories to principles of the Foundation Phase curriculum.

There are many texts available that explore theories and theorists associated with early childhood education. However, this chapter has been selective in choosing the theories and theorists that underpin the principles of the Foundation Phase (FP). The principles discussed are: a play- based active learning approach; observation; use of the outdoors; planning for individual needs; and future initiatives. The discussion of influential thinkers is not in chronological order but is examined in relation to the specific Foundation Phase principles outlined above.

A play-based, active learning approach

According to WAG (2008c, p. 12), 'The Foundation Phase requires a teaching approach that is best suited to the active learning that characterizes this phase of education and the multiple ways in which children learn.' In agreement with this, Professor Janet Moyles (2005, p. 9) writes that:

> Anyone who has observed play for any length of time will recognise that, for young children, play is a medium for learning and practitioners who acknowledge and appreciate this can, through provision, interaction and intervention in children's play, ensure progression, **differentiation** and relevance in the curriculum ...

In fact a play- based approach to Early Years education has had a long and interesting history. In the sixteenth century **John Comenius (1592–1670)** proclaimed that 'Children should experience learning through pleasurable activity' (Andrews, 2012, p. 46). He made the link between play and the environment. This was supported by **Jean-Jacques Rousseau (1712–78)** who, in the eighteenth century, argued that play was the right of the child (Andrews, 2102b, p. 47). The theories of Rousseau were put into practice by **Johann Pestalozzi (1746–1827)**, who emphasized play as being spontaneous and a self-activity. He established a successful school in 1805 and argued that children needed to find out things for themselves through seeing, doing, judging and reasoning (Silber, 1965; Smith, 1997).

Friedrich Froebel (1782–1852) trained at Pestalozzi's school but went on to develop his own educational theory. Froebel is famous for saying that play is a 'child's work' (Pound, 2005, p. 14). His influence can still be seen today in the Foundation Phase as he emphasized play and a child-centred approach to learning. For Froebel, play represented enjoyment and **emotional well-being** and was of great benefit to a child. Through observing mothers with their children, Froebel recognized the importance of the mother's role in learning and believed that parents should be closely involved in their children's development and education. As a result of his observations, he recruited female teachers at a time when teaching was largely seen as a male profession.

In a Froebelian education, play and the outdoors were considered of the uppermost importance and Froebel was the inventor of the 'kindergarten'. Kindergarten can be translated as both 'garden of children' or 'garden for children'. In Froebel's kindergarten each child tended a piece of land and there was also a community garden. Froebel pioneered outdoor education, giving it the same status as indoor learning (Milchem, 2010; Tovey, 2007).

Froebel considered the development of the whole child through play and active learning. His pre-school curriculum was carefully planned and based on key learning experiences. This holistic, integrated approach promoted four basic ideas: play and language, actions, feelings and thought. He offered structured teacher-directed activities within which children had the opportunity to play. These activities included playing with a set of objects called 'gifts', such as spheres, cubes and cylinders. He also developed graduated exercises which he based on the games he had observed children playing. Froebel promoted the use of wet sand, clay and drawing with crayons and he designed occupations to develop children's manual dexterity such as weaving, paper pricking, cutting and sewing (Bruce, 2011b). He also encouraged teachers to begin where the learner is, therefore promoting the notion of 'readiness to learn' as advocated in the Foundation Phase today (WAG, 2008b).

A criticism of Froebel is that although he advocated nature walks and outdoor play, the importance of **gross motor skills** development was undervalued in his kindergartens. Also, there has been some criticism that his kindergartens were essentially middle class (Pound, 2005).

John Dewey (1859–1952) also argued that children learn best through a hands-on approach: that is, learning by doing. He postulated the theory that:

- Children should learn by doing.
- Education should be based on real-life experiences.
- Experimentation and independent thinking should be fostered.

Dewey has become associated with the idea of a child-centred educational approach (Gray and Macblain, 2012). This is the ethos of the Foundation Phase curriculum, where the child is at the centre of the learning and there should be a balance between child-initiated and adult-directed learning. He felt that practitioners should, 'know their children well and observe children and plan from what they learn of them' (Pound, 2005, p. 22).

Dewey felt that children needed to develop their own interests and have hands-on experiences that would help to contribute to their understanding of the world. He believed in a cross-curricular approach, an example of which in today's Foundation Phase would be described as follows:

Case study

A parent comes into the setting to make bread with the children. All children take turns in making bread and the finished products are evaluated and taken home. The following week a bread company come in and talk to the children about making bread commercially and allow the children to taste different types of bread. Children discuss their favourites and a graph is made to show the results. They write about their experiences and take photographs to be made into a class book.

The teacher's role was to ask questions, discover what the children already knew and to then plan experiences for them to discover things they did not know. She used her knowledge to set up age-appropriate experiences for the children and observed the children throughout, documenting her findings to help her with future planning. The activities were cross-curricular as they focused on knowledge and understanding of the world, language, literacy and communication skills, mathematics, personal and social development and cultural diversity. Dewey has also been credited with the notion of reflective professional practice and the reflective practitioner. Again, this way of teaching and learning fits in with the Foundation Phase notion of a curriculum that should embrace partnership with all stakeholders.

A criticism that is sometimes made of John Dewey is that a cross-curricular approach could mean more emphasis on some subjects at the expense of others. However, it can be argued that by adopting a cross-curricular approach more team work is embraced and partnership collaborations developed and fostered. The Foundation Phase advocates a cross-curricular approach to learning based on topics or themes.

Rudolf Steiner (1861–1925) was another key figure in promoting a play-based approach to learning. In 1919 he formed the first Steiner-Waldorf school and 'today there are 1,087 nurseries and 640 schools in fifty countries for children aged three to eighteen' (Pound, 2005, p. 26). Steiner believed the spirit of the future child would emerge in play. If play were repressed then the child would become constrained (Andrews, 2012b).

Steiner focused on all aspects of growth and development including spirituality. He wanted children to experience arts and sciences. He believed that there are three seven-year cycles of development. Practitioners need to work with the children's differing abilities and needs in each of the cycles. Steiner believed that these stages or cycles were:

- Birth to 7, child responds to his world through will.
- Seven to 14, children live in the emotional realm.
- Fourteen to 21, adolescents enter the realm of ideas and ideal.

(Bruce, 2011a).

Steiner argued that if children were pressurized to succeed at too early an age they would lack motivation in later life. This fits in with the ethos of the Foundation Phase where the emphasis is on stage of readiness not the age of the children.

Steiner-Waldorf schools place great importance on the learning environment. Again, learning is cross-curricular with an emphasis on play, and the pace of learning is set by the child. This is the same child-centred, play-based approach used in the Foundation Phase. In the Steiner curriculum, creativity and practical experiences are combined. Unlike the Foundation Phase, children in Steiner schools are not shown printed words until the age of seven when formal schooling begins. Instead, there is a great focus on the spoken word, with stories being told over and over as this allows children to appreciate the rhythm of language. This contrasts with many mainstream educational practices but actually supports, in some parts, the Foundation Phase concept of a 'stage not age' approach to development and learning. However, children in the Foundation Phase are given opportunities to see books and print but should not be 'forced' into reading and writing until they are ready.

In a Steiner setting, children are encouraged to participate freely in creative play. There is a sense of routine as they believe children need continuity and the setting has a home-like feel. The rooms are painted in warm colours and furnished with soft muslins to separate areas and to give softer lighting (Pound, 2005). There is rhythm and repetition in the setting to establish continuity and memory.

There have been criticisms of not introducing children in Steiner-Waldorf settings to any formal literacy until the age of seven. Also, the absence of any up-to-date technology raises the question as to whether Steiner-Waldorf education equips children for life in the twenty-first century (Taplin, 2011).

Jerome Bruner (b. 1915) advocated an approach to learning that embraces children actively playing. He also emphasized the importance of the role of the adult in supporting children's play. Bruner identified two functions of play: the first allowing children to test out their actions without threat and fear of failure; the second allowing them to engage in behaviours free from adult pressure (Llewelyn Jones, 2004 as cited in Maynard and Thomas).

His theory supports the idea of the importance of play as a process. Bruner identified three stages or modes that children go through in the learning process:

- The enactive mode, which involves physical action.
- The iconic mode, which involves images and pictures.
- The symbolic mode which involves children representing experiences through a range of symbolic systems.

(Gray and Macblain, 2012).

Bruner believes that the chosen mode depends on the level of experience and that children move between modes. If something is new to a child then he/she will more than likely choose the enactive mode, gradually moving towards the symbolic mode as they become more experienced. Again, this theory would link to the concept of 'readiness for learning' of the child. The application of Bruner's theory to these stages of development can be seen in the Foundation Phase classroom today by practitioners encouraging children to represent their ideas and experiences through their individual play.

Bruner has increasingly emphasized the importance of the supporting role of the adult, which he calls '**scaffolding**'. He states that adults need to support the children in moving from where they are now to where the adult wants to take them (Bruce, 2005). Adults do this by supporting the child whilst simultaneously challenging them to re-examine and extend their understanding (Bruner, 1990). Bruner also introduced the idea of the **spiral curriculum**, where children revisit topics and resources as their thinking skills develop. This work has been further developed by Janet Moyles (see below). Bruner also emphasizes the importance of children learning through the process of enquiry and that practitioners need to accept and be comfortable with intuitive thinking (Gray and Macblain, 2012).

However, critics have sometimes cited disadvantages of Bruner's work, including:

- creation of cognitive overload;
- potential misconceptions for the child;
- teachers may fail to detect problems and misconceptions by allowing children to learn independently.

(*Learning Theories*, 2007).

Nevertheless Bruner's theory of 'learning by doing' fits in well with the idea of a kinaesthetic **learning style** which is favoured by most children at a young age and relates to the experiential principles of the Foundation Phase.

Bruner's theory of the spiral curriculum has been further developed by **Janet Moyles**. Previously Professor of Early Childhood Education and Research at Anglia Ruskin University, Moyles is a prolific writer focusing on Early Years and primary education. She is particularly well known for writing on play, producing in 1989 the book *Just Playing*, followed by *The Excellence of Play* in 1994.

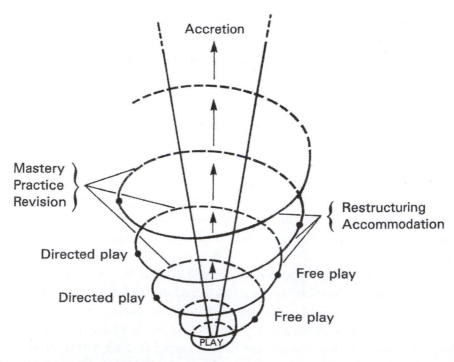

Figure 2.1 The Play Spiral (Moyles, 1989, p. 16)

In 1989, Moyles introduced the concept of the '**play spiral**' which has much in common with Bruner's 'spiral curriculum'. In Moyles' play spiral (Figure 2.1), children engage in exploratory free play which spreads upwards into wider experiences for the child until accretion is reached. Again, this links with the concept of a child's 'readiness to learn' in the Foundation Phase, as they would continue to revisit play and learning experiences until they felt ready to move onto the next level. Moyles (1994) believes that practitioners are the best people to observe and channel children's play into learning opportunities.

The following case study illustrates Moyles' play spiral.

Case study

The children in the reception class have visited the local farm as part of their topic on animals. On returning to the class, some children ask to play with the toy farm set. Previously their play was mainly on the carpet but now they want to take the farm outdoors as they state that animals live outside in fields. The children are keen to put the different animals in different fields and not altogether as they did previously. Some children collect grass to feed the toy animals and have asked the head teacher can they have some real chickens to look after because they 'will give us lots of eggs'.

Here the children had some prior knowledge of farms and farm animals before the visit. However, the visit to the farm has triggered deeper thinking and learning as the children now want to put into practice what they have seen on their trip. The children had previous experience of playing with the farm set but now their knowledge has expanded and new thinking has emerged with the request to the school to have their own chickens. Moyles' thinking can be seen in the Foundation Phase which is a play-based, holistic curriculum. Children learn and develop through exploratory and investigative activities, where adult-directed and child-initiated play are of equal importance.

There are many opportunities throughout the Foundation Phase for learners to revisit previous play experiences and resources, bringing new ideas and putting prior learning into practice. This encompasses the whole ethos of the play spiral and spiral curriculum as postulated by Bruner and Moyles.

Another current influential thinker on children's play is **Tina Bruce**, who, along with Janet Moyles, is widely regarded as an expert in the field of 'play'. Bruce originally trained at the Froebel institute as a primary teacher and has taught in both mainstream and special needs schools. Currently she is an honorary visiting professor at Roehampton University. Bruce describes herself as a 'social learning theorist influenced by the work of Froebel' (Pound, 2009, p. 12). She favours a holistic approach to teaching young children which has its focus on creativity, play and hands-on learning experiences. Bruce identifies ten principles of early childhood education that draw on the theories of Froebel, Montessori and Steiner. Pound (2009, p. 12) writes that the ten principles are as follows:

- A child's need to be a child.
- The holistic nature of development and the integrated nature of learning.
- The importance of opportunities to act as an independent learner, making choices and mistakes with an emphasis on self-motivation.
- Receptive learning periods – practice will not help until the brain and body are sufficiently developed.
- A focus on what children are able to do – taking that as the starting point for learning.
- Imagination and symbolic representation which support development.
- The central role of relationships with others in children's development.

The ethos of the Foundation Phase curriculum as stated in the *Framework for Children's Learning for 3 to 7-year-olds in Wales* encompasses all the above: 'At the centre of the statutory framework lies the holistic development of children and their skills across the curriculum building on their previous learning experiences, knowledge and skills.' The document goes on to state that 'Children learn through first-hand experiential activities with the serious business of "play" providing the vehicle' (WAG, 2008b, p. 4). This echoes Bruce's theory of starting where the child is and providing an integrated approach to play and learning.

The theorists discussed so far have all advocated the importance of a play-based approach to learning, and the holistic and child-centred approach of the Foundation Phase has embraced these ideas. However, since 2008 when the Foundation Phase curriculum became statutory there have been several changes introduced that could be seen as detrimental to a play-based pedagogy. These include the National Literacy and Numeracy test for all 7- to 14-year-olds and the Literacy and Numeracy Framework (LNF) – these will be discussed in more detail throughout the book.

Theories of observation

Methods of observation in the Foundation Phase are discussed in detail in Chapter 5. This section, however, will consider how theories and theorists have influenced this practice. In the Foundation Phase curriculum (WAG, 2008c, p. 4) it states that:

> By observing children while they are involved in activities, practitioners will find out how children's skills are developing and what they are able to do.

However, observation and observing children is not a 'new' idea; for centuries, theorists have discussed the importance of observing children in order to meet their individual needs. **Maria Montessori (1870–1952)**, who was one of the most influential pioneers of Early Years education, based her educational theories on scientific observations. She stated that education begins from birth and children have periods where they are eager to learn. She believed that children learn independently through hands-on learning experiences, using resources that are designed for a particular purpose. Montessori believed in a planned learning environment and she introduced child-sized furniture. In addition, she believed that 'decorations should be kept simple' (Bradley et al., 2011, p. 78). Montessori felt that neutral colours would not distract a child from learning; this is in contrast to most Foundation Phase classrooms where bright colours and displays of children's work adorn the walls.

Like Froebel, Montessori also believed in active learning and the development of the whole child. Children were free to move about and choose what activities interested them. The outdoors should be seen as an area for work, with children moving freely between the indoors and outdoors. This is seen today with the proposed free-flow approach between the indoors and outdoors in Foundation Phase settings. However, in contrast to the Foundation Phase, Montessori did not believe in developing the child's imaginative play, but focused instead on the intellectual development of the child (WAG, 2008a).

Montessori believed in adults observing the children on a regular basis and that children move through four main developmental stages. These stages were from conception to age 6; age 6 to 12; age 12 to 18; and early adulthood from 18 to 24 (Bradley et al., 2011).

Through her regular observation of children, Montessori believed that learning should be linked to movement and that children learn best through their senses. Reading, writing and numbers could be introduced at an early age but only when the child is ready and showed an interest; Montessori also taught language development through phonics. Montessori schools are still in existence today, with the modern Montessori curriculum supporting all aspects of the child's personal and social development. This matches the ethos of the Foundation Phase framework where personal and social development is at the heart of the curriculum.

Montessori schools have a focus on caring for the environment and the community and exploration of the world through the senses. Language development is taught through a phonic-based approach and mathematics through an understanding of the concepts of numbers (Pound, 2005). Practitioners working today in Montessori settings claim this method of teaching allows children to develop in a balanced way, becoming independent thinkers, decision-makers and confident learners.

A criticism of Montessori and her approaches to teaching and learning would be the rejection of role play and imagination in learning and that she did not see play as an important part of the curriculum.

Susan Isaacs (1885–1948) was a contemporary of Maria Montessori. She used systematic observations to develop understanding of children's intellectual growth. Isaacs believed in the importance of play and, like Froebel, believed in children learning by doing. She believed that play was not only about learning but also a way of expressing oneself and a way of emotional relief (Palaiologou, 2012). Isaacs taught at the Malting House School in Cambridge and paid great attention to the children's emotional needs. She pioneered narrative observations in the Malting House, the children were encouraged to follow their own interests and there was no fixed curriculum (Bruce, 2011a). Isaacs set up the first Department of Child Development in 1933 at the London Institute of Education and she believed in the importance of working with parents.

Isaacs was critical of Montessori's phonic-based approach to reading. She felt that because Montessori schools lacked other games and resources to teach reading that was the only reason the phonic approach worked. Criticisms of Isaacs lie in the fact that her experiences were with a small group of children and those children were from rich, well-educated families (Pound, 2005).

Jean Piaget (1896–1980) is considered to be one of the most famous pioneers of Early Years education. Piaget, like Montessori, was famous for his theory that children go through four stages of development. These four stages were from birth to adulthood and are as follows: the sensori-motor stage covers the first two years of a child's life, followed by the pre-operational stage from the age of two to seven years. The next stage is the concrete operational stage from seven to eleven years, and finally the formal operations stage from twelve to adulthood.

Piaget stated that a child must progress through each stage in turn, and cannot skip a stage nor return to an earlier stage. He believed that children are active participants who construct their learning by interacting with their environment and making concrete links between their new and previous learning. He also contended that children's thinking begins even before they have the language skills to express this thinking. For Piaget, language was merely a tool used to develop and enhance thinking (Gray and Macblain, 2012).

Although Piaget did not explicitly specify his theory in terms of changing educational practices, the idea that there was a sequence in which children learn new concepts was soon adopted by educationalists. This allowed practitioners to align their pedagogy with the cognitive levels of the children they were teaching, and there was a recognition that a readiness to learn was something that could not be hurried. Conversely, this has been the feature of Piaget's theories that has been the most criticized and challenged. The criticism of Piaget's stage theory centres on the fact that the stages are linear in progression, and that one stage replaces another.

Piaget also postulated the idea of equilibrium, accommodation and assimilation. He believed that we assimilate new information and when that new information is called into question we need to rethink our original idea – this is called accommodation. Once thinking has been readjusted and starts to feel comfortable, equilibrium has been reached. An example of this is when a child has understood what a horse is but then sees a zebra for the first time. Initially the child thinks it is a stripy horse, but as the child gains more knowledge about the zebra he/she comes to realize it is a different animal altogether. At this stage the child has achieved equilibrium.

Piaget used the term schema to describe the cognitive and mental represent- ations a child develops as they have new experiences (**schemas** are discussed in more detail at the end of this chapter). He observed his own children and these observations shaped his understanding about how children construct knowledge. In the Foundation Phase, observations are linked to assessment and planning to meet children's individual learning needs. One of Piaget's observations involved his daughter at seven months when he hid a toy duck from her. At this stage in her development she watched the duck disappear but no longer looked for it. Several months later, Piaget repeated the observation using a coin, and now when he hid it, his daughter looked for it – Piaget called this 'object permanence': the realization that objects have their own existence (Crowley, 2014).

Piaget also carried out observations on the concept of conservation. He asked children to compare two sets of coins in two lines. Both sets had the same number of coins but one line was more spread out than the other. Preoperational children always stated that the line with the coins further apart had more (Garhart and Mooney, 2013). Experiments such as this show if a child has grasped the idea that certain physical characteristics remain the same even if outward appearances change.

Today Paiget's ideas are known as 'constructivist theories', as they are based on the belief that children construct their knowledge and learning through interacting with the environment and making connections between old and new learning. This emphasis on building on prior learning is a cornerstone of the Foundation Phase curriculum. Piaget believed that children are active learners and through obser- vation practitioners could provide first-hand learning experiences that challenge and motivate children to expand their knowledge. He encouraged practitioners to examine the processes children go through to arrive at their answers. By using this approach, teachers could identify the child's stage of 'readiness' to learn (Crowley, 2014).

Piaget's theories can be seen in the Foundation Phase classroom through regularly observing the children and using these observations to understand individual needs. Practitioners identify what the next learning step should be and where children need support, and match the curriculum to each individual child's stage of development. Piaget stated that teaching should be matched to individuals needs and that children need to experiment and play with materials as learning is matched to action. Practitioners need to provide open-ended activities and allow children to have long uninterrupted periods of play and exploration. This is the child-centred approach underpinning the Foundation Phase curriculum (WAG, 2008d).

Nevertheless, there have been criticisms of Piaget's theories, mainly the stages of development as children's rates of development vary and, depending on the area of learning, they can operate at different levels. Susan Isaacs was also an early critic of Piaget. She argued that he tended to portray children in a negative light, with the emphasis on what they could not do rather than what they could do (Gray and Macblain, 2012). There has also been some criticism of the way Piaget worded questions to children. In addition, Piaget did not put enough emphasis on the importance of social and emotional learning, which is in complete contrast to the Foundation Phase which has personal, social and emotional well-being at its centre (Pound, 2005). Piaget stressed the need for children to be active in their learning approaches but did not place great emphasis on social interaction. He claimed that a child constructs knowledge by actively engaging, independently, with the environment. However, he did support collaboration between peers on tasks but that the tasks must be suitable for the stage of development the child was at. This is in contrast to the sociocultural theory of Lev Vygotsky who emphasized the need for more knowledgeable adults to support the children and to accelerate their learning.

Lev Vygotsky (1896–1934) extended the constructivist approach through the notion of the '**zone of proximal development**'. He believed that learners need to construct knowledge from their experiences, but unlike Piaget he emphasized the social interaction needed in those experiences in order to take the learning forward. The central idea in Vygotsky's theory is that all learning begins in the social context, with children constructing their own understanding (Whitebread, 2012). This is supported by Adams (2006), who postulates that in constructivist learning each learner will construct knowledge differently depending on how the individual interprets and organizes information.

Vygotsky argued that there were three stages in the relationship between thinking and language but that the stages were not one way. He stipulated that depending on the level of difficulty, children or adults may regress to an earlier stage. The first stage is external speech – here thinking is from outside the child. The second stage is private speech, where children talk to themselves as a means of directing their own thinking. In the final stage, termed internal speech, children will internalize their thought processes (Ford, 2004).

Vygotsky believed that communication between adults and children enabled children to achieve higher levels of understanding than they would otherwise. He called the gap between what a child can achieve independently and what they can achieve with adult support and guidance the 'zone of proximal development' (Garhart Mooney, 2013). This relies on detailed, regular observation of what a child can do and using that information to plan a curriculum that challenges them and their current capability. Vygotsky believed that language supports **cognitive development** and that social interactions benefit children's thinking due to the input of language. In contrast, Piaget believed that language was a system for representing the world and is quite separate from action that leads to reasoning and logical thinking (Smidt, 2009).

Vygotsky also valued play and believed that it made a deeply important contribution to the zone of proximal development. He believed that 'what a child can do with help today, she will be able to do by herself tomorrow' (Bruce, 2005, p. 43). An example of an adult supporting a child can be seen in the following case study.

Case study

Ellie, aged four, is fascinated with shoes and continually takes off her own shoes and puts on the 'play' shoes in the home corner. All of these shoes are the slip-on type, so Ellie is able to put them on and take them off independently. One of the practitioners has observed Ellie doing this and brings in some shoes with Velcro straps and some shoes with popper fasteners. Ellie quickly works out how to wear the shoes with the Velcro strap but finds the shoes with the fasteners more of a challenge. The practitioner sits with Ellie and shows her how to fasten the poppers on the shoes and then lets Ellie try herself. After a few attempts Ellie is successful and happily goes around the classroom showing everyone her 'new' shoes.

This is an example of how the adult noted Ellie's interest in shoes, observed that she was able to put on slip-on shoes but challenged and extended Ellie's development to allow her to now wear a different type of shoe. Piaget would disagree with Vygotsky on this point of the more knowledgeable other supporting learning and development. For Piaget there was little point in a child participating in an activity they were not ready for even if with a more knowledgeable other. He felt this would just lead to the more knowledgeable other imposing their views and would not benefit the other child (Matusov and Hayes, 2000).

In today's Foundation Phase curriculum the notion of matching tasks and activities to the child's current ability and scaffolding their learning comes directly from Vygotsky's work. Peer mentoring and the apprenticeship approach to learning are also linked to Vygotsky. An example is a parent helping a child to read and write. Here the child is the novice apprentice learning from the more experienced parent.

One criticism of Vygotsky is that his theories are incomplete and are based on hypotheses instead of empirical evidence, but this may be because of his early death at the age of thirty-eight (Daniels, 2005). Finally, Vygotsky focused on social and cultural influences but not on the biological aspect of cognition. His theory does not answer the question of how memory or problem-solving change children's social experiences and promote advances in cognitive development. Moll (1994) also argues that Vygotsky's theory does not explain exactly how children internalize their social experiences to move ahead in their mental functioning.

The rest of this chapter will focus on some of the other philosophies and initiatives that underpin current pedagogy in the Foundation Phase and the theories that support them.

Outdoor learning and play

As discussed previously in Chapter 1, there is much more of a requirement in the new Foundation Phase for children to be actively engaged in outdoor learning. In fact the outdoors should be viewed as equally important for children to learn as the indoors. A recent study conducted by Maynard et al. (2013a) found that those children perceived to be underachieving by teachers, when engaged in child-initiated learning outdoors behaved differently and the perception of underachievement was reduced.

The Foundation Phase outdoor learning handbook states that:

> Wales leads the UK in its development of learning outdoors and the Foundation Phase will further ensure that we are in the vanguard of experiential learning, of which outdoor learning is such a vital element.
>
> (WAG, 2009a, p. 2)

Many of the theorists already discussed also recognized the importance of learning outdoors. Froebel saw kindergartens as the best environment for young children to learn and develop and Susan Isaacs encouraged children to use the outdoors for exploration and enquiry. Rudolf Steiner emphasized meaningful life experiences such as gardening and an appreciation of nature and the seasons, while Maria Montessori advocated 'freedom of movement and choice' (Bradley et al., 2011, p. 78). Montessori believed children should be able to move between the outdoors and the indoors and that the outdoors should be seen as a place for purposeful work as well as play.

Margaret McMillan (1860–1931) drew on the work of Froebel and placed great emphasis on the importance of the garden. She and her sister Rachel believed young children needed time and space to develop, as well as for their health and well-being. It has been claimed that McMillan invented the nursery school. In 1903 she became manager of a group of Deptford schools where there was a strong emphasis on being outdoors. The schools in Deptford had large beautiful gardens, were light and airy and carried the expectation that children would develop a love of working and playing outdoors (Blackwell and Pound, 2011). The McMillan sisters are credited with the establishment of the school medical service and the school meals service, the legacy of which still exists in the UK today.

Their educational philosophy drew on Froebel's work and placed great emphasis on using the garden as a place children could learn and play. Criticism of Margaret McMillan focused on the long hours offered at her school, which was considered by some an example of professional parenting (Pound, 2005).

Today, in twenty-first-century Britain, learning outdoors can be seen as equally, if not more, important than ever before. Modern society has seen a rapid decline in children playing and learning outside. This can be linked to many factors including lack of open space to play in, fear of strangers, road safety concerns and too much TV and electronic games. This decline in playing and learning outdoors has in turn led to problems with childhood obesity, an increase in health problems such as asthma, a decrease in physical development and a lack of imagination and independence and problem-solving abilities. These are just some of the reasons why learning and playing outdoors has become top of many educational agendas, including the Foundation Phase in Wales. The policy states that children should spend time outdoors every day regardless of the weather – there is no unsuitable weather, only unsuitable clothing! All seven areas of learning can be delivered outside and children are encouraged to take supervised risks that both stimulate and challenge them, an example of which follows.

Case study

The children in the reception class have been studying the topic of teddy bears. They have been reading many stories about bears and one of their favourites is *We're going on a bear hunt* by Michael Rosen and Helen Oxenbury. Today the children are going to re-enact the story outdoors. Prior to this the children have made bear masks and costumes; they have made a cave for the bear and maps for the journey. The staff have provided the children with various resources to represent the different parts of the journey and the children will work together to find the cave where the bear is sleeping.

The children spend most of the morning outdoors role-playing the story. Staff observe the children, noting how they communicate with each other, their physical development, how they work as a team and their ability to follow the maps to find the bear. At the end of the morning the children sit outdoors to have a teddy bears' picnic, wearing their bear masks.

This is just one example of how using the outdoors can stimulate and enthuse children's learning.

Today many additional initiatives have been introduced to support outdoor learning. Examples include the Forest School initiative, where children are taught to use tools and how to light fires in a supervised environment (this will be discussed in more detail in Chapter 3). Eco schools are another way of engaging children in outdoor learning. Here schools form an Eco committee and work towards different Eco awards, leading to the Green Flag. This is part of the healthy schools initiative, along with the walking school bus and healthy school meals and fruit tuck provision. Information on the Eco-school initiative can be found through the following link: http://www.wasteawarenesswales.org.uk/ecoschools.html.

Planning for individual learning needs

Learning styles

As our knowledge of how the brain processes information has increased, this has led to a greater interest in the role of the senses in learning. Some would take the view there are three main learning styles, namely visual, auditory, and kinaesthetic (WAG, 2008d). It has been argued that if practitioners cater for all styles through a range of activities then we are catering to learners' individual needs. This can be done through visual aids, songs, stories and active learning in the Foundation Phase curriculum.

However, it is important to note that there have been criticisms of the concept of learning styles, notably by Professor Frank Coffield. He has stated that the majority of tools used to measure learning styles are invalid and unreliable (Coffield, 2005). Coffield's criticisms followed an eighteen-month investigation of learning styles and their implications for methods of teaching, which he and his team carried out for the Learning and Skills Development Council in England. Though this investigation was carried out in 2005, Professor Coffield disputes the concept of labelling children with a given learning style and feels practitioners should instead look at the strengths and weaknesses of an individual rather than their 'style of learning'.

Schemas and schematic play

Schemas or schematic play is not a new concept. Educational pioneers such as Froebel, Steiner, Piaget and Montessori all recognized the significance of schema-type behaviour in children's development, learning and play (Louis et al., 2008).

One definition of schemas by Chris Athey (2007, p. 5) states that they are 'patterns of behaviour and thinking in children that exists underneath the surface features of various contexts and specific experiences' and as 'patterns of repeatable actions'. There are different types of schemas and children may exhibit one or more type at any given time. An example of a 'transporting schema' would be a child who continually moves things, for example carries sand into the water tray or carries bricks from the construction area to the role-play area.

Cathy Nutbrown (1999), a **proponent** of schema theory, believed that play needed to be at the heart of the Early Years curriculum as play underpins the process of learning. She also introduced a number of principles for working in partnership with parents. Nutbrown stated that parents need to be informed of children's schemas so they can work in partnership with practitioners to build upon and enhance children's lifelong learning. This links to the Foundation Phase curriculum in terms of the promotion of purposeful play and active partnership with parents.

Recognizing and promoting children's preferred schemas is important because it allows practitioners to understand children better and to become sensitive to their ideas, thoughts and physical needs (Bruce, 2011). The Foundation Phase emphasizes the need for practitioners to observe children on a regular basis, and these observations could allow practitioners to identify children's preferred schemas and to plan appropriate activities to accommodate them.

Schemas also provide another lens through which to view children and to meet their individual learning needs (Bruce, 2011). However, at the time of writing the Foundation Phase documentation only makes one reference to children's schemas: in the '*Foundation Phase Child Development Profile*', p. 19 (WAG, 2009b). In addition, there seems to be little training available for Foundation Phase practitioners on schema theory. Further information on schemas can be found at the end of this chapter.

Conclusion

This chapter has allowed the reader to reflect upon the connections between the modern day Foundation Phase curriculum and the theories espoused by both past and present thinkers on Early Years education. Strengths and weaknesses of the theories, theorists and initiatives have been discussed to evaluate the links between theory and practice. What is evident is the recurring theme of the importance of a play-based approach to learning with a balance of child- and adult-initiated learning needed. This is backed by Sylva et al. (2004), who argue that a combination of child-led and adult-led activities provides the best outcomes for children. Children should be encouraged to learn at their own pace, and through observation, practitioners should be able to start where the child is and plan for individual learning needs. Teamwork and partnership between all stakeholders should be embraced, with an emphasis on more able learners helping less able learners to succeed – an argument supported by Vygotsky, Bruner and Dewey. By applying these principles to practice then the Foundation Phase could truly become an holistic approach to teaching and learning.

Chapter summary

- The play-based, child-centred Foundation Phase embraces many of the philosophies and principles of both past and present influential thinkers in Early Childhood education. Outdoor learning, teamwork, cross-curricular approaches and purposeful play are all philosophies of the Foundation Phase curriculum in Wales that can be linked back to educational pioneers.
- Understanding of how children learn and develop is continually evolving and expanding (e.g. schemas and learning styles). As this knowledge expands and changes, Foundation Phase practitioners will need to reflect upon and evolve their practice to keep pace. There should be a balance between adult- and child-led activities in settings.
- Children should be taught holistically by empathetic and passionate practitioners, who believe in ensuring that the child's well-being is at the very centre of their practice. Practitioners and more able peers need to scaffold children's learning and provide opportunities for reflection and thought.
- Observations of children should be ongoing and used to plan for individual learning needs. Children need time to apply new learning to past experiences. Janet Moyles advocates the notion of a 'play spiral' where children revisit and build upon past experiences.

Access the following link online to take part in a short 'Who am I?' quiz about this chapter:

www.bloomsbury.com/an-introduction-to-the-foundation-phase-
9781474264273

Thought-provoking questions

- What do you think the pioneers of Early Years education would think of the Foundation Phase curriculum?
- Which pioneer would you agree/disagree with most and why?
- If you are a practitioner then consider how you can refine your understanding between theory and practice. Do you apply any of these principles in your practice?
- Can you recall seeing any examples of children in your setting exhibiting any of the theories discussed above?

Further reading and information

Athey, C. (1990), *Extending Thought in Young Children*. London: Sage.

Froebel information: http://www.froebeltrust.org.uk/.

Howard, L., E. Wood and P. Broadhead (eds) (2011), *Play and Learning in the Early Years*. London: Sage.

Learning styles, criticisms of: http://www.tes.co.uk/article.aspx?storycode=2142655.

Louis, S., C. Beswick, L. Magraw, L. Hayes, and S. Featherstone (eds) (2008), *Again! Again! Understanding Schemas in Young Children*. London: A&C Black.

Montessori information: www.montessori.org.

Mooney, C . G. (2000), *Theories of Childhood: An Introduction to Dewey, Montessori, Erikson, Piaget and Vygotsky*. St Paul, MN: Redleaf Press.

Moyles, J. and S. Adams (2001), *StEPs (A Statement of Entitlement to Play: A Framework for Playful Teaching)*. London: Open University Press.

Rudolph Steiner information: www.steinerwaldorf.org.uk.

Woods, A. (ed.) (2013), *Child-Initiated Play and Learning*. London: Routledge.

3

International Perspectives
on Play

Chapter aims

To explore features of international curricula from a New Zealand, Northern Italy, North America, Wales and Scandinavia perspective.

To discuss the role and status of play within each country.

To consider the role of the adult and different views of childhood.

To briefly explore the challenges and barriers to outdoor play.

It is important to note early on in this chapter that 'getting a broader perspective, looking at international patterns and keys to success, is important but there is no blue print' (Tornberg and Lindholm, 2009, p. 33). Practitioners need to understand that there are many ways of implementing a curriculum and the delivery is inextricably linked to how play and childhood is understood and valued. Most of the countries selected for discussion in this chapter were chosen because of their relevance and contribution to the Foundation Phase (Siraj-Blatchford et al., 2005), for example New Zealand for its bilingual element and a Nordic perspective for the outdoor element.

How is play understood across cultures?

For thousands of years play has fascinated many stakeholders such as philosophers, educationalists, psychologists, anthropologists and sociologists (Bruce, 2004), and especially over the last 150 years numerous writers have attempted to define play but as yet there is not one single coherent definition (Brown, 2008). It is thought that 'an understanding of play can be derived from perspectives of developmental, cognitive, behavioural and social psychology as well as theories of education' (Sayeed and Guerin, 2000, p. 9). For Bruce (2004), play aids logical reasoning and develops interpersonal and intrapersonal skills. It is thought that 'play is what children are involved in when they initiate the task and work is what they do when they fulfil a task required by an adult' (Bruce, 1987, p. 17), and for some educators as soon as an adult plans an activity or has a play agenda then the child is not playing but doing work for the adult (Fisher, 1996). According to Bruce (1987), adults should develop appropriate skills that enable them to enter into a child's play and view themselves as a shared partner in the play process.

According to Sayeed and Guerin (2000) the role and value of play is continuously changing and is a reflection of the socio-cultural values and perspectives of a particular society (Fromberg and Bergen, 2006). Soler and Miller (2003) and Sayeed and Guerin (2000) suggest that many professionals and politicians feel strongly about what is appropriate for young children and often have conflicting views about curricula. Melhuish and Petrogiannis (2006) argue that numerous social factors influence the content of a policy on early childhood care and education.

Curtis (1994) and Bennett, Wood and Rogers (1997) argue that play is at the heart of many international curricula but the way it is interpreted and understood may be quite different. Furthermore, 'research shows that there is an immense gap between the rhetoric and the reality of play being at the heart of the Early Years curriculum' (Fisher, 1996, p. 95). Bennett et al. (1997) point out that play is closely linked to learning but the pedagogical principles are often complicated and this frequently leads to misinterpretations. Fisher (1996) strongly argues that regardless of any complications, play should be regarded as a necessity in early childhood and its status should be guaranteed by everyone.

A New Zealand perspective

The 'Te Whāriki' (the woven mat, Figure 3.1) Early Years curriculum has recently been established as the first national curriculum guidance, aimed at children aged between 0 and 5 years in New Zealand (Ministry of Education, 1996). Guidance is given throughout the document for infants, toddlers and young children and consists of principles (four), strands (five) and goals. Each strand has goals with specific learning outcomes. For example, the first goal in strand five, known as 'Exploration', states that 'children experience an environment where their play is valued as meaningful learning and the importance of spontaneous play is recognised' (Ministry of Education, 1996, p. 16).

In New Zealand, practitioners are expected to have a thorough understanding of play and are able to facilitate it by careful intervention. Practitioners believe that children learn by being actively involved in tasks, socializing with others,

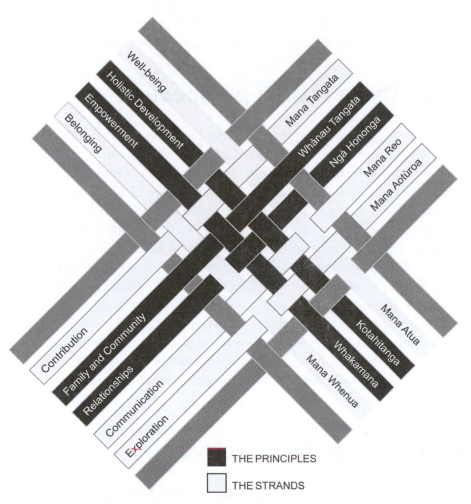

THE PRINCIPLES

THE STRANDS

Figure 3.1 Te Whāriki Principles and Strands (http://www.education.govt.nz/early-childhood/teaching-and-learning/ece-curriculum/te-whariki/principles-strands-goals/). Published by the New Zealand Ministry of Education, copyright © Crown.

questioning ideas and events and by using resources in a creative and innovative way (Ministry of Education, 1996).

The 'Te Whāriki' curriculum document states that 'a reference library should be available for both children and adults as well as information for parents on … the value of play in learning and development' (Ministry of Education, 1996, p. 83). It is widely known that in many countries parents acknowledge that children play but they don't always appreciate that their child is capable of learning through play (Curtis, 1994). Both the New Zealand and Italian approaches place greater emphasis on working with and building positive relationships with families, perhaps because they understand that when parents are more involved the quality of play is improved and enhanced (Sayeed and Guerin, 2000). Especially in the early years, it is unquestionable that Italian society places high expectations on parenting (Musatti, 2006).

A Northern Italian perspective

The Italian 'Reggio Emilia' approach was founded in 1963 by Loris Malaguzzi and caters for children from birth to 6 years of age (Abbott and Nutbrown, 2001). Reggio Emilia (a city near Parma in Northern Italy) practice began in 1945 when the Second World War ended and it was generally felt that children needed to be educated to understand democracy and act as innovative thinkers (New, 2000). The contributing educator, Loris Malaguzzi, mirrored John Dewey's main principles: effective collaboration between adult and child, active participation and worthwhile involvement in the learning and thinking process (Soler and Miller, 2003). New (2000) explains that play is highly regarded as promoting holistic development. However, it is not any more significant than the long-term projects that the children get involved with. Play is viewed equally alongside drawing, drama, movement and painting, and documentation, such as, photos, videos and paintings, help children remember what they have done and can be revisited at any time for any reason (Edwards et al., 1998) which is similar to the 'High/Scope' model where children are encouraged to review their work.

An American perspective

The 'High/Scope' approach (Figure 4, below) is based on three main concepts: planning, doing and reviewing. The children are encouraged to plan their own activities, carry them out and reflect on them with others (Schweinhart et al., 1993). It is thought that when children are given opportunities to choose activities, learning becomes more meaningful and memorable (Bennett et al., 1997). The High/Scope model originated in North America in 1962 and was founded by Dr Weikart. Essentially, 'it is a philosophy of Early Years education comprising a developmentally appropriate curriculum which advocates active learning' (Northern Ireland Childminding Association (NICMA), 2004, p. 2). The model highlights the importance of the process of play (Moyles, 1989; NICMA, 2004).

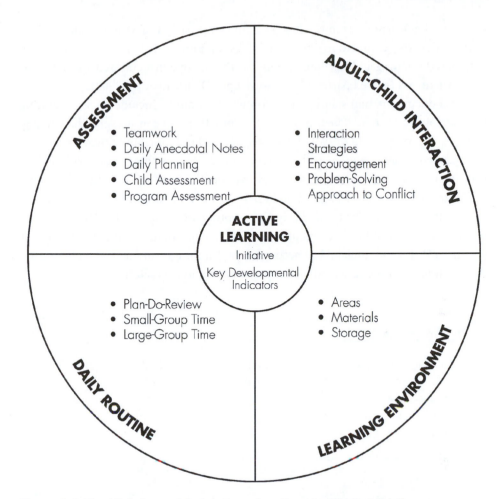

Figure 3.2 The High Scope Model. From Ann Epstein (2014), 'HighScope Preschool Wheel of Learning', in *Essentials of Active Learning in Preschool: Getting to Know the HighScope Curriculum,* 2nd edn, Ypsilanti, MI: HighScope Press, p 9. © 2014 HighScope Educational Research Foundation. Used with permission.

A Welsh perspective

The Foundation Phase in Wales for 3- to 7-year-olds, which was rolled out between 2008 and 2011, regards 'play' as a fundamental, meaningful aspect of the curriculum. It emphasizes the importance of play being understood by all stakeholders and that it should be recognized and accepted as an essential element of a curriculum for young children (WAG, 2008b). However, the *Play/Active Learning* document appears to refer more frequently to the adult planning children's play rather than supporting or facilitating learning, as in the Reggio Emilia approach. Clarke and Waller (2007) suggest that the Foundation Phase in Wales supports a balanced programme of play-based teaching and learning activities with the hope that children are viewed as co-constructors (shared partners) of knowledge (Dahlberg et al., 2007).

WAG documentation states that 'children's ideas can be included when planning topics/projects' (WAG, 2008a, p. 13), yet in practice this can be very challenging. Interestingly, on page 13 of *Play/Active Learning* a developmentally staged approach is described, where children will progress and move at different rates within their learning (WAG, 2008b). First, this implies a view of the child as a scientific object that moves through biological stages (Dahlberg et al., 2007), and second, it implies a 'step ladder' approach, similar to the Early Years Foundation Stage in England and very different to the Te Whāriki curriculum. Welch (2008) points out that the particular system in Wales and England has 'accountability' at the core of the curriculum rather than a child's best interests, individual personality and characteristics.

Reflective task

If you are working within the Foundation Phase, reflect on what is at the heart of your practice. Insert the important features of your practice in the concentric circles. Decide what will help you improve your work with children and what hinders your practice. The child should be in the centre circle.

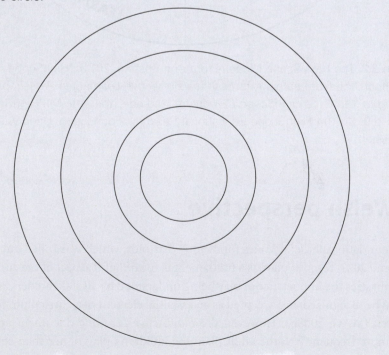

The Foundation Phase has been developed from ideas and features from the Italian Reggio Emilia approach, the New Zealand Te Whāriki curriculum and the North American High/Scope model (Siraj-Blatchford et al., 2005), but it is thought that practitioners both in the UK and the USA tend to manipulate the play in which they engage with young children, in contrast to the practice in mainland Europe where adults have less of a tendency to dominate and control play (Kalliala, 2004). Possibly this is because in Europe 'play is considered to be such an educationally powerful process that learning will occur spontaneously, even if an adult is not present' (Bennett et al., 1997, p. 1).

The Welsh Government advocates a play-based curriculum in the Foundation Phase where children should have equal opportunities both indoors and outdoors, yet this has been challenging for some settings. Estyn (2011) report the following in evaluating outdoor learning in the Foundation Phase:

> Most schools and settings are making at least adequate use of the outdoors … In most cases, children's enjoyment, wellbeing, behaviour, knowledge and understanding of the world, and their physical development improve, as a result of using the outdoors. However, the outdoors is not used enough to develop children's reading and writing, Welsh language, creativity, or their ability to use information and communication technology (ICT).
>
> (Estyn, 2011, p. 1)

They further report that:

> Teachers tend to assess children's learning less often and less well outdoors than indoors. They do not track the progress children make in developing their skills outdoors well enough. With children spending more time outdoors, this means that important milestones in their development may be missed.
>
> (Estyn, 2011, p. 1)

Estyn also comment on leadership and learning in the outdoors, observing that 'the vision of leaders and their commitment to making the best use of outdoor learning are key factors in overcoming obstacles [and] a few schools and settings are sceptical about the benefits of outdoor learning for children' (Estyn, 2011, p. 2).

More recent findings from the Welsh Government's three-year evaluation linked to the outdoor environment found that children were observed outside more regularly by teaching assistants than teachers and that children said they rarely did any learning outside (Rhys et al., 2014b).

Experiencing the outdoors

Williams-Siegfredson (2005) strongly believes that playing outdoors aids a happy and healthy childhood and experimenting with mud, looking for minibeasts, taking risks and climbing are genuine learning experiences (Hammond, 2007) and for young children 'desirable equipment experiences include swinging, sliding, spinning, springing and scrambling or climbing' (McConaghy, 2008, p. 18). Jenkinson (2001) explains that diabetes and asthma could be increasing because children do not have enough exposure to the microbacteria in mud. A study carried out at the University of Reading by Professor Derek Clements-Croome found that the higher the levels of carbon dioxide in the classroom the slower the reaction times from the children, and they tended to be drowsier and were less likely to complete difficult tasks because the classroom was simply too hot and stuffy (Bilton, 2010). The study concluded that carbon dioxide and heat levels needed monitoring in classrooms to help improve performance. Therefore, being outside in the fresh air can have many health benefits (Bilton, 2010).

Maynard (2007a) explains that free-flow access to the outdoors which the Welsh Government advocates is meaningless unless it is combined with well-trained, competent, knowledgeable and enthusiastic staff (Ryder-Richardson, 2006) and this is the key to recognizing the potential of a natural outdoor environment. There are significant physical differences between the indoor and outdoor learning environments, the outdoors offering children quality, first-hand sensory (weather) experiences and freedom to move and explore (Ryder-Richardson, 2006; Tovey, 2007).

Play spaces

Jenkinson (2001) claims that practitioners need to look closer at what children do and how they utilize their space and respect what they see, and that they should regularly review the outdoor play space to gain a feel for its success and observe children focusing on the range of play types, the most and least favourite play resources or equipment and the way the children change or adapt their outdoor play space (Casey, 2007). Ultimately, practitioners should 'develop qualities reflecting eagerness, energy, curiosity and playfulness' (Clements, 2004, p. 77). It could be argued that to develop such qualities in young children, adults need to be well trained and knowledgeable about child development. Joyce (2012) argues that 'people who work with young children have to be highly trained ... this is a prerequisite to quality care' (p. 80). Consider at this point your training to date. If you are in a managerial role then consider how well trained your staff are.

Moore (1986) suggests that it is pointless making decisions about resources and allocating money to equipment when practitioners have not considered what the children enjoy doing, where they play and the reasons for their play. What is worrying is that those children engaged in play tend not to be observed or noticed by staff (Bishop and Curtis, 2001). Ward (1990) reminds us that practitioners will assign play areas but undoubtedly children will not use it as planned, and Clements (2004) states that one of the most valuable outdoor experiences for children is when they choose their agenda, which leads to fulfilment and motivation. According to Casey (2007), children are very good at utilizing play equipment correctly to please adults but very quickly revert to using equipment in a different manner. It has been suggested that 'the landscape might have a functional impact on children's behaviour and play performance' (Fjørtoft, 2001, p. 115). Corsaro (1997) explains that children are persistent in climbing to the top of structures and have a desire to be bigger, which allows them to look down on adults so they can regain power. He also suggests that children prefer climbing-type structures because of their unique size, a factor that does not permit adults to use them. In 2009, one of the authors conducted a study as part of a Master's thesis where nursery and reception children were asked to photograph their favourite aspects of their outdoor play, and the most popular categories of photographs taken by the children turned out to be the climbing and fixed structures. This may suggest that the children were regaining power by climbing high and using fixed structures that were not permitted for use by adults. It is known that 'children's time and space are increasingly organised by adults in homes, nurseries and schools, public streets and leisure spaces' (Alderson, 2008, p. 211).

In 2005, Alison Clark and Peter Moss conducted a study with 3- and 4-year-olds to investigate the use of outdoor provision. They state very clearly at the beginning of their study how the children are viewed, for example as 'experts in their own lives … skilful communicators … rights holders and as … meaning-makers' (Clark et al., 2005, p. 5). Furthermore, children are listened to and become involved as active participants in the research and are viewed as 'beings' rather than 'becomings' (Clark and Moss, 2001). A key component of the approach is the aim of achieving a balance of power between adults and children (Clark and Moss, 2005). This particular way of viewing the child is at the heart of the Reggio Emilia approach, and the contributing educator, Loris Malaguzzi, mirrored John Dewey's main principles: effective collaboration between adult and child, active participation and worthwhile involvement in the learning and thinking process (Soler and Miller, 2003).

Clark Kjorhølt and Moss (2005) explicitly discuss Reggio Emilia preschools when mentioning the child as a 'skilful communicator' and place strong emphasis on the adult helping the child present their feelings through a variety of media. This particular approach allowed Clark et al. to gain an insight into the perspectives of children in Early Years settings by using creative and innovative ways of collecting data. The approach they developed is known as the 'Mosaic approach' (Clark et al., 2005). A key component of this approach is viewing children as rights holders with a particular focus on two particular elements of the United Nations Convention on the Rights of the Child (UNCRC): Article 12 (the right to express views freely if capable of doing so) and Article 13 (the right to a range of media to receive information and the right to express ideas in any form chosen by the child) (Clark et al., 2005). However, many adults find it difficult to accept that young children have rights (Alexander, 1995) and the UNCRC is not yet thought about by many people because the way a child is viewed is often very traditional (without rights) (Casas, 1997). Unfortunately, 'the welfare model of childcare has perpetuated the view that children lack the capacity to contribute to their own well-being or do not have a valid and valuable contribution to make' (Lansdown, 2001, p. 93).

Understanding pedagogy

Tovey explains that the key issue about quality outdoor play is not the physical environment but rather the pedagogy (Tovey, 2007), which is the relationship between the learner (child) and pedagogue (trained adult) (WAG, 2008a). Pedagogy can also be defined as 'the performance of teaching together with the theories, beliefs, policies and controversies that inform and shape it' (Alexander, 2000, p. 540). Moreover, the way children and the curriculum are viewed determines the provision, care and pedagogy of an Early Years setting (Dahlberg et al., 2007). Rosaleen Joyce (2012) states that there has been much debate about whether pedagogy actually exists in the UK! She continues to argue that there appears to be no pedagogical discourse or engagement compared to Sweden: 'Pedagogy, sustained critical thinking about practice, needs to be at the centre not the periphery of education' (Joyce, 2012, p. 102). The authors often wonder what *is* at the core of Early Years practice in Wales. Put simply, what do practitioners (and other stakeholders) value in their practice and what is really at the heart of what they do? Huggins and Wickett (2011) argue that what is needed is a 'shared effective pedagogy for the outdoor learning environment' (p. 30). Furthermore, the recent three-year evaluation report about the Foundation Phase by Maynard et al. (2013b) suggested that adults tend to have different expectations of children when they play outdoors, with adults being more at ease.

Reflective task

?

If you are working within a Foundation Phase setting, consider as a team your shared pedagogy for the outdoor learning environment. First, individually write down your vision for outdoor play, and second, compare the responses. Last, write collaboratively your pedagogy for outdoor learning and share it with parents and other staff (e.g. Key Stage 2 if you work in a primary school). You may like to share your values and beliefs in a policy and consider evaluating your policy (or writing one) on outdoor play provision in your setting. In 2005, two organizations (Early Education and Learning Through Landscapes) conducted a survey to gain an insight into outdoor provision in the UK. Of the 620 responses that were analysed, less than a third currently had a policy on outdoor provision and just under 55 per cent communicated that they had undergone training linked to play provision outdoors.

The Foundation Phase documentation implies that learning in the outdoors should be a significant characteristic of an Early Years curriculum as well as free-flow access between the indoors and outdoors, and is beneficial to holistic development, health and well-being (WAG, 2008b). It claims that 'the importance of outdoor play to health, development and learning is well recognised' (WAG, 2008b, p. 34). However, there is a general perception that the outdoors is good for our health but the benefits linked to outdoor play and specific play areas are under-researched (Muñoz, 2009). Siraj-Blatchford et al. (2005) remind us that one of the main principles under-lying the Foundation Phase is ensuring that a well-planned learning environment outdoors is provided.

For learning to take place outside, settings must have clear, focused aims and well-planned activities which would apply to any learning environment regardless if it is inside or outside (Ouvry, 2003). It is thought that 'adult planning, structuring and sometimes directing children's first-hand experiences outdoors is essential' (Tovey, 2007, p. 122), and Bilton (2010) asserts that it is unacceptable to have planning (written) for indoor provision and not to have it for outdoor provision. The kind of thought processes that practitioners go through for planning and providing learning opportunities indoors should be applied to the outdoors (Edgington, 2003).

Edgington (2003) continues to claim that *all* practitioners should have positive attitudes towards outdoor play, be *willing* to get involved with the children and plan for learning to take place *as they would inside*. Ouvry (2003) explains that the outdoor environment is best utilized when staff have a shared understanding about the importance and use of the outdoors and have an awareness of their role in developing learning. The inside and the outside environment needs to be viewed in the same way by staff, as denying one to children would be depriving them of that environment and it is their right to have access to both environments (Bilton, 2010).

Challenges and barriers to outdoor play

An evaluation report about the implementation of the Foundation Phase in Wales, conducted by Siraj-Blatchford et al. (2005), found that the outdoor environment was utilized more because of the increased number of adults within their setting. They further reported that the majority of practitioners had interpreted the term 'active' as physically active and made more changes to their practice outdoors. Comment was also made on the terminology used in the Foundation Phase and highlighted that the 'outdoor classroom' is often misunderstood and misrepresented. One of the difficulties that settings faced in meeting the requirements of the Foundation Phase (during the pilot) was providing outdoor experiences in all weathers. Interestingly, Estyn (2007) reported three years after the Foundation Phase had been piloted (in forty-two settings) that outdoor play was occurring more frequently since the start of the initiative, but in most settings practitioners were not convinced of the benefits and worried about dealing with parental concerns about children being outside in poor weather.

A few documents have been produced by the Welsh Government to support practitioners in settings. For example, in 2007 the Welsh Assembly Government published a document titled *Out of classroom learning: Making the most of first hand experiences of the natural environment* aimed at motivating staff and helping them understand the learning potential of an outdoor environment. The document, if used successfully, aims to construct more 'active and sustainable citizens' (WAG, 2007). In 2009, *The Foundation Phase Outdoor Learning Handbook* was produced and provides guidance to all staff working with 3- to 7-year-olds on making the best use of their outdoor learning environment. It is a useful handbook that covers a range of topics from managing risk, the benefits of outdoor learning, the forest school approach and general issues relating to organization and storage of resources.

Weather

Parents and practitioners often blame the weather for children getting colds, yet research suggests that 'cold viruses do not live in fresh air, they live in us' (Bilton, 2010, p. 18). A study carried out at the Common Cold Centre in Cardiff in 2005 suggested that when someone gets chilled they are twice as likely to get a cold, therefore it is imperative that when children play outdoors in very cold weather they are dressed in warm clothing to prevent getting chilled. It seems appropriate here to state a famous Nordic saying, that 'there is no such thing as bad weather, only bad clothing' (Joyce, 2012, p. 105).

Non-committed staff

Bilton (2010, p. 102) strongly states that 'if you are more concerned with the state of your nails, the straightness of your hair or the height of your heels, then go and do something else'. Edgington (2003, cited in Bilton, 2010) asserts that 'if you are not interested in outdoor play you should not even consider working with young children' (p. 102). All staff should be supportive of outdoor play if it is going to be successful. Problems may arise if staff do not understand their role when outside. Findings from a Master's thesis in 2009 clearly showed that staff understood and viewed outdoor play differently and it was expressed that not all staff were positive about outdoor play and did not work together, which may be explained by discussing some of Janet Moyles' ideas in her paper entitled 'Passion, Paradox and Professionalism'.

Moyles (2001) suggests that when staff feel pressured into continuously justifying and explaining the value of outdoor play to other professionals and parents they start to lose their passion and eventually sink into the 'black hole' (the centre of a concentric circle). She further suggests that staff should allocate time to discuss issues that evoke thoughts and feelings, but many settings do not allocate time to reflect (MacNaughton, 2005). Brunson Phillips and Bredekamp (1998) remind us that time for professional development is an important feature of Reggio Emilia practice in Northern Italy, where practitioners become involved in meaningful discussion about their daily work with children. Tovey (2007) suggests that staff need to be prepared to confront their judgements and their rigid views about children's play. However, to do this 'it requires high levels of professional knowledge coupled with self-esteem, self-confidence, paradoxically lacking in many early years, female practitioners' (Moyles, 2001, p. 89). A comment about 'better suited staff' was focused on improving the outdoor learning, possibly suggesting that staff need to show a more passionate understanding or require further professional training (or both), which might make them 'better suited'. There is always the potential for disagreements, lack of commitment and vision and uncertainty when discussing outdoor play (Ouvry, 2003). There was an obvious tension between members of staff relating to their feelings about outdoor play, particularly about team work and the organization, planning and management of resources, which were reflected in the results. Overton (2009) suggests that staff tend to feel disempowered, devalued and disheartened by other staff members' deliberate or inadvertent actions towards (in this case) outdoor play.

According to Huggins and Wickett (2011, p. 28), 'practitioners with a deep knowledge of child development and an understanding of the ways that very young children learn most effectively will be able to see the unique potential in any outdoor learning environment'. This implies that practitioners who do not have a deep understanding of child development also do not fully understand the benefits of children learning outdoors. In 2006, a study carried out by Waite and Rea (cited in Waite and Pratt, 2011) found that staff demonstrated a lack of understanding and awareness of the outdoor environment in Welsh schools. Furthermore, in 2011, Estyn urgently reported that schools, settings and Local Authorities need to provide training for *all* staff so they become knowledgeable and confident about the benefits of learning in the outdoors. Therefore, it could be questioned whether *all* practitioners working within the Foundation Phase have a deep knowledge of child development. The report further stated that 'Senior leaders and managers have not always received enough training on the Foundation Phase to identify good practice, challenge less effective practice, or make cost-effective decisions on improving outdoor provision and facilities' (Estyn, 2011, p. 1). Similarly, a point was made two centuries ago about effective training by Froebel and Pestalozzi who argued that to make full use of the outdoors, practitioners needed to be well trained and educated about the benefits of the outdoors (Joyce, 2012).

Organization

Timetabling play outdoors and interrupted play outdoors can often hinder the learning that takes place. Bilton (2010) reminds us that it can be very frustrating having started something and being engrossed with what we are doing to then be told by someone to stop; at times it can be very difficult to return to the task in question. The concern that Helen Bilton (2010) has is that children spend far too much time revisiting activities rather than spending valuable time in learning new concepts and developing and refining skills and it is thought that children's skills may regress as a result. Observations from an Master's thesis in 2009 showed that practitioners adopted a behaviourist approach to outdoor play because they decided on the amount of time children played outside, dominated by learning goals, outcomes and intentions of the adult – inevitably more interruptions occurred. By contrast, with a social constructionist approach the time could have been negotiated with children who could have then decided whether to continue to rest, work or play (MacNaughton, 2003). Huggins and Wickett (2011) argue that 'children need long periods of uninterrupted time in order for them to become engrossed in their play and learning' (p. 37). Timetabling play outdoors can give children clear messages about how staff value outdoor play. Consider the example below, written from a child's point of view, and how having free-flow access could improve the children's learning experiences.

Case study

I arrived at school at 9 a.m. and everyone seemed really happy. I saw Harry and we played with the cars before Mrs Control called us to the carpet at 9.30 a.m. We had register time and then a story, but a spider making its web just outside the window caught my eye and I couldn't wait to go out and watch it more closely and find more spiders. 'What was your favourite part of the story?' asked Mrs Control. I simply shrugged my shoulders as I didn't have a favourite part. 'Try to listen more carefully next time' she said sternly. Yellow group was called and that was me for maths. We were asked to count the plastic animals and find the number on the card. I asked Mrs Domino, 'Do you have spiders I can count instead.' I wanted to know more about spiders and I really wanted to go outside. When I finished, Mrs Domino said, 'You can go and choose now.' I wanted to play with Harry but he was still working with Mrs Control and she was getting cross with him. I decided to watch the spider at the window and wait for Harry. Then it started to rain and I thought it would be great not only to find spiders but go out in the rain and find spiders. Mrs Control started singing the tidy up song and told us 'It's raining, no playtime today, line up for the hall.' I never got to play with Harry, or find spiders or go out in the rain – I hate school sometimes.

Bilton (2010) states that it is cruel to tell children they can go off and play when they have finished their work, as she worries about the child who never actually gets to finish their work and consequently never gets to play! It has been stated that 'if we truly cared for children we would keep them away from schools altogether and just allow them to play' (Joyce, 2012, p. 23).

Access

Good practice is free-flow easy access to the outdoor environment, but this is not always possible (because historically outdoor spaces have been changed or adapted to save money and the indoor classroom prioritized), and staff need to work together to find a solution. According to Bilton (2010), unless there is a will to make something work then it will not happen.

A Scandinavian perspective

Garrick (2004) points out that locally there is a significant difference between settings in relation to quality resources, staff training, daily use and learning opportunities offered outdoors, and on an international level 'the significance of outdoor play and learning is not universally recognised' (Garrick, 2004, p. 2). It should be stated again that 'getting a broader perspective, looking at international patterns and keys to success, is important but there is no blue print' (Tornberg and Lindholm, 2009, p. 33). Apparently, early childhood education and care in Sweden is known throughout the world to offer exemplar practice (Martin Korpi, 2007) and according to Melhuish and Petrogiannis (2006, p. 2) 'their Early Childhood Care and Education is amongst the most developed in the world'; so for this reason we will give some consideration to the Scandinavian countries (Norway, Sweden, Denmark, Finland and Iceland).

It is worth noting that Early Years education and care in Nordic countries is financed differently to that of the UK, and practitioners are well trained, often to Master's level, and autonomy is welcomed within the system. The government does not provide prescriptive guidelines, and settings are trusted to provide a curriculum that is unique, with both practitioners and parents expected to evaluate its effectiveness (Penn, 2008). Joyce (2012) claims that the Swedish system strives towards meeting goals whereas in the UK, goals have to be met. According to Einarsdottir and Wagner (2006), the perception of early childhood in Nordic countries is embedded in cultural, historical, social and economic traditions. Joyce (2012, p. 8) argues that 'the Norwegian approach is culturally specific and not readily transferable ... being outdoors is an important part of being Norwegian'. This is an extremely important point when considering some of the challenges and barriers that have been discussed above.

One of the focal theories of the Danish Early Years curriculum is the development of competency in children, and regular access to outdoor play helps to achieve this (Williams-Siegfredson, 2005). Forest School is a new initiative that is growing fast in Wales but which originated in Denmark in the 1980s. It encourages children to take risks, work collaboratively, initiate ideas and become confident and competent learners (Knight, 2009). The adult's role in Forest School is to facilitate not to lead or dominate. A study carried out by Whitebread in 2008 (cited in Bilton, 2010) found that children who were instructed to do things were less inventive, less creative and became disinterested and demotivated, whereas children who were allowed to play freely and initiate ideas were more creative, successful and motivated. 'Forest School is an inspirational process that offers children … regular opportunities to … develop confidence and self-esteem through hands on learning experiences in a local woodland' (Forestry Commission, 2001, p. 3). Maynard (2007b) suggests that the growing interest in Forest School in the UK could be related to the decline in children's play.

In Finland there is a significant focus on developing self-esteem, self-confidence and a child's personal and social development rather than formal academic learning outcomes (Niikko, 2006). In Sweden, children are encouraged to discuss with staff what they would like to do, investigate or learn more about, and there is a very strong emphasis on listening to the child and respecting them. It is very common in Sweden for children to choose whether they want to spend most of their day outside or inside (Sheridan and Pramling Samuelsson, 2001). Their ideology is 'believing that teaching is not merely the transmission of knowledge, but that the teacher is a facilitator of the child's learning' (Bennett, 2001, p. 1). The term 'facilitator' is echoed within the Foundation Phase.

Similarly, Fjørtoft (2001) explains that there are preschools in Scandinavia that allow children to spend most or all of their time outside in a natural learning environment because it is believed that children benefit from physical strength and stamina and imaginative and social play. In Iceland, 'children play outdoors in every type of weather for 1–4 hours daily' (Einarsdottir, 2006, p. 169). When Johanna Einarsdottir conducted an ethnographic study in Iceland, she concluded that outdoor play was an integral aspect of the curriculum where children are mainly encouraged to exercise and have freedom to play. Climbing trees, swinging from branches and using tools such as sharp knives, drills, saws and hammers are activities associated with a Nordic childhood. More importantly, children are trusted to be competent beings (Einarsdottir and Wagner, 2006).

Interestingly, Einarsdottir and Wagner (2006) compare a Nordic childhood with an American one and explain that early American childhood experiences are governed by practitioners who take on the role of the 'boundary police'. Einarsdottir and Wagner (2006) further suggest that when an environment is surrounded by fearful staff, accidents are more likely to happen. There is a strong belief in democracy and equality in the Nordic countries (Niikko, 2006) and much of the tradition is about valuing children's perspectives and viewing them as co-constructors (shared partners) of knowledge and experts in their own lives. Furthermore, children become actively involved in a democratic society before the age of eighteen (Broström, 2006).

Comparison of approaches

Gonzalez-Mena (1993) and Freeman (1998) point out that Eastern cultures (China) promote collaboration with others, teamwork and making connections with society whereas Western cultures (USA, UK, New Zealand and Italy) are keen to encourage individuality, independence, personal progress and achievement. However, it is worth noting what Lilian Katz reports: 'I am always amazed at the similarities across countries … at least in the field of early childhood education; [the] low status, low pay, and poor or insufficient training that is commonly found' (Katz, 1999, p. 1).

O'Keefe (2001) describes her impressions and views of early childhood education in China and mentions that when children are given opportunities to play freely the most obvious feature was spontaneity of actions and movements. She also writes that in China there seemed to be more structured, teacher-led activities, larger classes, and a distinct difference between teaching art in China and in the USA. However, she concluded on a positive note: 'I think we have a lot to learn from each other and it is clear that we care deeply about our children and want them to have the best learning experiences' (O'Keefe, 2001, p. 3).

Bottery (1990) suggests four main models of the school education system and points out that a 'child-centred' approach and 'social-reconstruction' model (adopted mainly in Reggio Emilia and High/Scope approaches) disregard the needs of society, and by encouraging children to focus on their personal interests creates a narrow Early Years curriculum. In China, Bottery (1990) links school education to the Gross National Product (GNP) model where the main focus is on training children to match the needs of the economy, with the interests of the children often ignored and forgotten.

When Nancy Freeman (1998) visited China she observed children acting like robots: everyone was working on and completing exactly the same activity with little room for creatively or individuality. She pointed out that 'teachers expected conformity and a willingness to work toward the completion of a task that was chosen by the teacher rather than the child' (Freeman, 1998, p. 1). Shenglan (2006) describes a typical day at a Chinese kindergarten and notes that children would generally start at 7.50 a.m. and finish at 4.00 p.m. with a very structured timetable in between, and it is made clear that the children only have one hour 'free activity' in an eight-hour day. This seems significantly different from Reggio Emilia and High/Scope practice where children are immersed in a child-initiated environment and free from an adult play agenda. However, Freeman (1998) highlights the importance of being non-judgmental when observing practice that seems very different.

Reggio Emilia and High/Scope are quite different to the other approaches in that they do not have a framework or formalized component with determined outcomes (Soler and Miller, 2003). Schweinhart et al. (1993, p. 34) explain that the High/Scope approach offers 'an open framework of educational ideas and practices based on the natural development of young children'. In contrast, the Reggio Emilia approach is based upon underlying principles of socio-cultural values and beliefs and is predominantly community based and supported by local people and government, which some may think offers a limited view of the wider world (Soler and Miller, 2003).

Role of the adult (pedagogue)

The role of the adult and the way children are viewed by adults differ significantly across the various approaches. For example, the Italians tend to view the child as an active social participant (with rights) rather than an empty vessel to be filled (Soler and Miller, 2003), or as Dahlberg et al. (2007) would suggest, as a co-constructor of knowledge. Their role is to work alongside the children over long periods of time and facilitate their learning. Adults ensure that children 'rise to new challenges … [and] express themselves in ways that are more creative, more communicative, and more thoughtful' (Tarini and White, 1998, p. 178). When one of the authors visited a Reggio Emilia setting, all the children aged between one and five seemed very independent – for example in making choices, getting dressed and eating. They had many opportunities to think for themselves, be creative and utilize resources, and appeared happy and calm. In Reggio Emilia the child is viewed as a powerful partner who 'actively co-constructs' the content of the curriculum with a more able 'other' (Soler and Miller, 2003, p. 66). The preschool children were mainly engaged in child-initiated tasks, and the relationship between adult and child seemed very positive. It is thought that when children are given opportunities to choose activities, learning becomes more meaningful and memorable (Bennett et al., 1997). Alderson (2008) reminds us that Reggio Emilia practices are widely discussed but are not adapted or copied in other parts of the world because of the economic, political and social power structures, which refuse to admit that children are talented, experienced, knowledgeable and creative.

Visiting a Reggio Emilia setting confirmed the author's understanding of the importance of valuing, respecting and working with children. Moyles (1989) suggests that teachers should take into account what is written in a prescribed curriculum but ultimately use their knowledge of child development, research and practice and do what they believe is right for the children in their care. The field trip motivated the author to improve her own practice as an Early Years teacher and challenge current practice, views and ideas in the UK, particularly Wales. For example, the structure of the day for young children, the way we view childhood and understand the true meaning of child-initiated learning were some of the main aspects to reflect upon. Moyles (1989) reminds us that there will always be some who refuse to consider play and education in the same sentence. She also points out that change does not happen immediately and takes time. Also, in light of the visit, the author thought considerably about her title as 'teacher' and whether it has been misunderstood (by so many) and instead should she be thinking of herself as facilitator of young children's learning as defined in the WAG documentation: '[C]entral to the Foundation Phase approach is the practitioner as a facilitator of learning, with the child at the heart of learning and teaching' (WAG, 2008a, p. 12).

The High/Scope model is based on ideas of Piaget where practitioners should stand back and observe and monitor progress to extend children's learning through play (Schweinhart et al., 1993). Piaget mainly saw the adult as an observer, interacting when appropriate knowledge had been constructed, and thought that play facilitated cognitive development, whereas Vygotsky and Bruner proposed that social interaction and playing with others aided learning and viewed adults as active participants, celebrating and embracing socialization (Bennett et al., 1997). It is thought that the Te Whāriki curriculum is underpinned by Vygotsky's view of childhood, learning and teaching (Soler and Miller, 2003), and according to Dahlberg et al. (2007), practitioners view the child as a knowledge, identity and culture reproducer.

The New Zealand Early Years curriculum is a combination of two cultures (bicultural) – Māori and Pakeha – a holistic view of the child and a child-centred view (Soler and Miller, 2003). Similarly, in Wales there is the bilingual dimension, where 'children should appreciate the different languages ... and gain a sense of belonging to Wales, and understand the Welsh heritage, literature and arts as well as the language' (WAG, 2008a, p. 39). Recent findings from the three-year evaluation highlighted that '42% of Foundation Phase leaders believed that the introduction of the Foundation Phase had meant an improvement in developing children's Welsh language skills' (Rhys et al., 2014c, p. 1). Rhys et al. further report that 'incidental Welsh was prevalent in the majority of English-medium schools, and was present verbally (e.g. at lunchtime) as well as non-verbally (e.g. on wall displays) around the school'. The report also found that English-medium schools tended to develop children's Welsh language skills explicitly rather than integrated across the curriculum (Rhys et al., 2014c, p. 1).

The Early Years curriculum in Wales and New Zealand has been developed in relation to a National Curriculum in primary schools (Soler and Miller, 2003), with an essential focus on play. It appears that both the Te Whāriki and Foundation Phase have prescribed goals and targets in place for children to achieve, contrary to the Reggio Emilia and High/Scope approaches. Soler and Miller (2003) suggest that when a curriculum is predominantly prescribed then children become less active, less involved in sharing their thoughts and ideas and have less power to co-construct a curriculum. It is concerning that England *still* has a prescribed National Curriculum in place for its youngest learners at age five and does not advocate a play-based curriculum. Therefore, the role of the adult in providing a playful pedagogy within the National Curriculum will depend on the quality of the training and knowledge and understanding of the staff. The Early Years Foundation Stage in England (for children aged 0 to 5) advocates that children's play should be purposeful, and consists of adult-led and child-led activities. It states that 'play is essential for children's development [and] children learn by leading their own play' (DfE, 2014, p. 9). This is a very similar message to that of the Foundation Phase in Wales, yet it does not apply to children aged five and above in England.

There is a view that in the UK the services that are provided and available for young children are essentially associated with a lack of status for professionals, a poor understanding of children's development and a limited view of childhood (Alexander, 1995). Apparently, 'if the field of early education is to advance in any innovative, creative manner, we need to be intellectually involved in imagining different existences, constructing multiple new identities, while thinking well beyond where we are right now' (Johnson, 1999, p. 74).

Conclusion

It would appear that the Foundation Phase has developed some of its ideologies from other international approaches, and the focus on delaying formal approaches to learning until around the age of seven is evident in many European models. Play is a very controversial concept and the way it is understood varies across cultures, but essentially the ideologies that are applied depend on how governments and societies view early childhood education and care. It is clear that the role and status of play is underpinned by how childhood is constructed. Indoor and outdoor play experiences should be provided for children by staff who value them both equally, and this is something that the Welsh Government advocates in the Foundation Phase. The challenge for practitioners in Wales is to rethink the value of play and consider how it can be used on a daily basis to facilitate children's learning. Essentially a curriculum that has been designed for young children should have a strong belief in play and if this is not a true underlying principle of a curriculum, then it is up to you if you are a practitioner to ensure this becomes a reality. Ultimately children, regardless of where they live, play, grow and develop, have a right to play.

Chapter summary

- Play as a concept is difficult to define and appears to be at the heart of international curricula, but the way it is interpreted may be quite different. Play is recognized as a tool for learning and teaching.
- Some international curricula are more prescribed than others, for example the Italian, American and Scandinavian models appear to have more flexibility and fewer constraints on children achieving specific goals than the models in Wales, New Zealand or England.
- Every learning area of the curriculum can be developed and enhanced outdoors, but for this to happen practitioners need to be knowledgeable, well trained, enthusiastic and willing to make a change in their practice so that the outdoors is viewed as equal to the indoors. This generally happens in Reggio Emilia and Scandinavian models.
- Children should be viewed as experts in their own lives, and practitioners should involve them in the process of changing, adapting or improving their play provision. This is a feature that could be strengthened within the Foundation Phase.

Access the following link online to take part in a short 'Where am I?' quiz about this chapter:

www.bloomsbury.com/an-introduction-to-the-foundation-phase-9781474264273

Thought-provoking questions

- How is play valued within your setting and is there a balance of child-initiated and adult-directed tasks provided to children during the day and/or week?
- What features from other curricula approaches discussed within this chapter could you adopt in your setting?
- What learning opportunities does your outdoor environment provide for the children you work with and is it comparable with the indoor environment?
- Do you and your team plan and observe for learning to take place outside?
- How often do you consult with the children in your setting about what they think about their learning environment?

Further reading and information

Bilton, H. (2010), *Outdoor Learning in the Early Years*. 3rd edn. London: Routledge.

Forest School research: http://www.forestry.gov.uk/forestry/infd-77ldzd.

Knight, S. (2011), *Risk and Adventure in Early Years Outdoor Play*. London: Sage.

Murray, R. and E. O'Brien (2006), 'A *Marvellous Opportunity for Children to Learn*': A Participatory Evaluation of Forest School in England and Wales. Forest Research, http://www.forestry.gov.uk/pdf/fr0112forestschoolsreport.pdf/$FILE/fr0112forestschoolsreport.pdf.

Perry Preschool research: https://www.ncjrs.gov/pdffiles1/ojjdp/181725.pdf.

Reggio Emilia visits : http://www.reggiochildren.it/?lang=en.

4

Characteristics of Effective
Classroom Practice

Chapter aims

To explore the importance of children's Social and Emotional Aspects of Learning (SEAL).

To explore the importance of working in partnership to improve children's outcomes.

To discuss the relevance of pupil voice, play and participation and the United Nations Convention on the Rights of the Child (UNCRC).

To explore what is needed for children to become effective thinkers.

Understanding SEAL

The Welsh Government advocates the use of specific interventions to promote **emotional literacy** such as SEAL (Social and Emotional Aspects of Learning) and PALs (Playing and Learning to socialize). Arguably, these initiatives allow children to build relationships and empathize with others, which links to personal and social development, well-being and cultural diversity, an Area of Learning which is (allegedly) at the heart of the Foundation Phase (WAG, 2008a). Supporting this, Daniel Goleman's theory states that if we understand our own feelings and the feelings of others, we can manage personal and social situations better (WAG, 2008a). This will lead to an increase in self-esteem, and learning and performance can be improved. However, Carol Craig (2009), who is Chief Executive for the Centre for Confidence and Well-being, discusses the work of an American psychologist Roy Baumeister. He set out to find the evidence that was missing in an explanation of self-esteem, and was most disappointed when he found that self-esteem was not linked to academic achievement. 'He also thought high self-esteem posed a larger threat to society, than low self-esteem' (Craig, 2009, p. 10).

The SEAL programme, designed to promote and develop children's social, emotional and behavioural skills (Hallam, 2009), is encouraged by policymakers and implemented in schools, but far too much time and money has been wasted on an intervention (£40 million between 2007 and 2011) that is based on very little supporting evidence (Craig, 2007). Craig (2007) states there are many aspects of the SEAL programme that could be very useful for children and young people, but disagrees with a universal teaching programme of social and emotional skills for all children. SEAL is a way of getting children to socially comply with a set of outcomes that outline the type of person they should become (Craig, 2007). What is more concerning is that:

> … the empirical data presented shows that SEAL had no impact on attendance and virtually no affect on academic performance. More worryingly, the empirical data presented on the impact on pupils shows that for most of the attitudes measured the results went down, not up, after the pilot, particularly for boys.
>
> (Craig, 2007, p. 7)

Despite an unsuccessful pilot, the DfES still went ahead and continued with the intervention (Craig, 2007). 'Government needs to be more realistic about what it can change and influence and what it cannot. This will lessen the chances that it will launch interventions which could be pointless or dangerous. Problems with young people's well-being are the result of an enormous number of social and cultural changes' asserts Craig (2007, p. 13). Craig (2007) cites the work of Bradshaw and points out that it is family breakdown that governments should be targeting not individual lessons on social and emotional skills. Her report (Craig, 2009) argues that there is no point in teaching universal emotional and social skills to children who do not need it. Morrison, Gutman and Feinstein (2008) state in their report that 'school characteristics can either exacerbate or buffer the interaction between different aspects of children's well-being' (p. 6) and therefore one intervention may not suit the needs of all schools. Humphrey et al. (2010) conducted a study into the SEAL (small group work) programme and found the intervention had a positive impact on children but the gains started to decline after a few weeks, which suggests the SEAL programme should be more intensive and carried out over a longer period of time.

Explicit teaching of SEAL – is this needed?

Craig (2009) discusses the work of Professor Martin Seligman and writes that:

> … as a psychologist he is aware that strong emotions such as anxiety, depression, and anger, exist for a purpose: they galvanize you into action to change yourself or your world, and by doing so to terminate the negative emotion. Inevitably, such feelings carry pain but they are an effective 'alarm system' which warns us of danger, loss, and trespass. So artificially trying to protect children from bad feelings will undermine their development, not aid it.
>
> (Craig, 2009, p. 11)

It appears there are those who support the explicit teaching of social and emotional skills that contribute to well-being for the short term and those that believe it is not the job of schools to take on the role of therapists, psychiatrists or psychologists. When Hallam (2009) carried out an evaluation of the SEAL programme she found that many school co-coordinators found it very challenging to understand the psychological concepts of the programme and this made the dissemination to other staff less effective. Hallam (2009) claims that 'teachers felt overwhelmed by the volume of material and this created stress and increased workload leading to inappropriate implementation of the programme' (p. 318). This finding supports the argument that educators are somewhat compelled to become psychiatrists or psychologists where the training has taken years, in comparison to an educator's training for SEAL which has taken weeks.

A service that is available for children in schools is Place2Be. This is a national charity that provides emotional support for children in schools. They work in partnership with a range of organizations and their website claims that 'the Place2Be team are leaders in the field of mental health and well-being and have a wealth of experience in counselling, education, child psychiatry and philanthropy' (Place2Be, 2015). Place2Be currently provide an 'integrated school based mental health service in 235 primary and secondary schools across England, Scotland and Wales' (Place2Be, 2015).

SEAL: Success or failure?

The question as to whether schools are actually helping or hindering children's holistic development when implementing interventions such as SEAL (by those often untrained) is a contentious one. Rones and Hoagward (2000; cited in Hallam, 2009) state that SEAL on its own is not effective; there are factors such as consistent implementation of the programme, input from parents, staff and peers and the integration of SEAL components into the daily curricula that make it more effective. This point was made in the National Assembly for Wales (NAfW) document *Everybody's Business* (2001), which states that 'a multifaceted programme is likely to be most effective, combining a classroom programme with changes to school ethos and school environment alongside family/community involvement' (NAfW, 2001, p. 58).

Parental involvement or parental engagement?

In 2008, the School Effectiveness Framework (SEF) was introduced by the Welsh Government to improve the learning outcomes and well-being of all children regardless of socio-economic background. They suggest that 'greater parental involvement in schools has a significant impact on pupils' well-being, which subsequently impacts on their learning and life chances' (WG, 2013b). This was also the case for a project funded by the Teaching and Learning Research Programme (TLRP), called the 'Home School Knowledge Exchange Programme' (HSKE), which found that when schools and parents worked more in partnership, attainments in literacy were higher than for those children who did not attend a HSKE school (TLRP, 2007). Morrison, Gutman and Feinstein (2008) also found in their study that well-being is more positive when there is more parental engagement. The Teacher Support Network (TSN) and Parentline Plus (PP) (charities) prepared a report entitled *Beyond the School Gate*, which advocated that every school should have access to a trained Parent Support worker who specifically deals with emotional and family issues. The report was published as a result of the volume of calls linked to concerns about parents and schools working together and a need to inform and improve policy (TSN and PP, 2007). There is a strong argument in the report about the distinct difference between 'parental engagement' and 'parental involvement', and the work of Harris and Goodhall (2007, p. 38) claims that 'what makes a difference to student achievement is not parental involvement in *schooling* but parental engagement in *learning* in the home'. It is believed that parental engagement has more impact on improving children's outcomes than parental involvement. Their findings from secondary schools found that when parents were actively engaged with their child's education there were significant gains in achievement.

Findings from Estyn on partnerships with parents

In a recent Estyn report it was stated that 'establishing closer links between home and school has a significant impact on learners' well-being' (Estyn, 2012a, p. 34). However, they state that it is a challenge in reaching some parents and engaging them with their child's education but in successful schools there are multimodal forms of communication and that one of the most effective ways of engaging parents is face-to-face contact (Estyn, 2012a). Also in 2012, Estyn produced a 'Best practice' flyer on a pre-school setting that provided 'sector-leading practice' and judged the children's well-being to be 'excellent'. To achieve this outcome, the setting adopts a holistic approach involving many multi-disciplinary services, an emphasis on involving parents, provision of cooking classes to encourage healthy eating, and implementation of a range of activities that promote children's feelings and emotions (for example, visual timetables and photographs that represent different emotions to stimulate discussion) (Estyn, 2012b). Arguably, if this is 'sector-leading practice' one queries what the provision was like in other Early Years settings that were not judged as excellent.

Factors influencing learning outcomes

Parental engagement is clearly a factor that influences children's outcomes, but in the Morrison Gutman et al. (2010) study, risk factors such as low parental education and stressful events were associated with three of the dimensions of well-being (emotional, behavioural and social) but not subjective school well-being. Out of the four dimensions, subjective school well-being showed the greatest decline through mid-childhood to adolescence. However, the study found a relationship between high-risk children who enjoyed school (subjective school well-being) and positive changes in behavioural and social well-being and argues that children who have unstable and stressful backgrounds benefit from schools that provide positive learning environments. Laevers (2005) suggests that the personality and temperament of the teacher are the most important factors that contribute to high levels of well-being in schools, and it is the adult engagement and involvement that has more impact on learning than the physical space of the classroom environment or resources used. Laevers (2003, p. 10) discusses 'the person of the teacher' and argues that it is this aspect of practice that has the most influence on high levels of well-being. Likewise, Roffey (2012) claims that schools function in very different ways due to the diverse nature of their social, physical and human capital; and it is social capital, such as the quality of relationships and interactions, that has the most impact on children's well-being and the learning environment.

Promoting and supporting emotional health and well-being

The characteristics of professionals were highlighted in the Effective Provision of Pre-school Education (**EPPE**) project that was conducted in England in 2004, and showed that when practitioners demonstrated warmth and were more responsive to the needs of individual children they made more progress (Sylva et al., 2004). However, Aasen and Waters (2006) argue in their paper that being a caring and warm practitioner is not enough to place well-being at the heart of a curriculum (particularly with the Foundation Phase in Wales). Instead, teachers and other staff need to rethink what they do and understand the shift in learning theories and pedagogical approaches if well-being is going to be at the heart of the curriculum. Estyn (2011) reported that the impact of the Foundation Phase in Wales has been positive on children's well-being, although they also claim that in a minority of settings where experiential learning both indoors and outdoors is not implemented, well-being is hindered. The recent Estyn annual report states that when activities are more creative and exciting, well-being improves. They also report that nine out of ten pupils achieved the expected level in personal and social development at the end of the Foundation Phase in Year 2 (6- to 7-year-olds) (Estyn, 2013). Some may deduce from this outcome that practitioners have placed well-being at the heart of the Foundation Phase. Sceptics might question how this outcome was reached and how substantial was the evidence on which this judgement was based.

The Organization for Economic Co-operation and Development (OECD) (2006) suggest two approaches to learning and teaching that are beneficial for children's well-being, namely 'a focus on the agency of the child, including respect for the child's natural learning strategies; and also the extensive use of listening, project work and documentation in work with young children' (p. 16). The OECD does not explicitly present a child's natural learning strategy, but one obvious strategy might be to consider play and its relationship to children's well-being. However, similar to studies on the relationship between well-being and education, it is difficult to provide a causal link between play and well-being (Gleave and Cole-Hamilton, 2012).

It has been argued 'that the three key actions and skills that will enhance well-being are: developing good habits, particularly the habits of regular exercise and being kind to others; developing positive ways of thinking, such as savouring the moment; and being motivated, i.e. having the energy to make things happen' (Huppert, 2007; cited in McLaughlin, 2008, p. 356). However, there are limited research studies that investigate how settings promote social and emotional well-being (Davis et al., 2010).

When Davis et al. (2010) investigated strategies to promote children's social and emotional well-being in targeted low socio-economic child care settings, they found that strategies were implemented on three different levels: the individual child, the setting and the community. The researchers also reported barriers to promoting children's social and emotional development, for example communication with parents and the children. Another barrier they reported was the inconsistency between staff when dealing with behavioural issues. The study also suggested best practice in facilitating social and emotional development, for example a team that share the same goals and aims for the children, an open door policy with parents and effective communication between a range of stakeholders.

The recent Estyn report (2012a) structures its findings around ten aspects of good practice that highlight strategies that schools use to help combat disadvantage amongst learners. One of the strategies that schools employ is to 'develop the social and emotional skills of disadvantaged learners where they understand the relationships between well-being and standards and often restructure their pastoral care system to deal more directly with the specific needs of disadvantaged learners' (p. 2). The report also states that it is not just the responsibility of schools to undertake such measures; the involvement of Local Authorities and the Welsh Government is also important in establishing a positive working relationship. The report observed that effective schools are those that integrate programmes throughout the school curriculum and embed a culture based on promoting social and emotional development and speaking and listening. Estyn (2012a) claim that 'establishing closer links between home and school has a significant impact on learners' well-being' (p. 34). It is a challenge to reach some parents and engage them with their child's education, but, as already noted, in successful schools there are multimodal forms of communication, one of the most effective being the engagement of parents in face-to-face contact (Estyn, 2012a).

However, it is thought by some (Craig et al.; cited in Watson et al., 2012) that when educators persistently focus on developing positive emotional health and well-being, they may be disadvantaging children and young people preventing them from experiencing a range of emotions (from positive to negative) that are needed for healthy, well-rounded development. This point is also supported by Dowling (2010) who states that for children to be able to understand their emotions they need to experience a range of them. It is also felt that teachers should pay more attention to fulfilling their role as teachers rather than trying to become or act as psychologists, therapists and/or counsellors. Some would argue that 'children need to experience negative emotions and low self-esteem in order to be challenged and motivated to succeed and to develop persistence and resilience' (Watson et al., 2012, p. 4). If teachers are going to make well-being one of their responsibilities in schools then they require specialist training (Watson et al., 2012). This is evident in the Student Assist Programme (SAP) that is used across many Local Authorities in Wales and which is led by a highly trained specialist team that aims to break down barriers to learning for targeted children. Nurture groups have also been set up in many schools across Wales that aim to 'support children who due to social, emotional and/or behavioural difficulties find it difficult to access the curriculum within a mainstream class … Children are highly supported within this environment in order to raise their skills and confidence levels. Its holistic approach has a definite impact on the child's self-esteem and emotional health and well-being' (WG, 2010, p. 19).

In 2010, the Welsh Assembly Government published a document aimed at educational settings to promote emotional health and well-being. It states there is 'major potential benefits' (p. 3) for schools in teaching and learning, behaviour, attendance, staff recruitment and retention benefits. They also state that when a rights-based approach is adopted, emotional health and well-being improves (WG, 2010). However, Welch (2008) argues that for many practitioners adopting a rights-based approach is not straightforward. The way childhood is viewed and understood determines whether adults fully support a rights-based approach. Unfortunately, 'the welfare model of childcare has perpetuated the view that children lack the capacity to contribute to their own well-being or do not have a valid and valuable contribution to make' (Lansdown, 2001, p. 93). According to Dickins et al. (2004) and Alderson (2008), adults who show a deep respect and appreciation for children's rights help to produce positive well-being and self-worth.

Pupil voice and participation

To celebrate Universal Children's Day, the Welsh Government launched 'Lets get it right' e-learning materials for children, young people and practitioners. Further information can be found on www.uncrcletsgetitright.co.uk. Wales was the first country in the UK to appoint a Children's Commissioner and some proponents would argue that Wales is leading the way in children's rights, although some would equally argue against this. Also of significance is the School Council regulation, and two new measures, namely the Children and Family (Wales) Measure 2010 and the Rights of Children and Young Persons (Wales) Measure 2011, which all place emphasis on promoting children's rights around participation, protection and provision.

Participation has been interpreted in many different ways by different people and consequently has diverse definitions (UNICEF, 2003). For Beers and Trimmer (2004) and Save the Children (2005), participation is about adults listening to children, allowing them to freely express themselves, taking on board their views and comments and doing something about them. The definition offered by Casas

(1997) implies that participation is a social activity, and that children should be involved at every stage of a process in which they are often invisible.

Genuine participation only occurs when ideas, issues, targets and aspirations come from children themselves (UNICEF, 2003). Moreover, 'participation implies playing, learning and working in collaboration with others. It involves making choices about, and having a say in, what we do. More deeply, it is about being recognised, accepted and valued for ourselves' (Booth et al., 2006, p. 3). UNICEF (2003) states, in a document titled *The State of the World's Children*, that participation can be very easily misconstrued by adults, resulting in children being manipulated and forced into making decisions. They argue that 'in its worst manifestations, child participation can be repressive, exploitative or abusive' (UNICEF, 2003, p. 5). Sometimes participation is viewed as an adult's activity and something not to be considered for children (Casas, 1997).

Listening to children

Lansdown (2001) explains that it is extremely important to listen to children, as they have a wealth of experience to draw on when making decisions about public policy and classroom practices. Even very young children should be listened to, respected and taken seriously. Lansdown (2001) continues to argue that education fails to listen to children and educationalists fails to grasp the concept of listening; education generally fails to ignore what is best for children. Interestingly, 'the government agenda in respect of children perpetuates the view that education is something that adults do to or for children ... it fails to recognize the obligation to respect children's human rights within the education system – the right to be listened to, to be respected, to learn through day to day experience about the meaning of democracy and human rights' (Lansdown, 2001, p. 96).

Promoting participation

According to Beers and Trimmer (2004), if practitioners want to successfully implement participation they need to thoroughly understand the UNCRC (which is discussed in more detail below), consider the historical nature of children's and human rights and reflect on childhood in society. It is important that participation is understood by everyone in an organization or institution and that it is led in creative and innovative ways (Funky Dragon, 2004) and it is imperative that participation is purposeful. If there is not a commitment from everyone involved to promote participation (within a school/organization) with children then it becomes **tokenistic** (Funky Dragon, 2004). It is good practice to collaborate on a working definition when children are going to be involved. However, there are some schools, organizations and institutions that oppose children becoming involved in making decisions and still adopt a hierarchical culture (Beers and Trimmer, 2004). Hence there is a need for Early Years settings, in particular, to face the challenge of listening, valuing and respecting what children say and do and fulfilling the participatory agenda for all children within the UNCRC (Thomas and Skeels, 2006).

Participation needs improving because it is problematic when adults misread children's expression and non-verbal communication and lack competence in looking at things from a child's point of view (Casas, 1997). Improvements need to be made 'in terms of respect, self esteem and listening to and hearing what children say' (Children's Commissioner for Wales (CCfW), 2007–8, p. 81). In Wales, for example, there are organizations that promote and provide opportunities for children to participate, such as youth forums, Funky Dragon and school councils (CCfW, 2007–8). Also in Wales many Local Authorities have now employed a 'Child's Participation Officer' to ensure that participation is understood by stakeholders and effectively implemented (Thomas and Skeels, 2006). The charity Save the Children (2005) suggest seven practice standards in participation, giving clear guidance on each standard, including why the standard is important and how to meet the standard effectively.

The Children and Young People's Partnership Consortium for Wales and the Partnership Unit were established in 2003 and received funding from the Welsh Assembly Government to support participation and decision-making. One of the key features is to promote training and achieve higher quality participation standards. One of its strengths is that it includes the work of twenty-one multi-agency bodies (Children and Young People's Partnership Consortium for Wales and the Partnership Unit, 2004), which supports Article 2 and the categories of discrimination. For example, Article 2 explains that the UNCRC applies to all children regardless of gender, ethnicity, ability, language, religion and family background, and the work of twenty-one multi-agency bodies helps to ensure that children are not discriminated against.

In 2004, a conference in Wales was held to improve and get participation from children aged between 0 and 10 years, and it was felt that the following factors were important elements in engaging young children: raising awareness, ensuring training and guidance is given, providing a participation tool kit, establishing strategies and a national approach and government funding (Funky Dragon, 2004).

The UK Children's Commissioner Report (2008) explains that since 2002 children's participation in the UK has greatly improved in practice and quality. However, the report also suggests that there are numerous barriers to participation, such as policy documentation, the attitudes and views of adults and limited training opportunities for professionals (Miller, 2003). Similarly, Alderson (2008) highlights a few barriers to consulting children and listening to their views and ideas. For example, it can be time consuming to consult with children rather than with adults. Adults may lack confidence in communicating with children and some adults may fear losing control or have an inability to answer children's questions or deal with sensitive issues.

Effective communication

Nigel Thomas (2001) suggests there are significant differences between children and adults when communicating. First, the style and skills are different; second, the power issue must be considered; third, there can be a reluctance to answer openly and honestly; and last, the age and experience of both the child and adult can influence the quality of communication. Thomas explains how he (along with some others) asked forty-seven children what they thought good communication between children and adults involved. They discovered that time, relationships, active listening, choice and preparation, support and encouragement, fun activities and child agenda were all major components of successful communicative strategies. Similarly, Dickins et al. (2004) suggest ten guidelines in relation to consulting children. For example, consultation with children should be fun and enjoyable and feedback should be given so that children know if their views have been taken into consideration. The most important skill for an adult to possess is having a true interest in what the child is saying and thinking and being able to show empathy. Children need to know that the person they are communicating with is genuinely interested in their point of view (Crompton, 1980; Dickins, 2008). According to Lansdown (2001), many mistakes have been made by adults on behalf of children when they have failed both to listen and to involve them in the decision-making process. Alderson (2008) suggests that effective communication between adult and child is vital when informing children about services. It is thought that parents, Early Years practitioners and children all benefit from listening (Thomas, 2001; Dickins, 2008), but research on the principle that 'listening to children [leads to] better decisions' is very inadequate (Thomas, 2001).

Lansdown (1995) explains that it is pointless listening to children if their views and ideas are not going to be taken seriously, and both Thomas (2001) and Lansdown (1995) argue that the most significant component in listening to children is 'respect'. According to Alexander (1995), practitioners have great difficulty in listening and encouraging children to make decisions for themselves, and this is an area of concern that needs addressing. Consequently, 'teacher training should include a mandatory element on children's participation and the role of school councils' (Funky Dragon, 2004, p. 4). Standard 5 of Save the Children's seven practice standards explains that staff need to be appropriately trained to be able to promote genuine participation (Save the Children, 2005). Miller (2003) suggests that settings should draw up a policy for participation with specific guidance on how it is going to be implemented and monitored. Lancaster (2003) points out that a simple resolution would be to 'add another chair' and consider the views and expertise of a child as part of the panel that makes decisions.

Creative consultation

Dickins et al. (2004) suggest that the most appropriate thing to do for children is to ensure they know how to voice their views effectively. There are a range of creative and innovative ways to consult with children, for example interviews, projective techniques (using persona dolls), drawing, graffiti walls (bricks on walls for writing views/opinions), suggestion boxes, photo-stories/tours, role-play, evaluations, key words, ranking preferences or mapping an event to how they want it to look or feel (Funky Dragon, 2004; Hyder, 2002; Dickins et al., 2004).

According to Sheridan and Pramling Samuelsson (2001), pre-school teachers are often faced with the dilemma and difficulty of knowing children's limitations in the decision-making process. Alexander (1995), Lancaster (2003) and Funky Dragon (2004) point out that policymakers find the age group between 0 and 8 years an 'awkward' one to deal with in this respect, and therefore participation is not straightforward. This is despite the acceptance that 'children, even when very young, can act, for example, as peer counsellors, mediators or mentors for other children' (Lansdown, 2001, p. 93). Lansdown (2001) argues that when children are given the opportunity to make decisions they can act as experts in meeting their own needs.

The importance of participation

Research suggests that making children aware of their rights and providing opportunities for consultation and participation has a positive effect on self-esteem, self-confidence and well-being, and also helps develops independence (Covell and Howe, 1999; Fajerman et al., 2000). It is thought that when children are engaged in participation their overall development is enhanced and they can offer new ideas and influence adult thinking. Also, when children are given the opportunity to participate, they contribute to world peace and a democratic society (UNICEF, 2003).

Alderson (2008) talks extensively about participation and notes three main benefits. First, the relationship between adult and child is strengthened and respect is generated. Second, abuse can be reduced or prevented. Third, policies, communities and societies can be improved and enhanced. It has also been noted that when communication with children is of a high standard, children become more competent beings and at times may astonish those adults who have already formed an opinion about their ability (Thomas, 2001).

It is thought that most children grow up having very little control over situations and have important decisions made about them without their thoughts and views being considered. Thomas (2001) argues that if children are listened to, consulted and involved in making decisions then they have more chance of making a more successful life for themselves because they feel more confident and in control of situations and are equipped with many more skills. It is expected that conflict will arise when children and adults are faced with making choices and formulating decisions, but this is an argument for lifelong learning.

One school that has implemented a children's rights approach noticed that 'the establishment of children's rights seems to have created more confident children, better learners and improved relationships in the school' (Fisher et al., 2005, p. 31). This kind of approach implies that all children, regardless of gender, disability, race or religion, have a right to be happy and content individuals. Research suggests that high self-esteem improves pupils' learning, and adults who show a deep respect and appreciation for children's rights engender positive well-being and self-worth (Dickins et al., 2004; Alderson, 2008).

The School Councils (Wales) Regulations 2005

Pupil voice and participation is becoming a common feature of practice in education and it is now a legal requirement that every school have a school council with children from Year 3 (ages 7 to 8) upwards. A minimum of six meetings are to be held each year and there is a secret vote for children to be elected to the school council. It is now very common for children to be included on interview panels for teaching jobs at a school, but some argue that such activities are often tokenistic and that the child's opinion is not fully endorsed. For more information about school councils in Wales, use the link at the end of this chapter. When children engage with their school council it could be said that Article 12 of the UNCRC is being promoted.

Understanding the United Nations Convention on the Rights of the Child (1989)

In 1989, the United Nations Convention on the Rights of the Child (UNCRC) was produced for children aged between 0 and 18 years, stipulating the 'basic necessities' for all children, but which so many do not receive (Alderson, 2008). This marked a significant advance in the concept of children's rights. In 1991 the UK ratified the Convention and integrated it into UK law. There are 54 articles in total in the UNCRC, of which Articles 43–54 explain how adults and the government have to work collaboratively and cooperatively to help ensure that children's rights are endorsed. Articles 1–42 tend to be grouped in three main ways, namely provision, protection and participation, commonly known as the three Ps (Welch, 2008). It is generally thought that for the UNCRC to be fully implemented there needs to be a dramatic change in the way that society and the law view children (Croke and Crowley, 2006). Casas (1997) explains that the Convention is not yet at the forefront of many people's minds, because the way a child is viewed is very traditional (i.e. without rights). Unfortunately, 'the welfare model of childcare has perpetuated the view that children lack the capacity to contribute to their own well-being or do not have a valid and valuable contribution to make' (Lansdown, 2001, p. 93). Furthermore, adults insist that young children are incapable of making decisions and lack maturity (Tomlinson, 2008), and many adults also find it difficult to accept that young children have rights (Alexander, 1995). There needs to be more of a focus on the voices of all young children: they should be heard, respected, listened to and valued and should be regarded very highly in society (Welch, 2008), as suggested in all the Articles of the UNCRC, but particularly in Articles 2 and 12.

Even though a country might ratify the UNCRC, the Articles do not automatically apply in practice (Tomlinson, 2008) and many countries simply ignore the the detail of the UNCRC (Archard, 2004). Apparently the UNCRC has not been as successful and accepted as the European Convention on Human Rights (Archard, 2004), but according to Hammarberg (1994, preface) 'the Convention itself is more than a dry document with some rules on how to behave. It has a vision'.

The UNCRC has been criticized by many because babies can be thought of in the same way as seventeen-year-olds, and the tension between parental rights and children's rights is heightened (Welch, 2008). The UNCRC reference to 'what is best for the child' is often vague and can be interpreted differently in different cultures (Archard, 2004). Moreover, the UNCRC does not expect adults to do what children demand; instead, it expects adults to listen carefully to children and be attuned to their needs. Adults should begin to understand the reasons why children say or do certain things (Thomas, 2001; Lancaster, 2003). It is thought that children's views in most European countries are taken more seriously than children's views in the UK, where they are discouraged from having an opinion (Davies and Fitzpatrick, 2000). Denmark, arguably, leads the way in listening to and engaging children in participation (Clark et al., 2005).

Beers and Trimmer (2004) explain that the Articles in the UNCRC are not gifts from adults to children, but instead are indicators that give adults opportunities to ensure that children participate, are provided for and are protected. Out of the fifty-four Articles in the UNCRC, Articles 12 and 13 are the most relevant to participation rights, but Articles 2, 3, 14, 15, 17, 23 and 29 also relate to participation, a topic discussed earlier in this chapter. The most contentious article linked to participation is Article 14, but for the purpose of this chapter Articles 12 and 2 will be discussed in more detail.

The UNCRC (1989) stipulates in Article 12 that '*1*. States Parties shall assure to the child who is capable of forming his or her own views the right to express those views freely in all matters affecting the child, the views of the child being given due weight in accordance with the age and maturity of the child.' It has been pointed out that part of Article 12 will be misunderstood and that children's views, opinions and ideas will not be taken seriously (Beers and Trimmer, 2004) when interpreting 'due weight' and 'age and maturity'. Welch (2008) argues that phrases such as 'best interest' and 'due weight' can potentially be misinterpreted. According to Save the Children (2001), the main reason for Article 12 being disregarded is because of the way childhood is constructed and viewed. Thomas and Skeels (2006) suggest that much work still needs to be done for Article 12 to be fully implemented, appreciated and understood.

The UNCRC (1989) stipulate in Article 2 that '*1*. States Parties shall respect and ensure the rights set forth in the present Convention to each child within their jurisdiction without discrimination of any kind, irrespective of the child's, of his or her parent's or legal guardian's race, colour, sex, language, religion, political or other opinion, national ethnic or social origin, property, disability, birth or family members.' Ultimately, Article 12 is underpinned by participation and Article 2 is underpinned by non-discriminatory practice and they are both very difficult to implement in practice, largely due to traditional values and attitudes (Lancaster, 2003). One of the main difficulties of the UNCRC is applying the four principles ('Article 2 – non-discrimination, Article 3 – best interests, Article 6 – life, survival and development, Article 12 – listening to children' [Save the Children, 2001, p. 53]) to policy and day-to-day practice. The following discussion explores some other Articles that link specifically to developing effective classroom practice.

A right to basic needs! (Articles 3, 6, 7, 19, 20, 24, 27, 31, 36)

Practitioners working with young children might already be familiar with Abraham Maslow's (1908–70) **Hierarchy of Needs** model which is represented as a pyramid. Maslow's Hierarchy of Needs states that practitioners should satisfy each need in turn, starting with the first, which deals with the most obvious need of survival itself. Only when the lower order needs of physical and emotional well-being are satisfied should practitioners be concerned with the higher order needs of influence and personal development. This can be linked to child development, since a child who is cold or hungry will not be able to respond and engage fully with planned activities.

Equally, a child who is upset, withdrawn and unhappy might find it difficult to participate in daily classroom activities.

Healthy children enjoy active play, a balanced diet and supportive relationships. There are many current initiatives such as breakfast clubs, the healthy schools initiative, the walking school bus and eco schools that support children's health and well-being. Further information can be found on the Welsh Government website or Local Authority websites.

A right to play! (Article 31)

Children's right to play is a central focus of this book and one that is now a focus particularly for 5- to 7-year-olds in the Foundation Phase (which replaces the

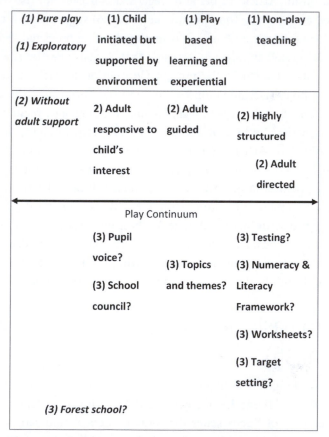

Figure 4.1 The Play Continuum

Key
Play Continuum = ⟷
Number 1 = Type of play
Number 2 = Role of the adult
Number 3= Educational polices/ initiatives

Desirable Outcome and Key Stage One of the National Curriculum). The challenge for most practitioners is likely to be in achieving a balance of child-led and adult-directed play tasks, which also involves the distribution of power between adult and child. To help the reader understand the importance, relevance and value of the right to play in the Foundation Phase, the authors have adapted the diagram above, which illustrates play on a continuum. If you are a practitioner, the diagram can be used to reflect on your position of play both pre- and post-Foundation Phase. The key is situated below the figure.

Reflective task

If you are a practitioner, use the table below to reflect upon play and learning in your setting.

What you believe? (espoused theory)	What you do or say (theory in action)
e.g. children have a natural ability to explore	e.g. Do not mix the sand and water (set boundaries)!
e.g. children learn best through play	e.g. You can go play after you finish this work!
e.g. children should be given risk-taking opportunities	e.g. Discourage children from climbing too high or riding bicycles too fast

According to Argyris and Schon (1978; cited in Andrews, 2012) there is a difference between what we believe we do (espoused theory) and what we actually do (theory in action), and this if often referred to as tokenism.

Opportunities to play and be outdoors

Children have a right to play both indoors and outdoors and one of the key features of the Foundation Phase was to ensure children had free-flow opportunities to play indoors and outdoors. There are significant physical differences between the indoor and outdoor learning environments, the outdoors offering children quality, first-hand sensory (weather) experiences and freedom to move and explore (Ryder-Richardson, 2006; Tovey, 2007). It has been suggested that the 'outdoor space can literally "free up" the body and the mind' (Tovey, 2007, p. 13). Many children prefer the outdoors as a learning environment because they are in control, they are making choices, they are managing and assessing risks and they are initiating play (Bilton, 2010).

The outdoors offers children a sense of security (that some children may not always feel) because of its patterned events, such as the seasons and life cycles in nature. Children playing outdoors are more likely to use gross motor movements, run around and play chasing games and exercise more vigorously, which contributes to overall health and well-being. It should be remembered that all areas of development can be advanced through outdoor play not just physical development (Tovey, 2007). The **Researching Effective Pedagogy in the Early Years (REPEY)** project found that the majority of practitioners viewed the outside mainly in relation to physical development (Siraj-Blatchford et al., 2002). Ouvry (2003) states that every single learning outcome from every Area of Learning can be developed and enhanced outside, as well as promoting health and well-being.

Tovey (2007) and Huggins and Wickett (2011) suggest that the outdoors creates awe and wonder, stimulates imagination and encourages discovery. Furthermore, the outdoor environment lends itself to more opportunities for problem-solving and teamwork and has the capacity for children to manipulate materials and resources and plan their play spaces more frequently than they would in the inside environment (Waite and Pratt, 2011). When children transform their outdoor play space in a way that suits them, it indicates that they are truly connected with it (Casey, 2007). However, 'when children feel they are controlled by others or that choice is taken away from them, then mastery motivation – their natural curiosity – is reduced or eliminated' (Maynard, 2007, p. 325).

According to Tovey (2007), there are ten different types of play spaces for children, from 'designated spaces' provided by adults to 'natural and imaginative spaces'. Also, Fjørtoft (2004) suggests that when children are offered a complex landscape they demonstrate a range of play types. Natural items such as fallen logs, planks of wood and grassy inclines help to develop children's imaginative play (Clark, 2007; Huggins and Wicket, 2011), and cardboard boxes are very popular play items for young children which can stimulate their imagination (Hammond, 2007). It could be argued that children tend to play more creatively in a natural outdoor environment (Fjørtoft, 2001).

Moore (1986) suggests that it is pointless making decisions about resources and allocating money to equipment when practitioners have not considered what the children enjoy doing, where they play and the reasons for their play. What is worrying is that those children engaged in play tend not to be observed or noticed by staff (Bishop and Curtis, 2001). Ward (1990) reminds us that practitioners will assign play areas but undoubtedly children will not use them as planned, and Clements (2004) states that one of the most valuable outdoor experiences for children is when they choose their agenda, which leads to fulfilment and motivation. According to Casey (2007), children are very good at utilizing play equipment correctly to please adults but very quickly revert to using equipment in their own way. Furthermore, it has been suggested that 'the landscape might have a functional impact on children's behaviour and play performance' (Fjørtoft, 2001, p. 115).

A right to think! Sustained Shared Thinking (SST) (Articles 2, 6, 12, 14, 28, 30, 31, 36)

Chapter 6 of this book discusses Assessment for Learning (AfL), and there is great importance placed on communicating with children, challenging their opinions and asking open-ended questions. In this way a practitioner can extend a child's thinking, and work with them as co-constructors in the learning process. The practitioner and the child can work together on a given problem, introduce relevant vocabulary, allow for reflective discussion and encourage reflection. Here the practitioner has a crucial role in helping the child to develop their thinking skills (WAG, 2008a).

A concept known as **Sustained Shared Thinking** (SST) can be defined as 'an episode in which two or more individuals "work together" in an intellectual way to solve a problem, clarify a concept, evaluate activities, extend a narrative etc.' (Chilvers, 2008, p. 19). According to Dowling (2005), children's thinking is different from adults: they apply the knowledge they have and extend it with new discoveries. Children's thinking can be seen in their chosen activities, in their questions and what they say. Research findings from EPPE (2003) and REPEY (2002) suggest that children improve their thinking skills in high quality Early Years settings. In settings that demonstrate high quality, staff provide opportunities to sustain and challenge children's thinking and model how children can share this with other children.

Practitioners can extend children's thinking skills by being aware of their interests and the adult and child can work together to develop an idea or skill, but to enable this to happen there needs to be appropriate contexts for thinking.

Cultural and contextual experiences

Contexts for thinking can include children becoming involved in activities and situations that interest and intrigue them. Access to a varied and rich provision is needed. Children need to be able to move freely between the indoors and outdoors. Time for reflection is needed, where children can apply what they have learnt, follow their interests and make connections. Concrete links between home and setting are important, as are opportunities to have their thinking made visible through records of their ideas in words and images.

Culture and language opportunities allow the children to embed their thinking. Adults who are successful at engaging in sustained shared thinking have established warm caring relationships with children, which encourage children to learn and develop their thinking skills.

Children should also be encouraged to share their thinking with one another, where the adults help children to listen to each other, act as a point of reference and if needed refocus thinking (Dowling, 2005).

There are different types of thinking. Children can:

- plan and think ahead;
- investigate and explore;
- solve problems;
- use logic;
- fantasize;
- reflect.

In addition to considering different types of thinking, it is worth noting that Howard Gardner, a professor of cognition and education at Harvard University who has worked in many areas of psychology, suggests there are different types of multiple intelligences. He has been strongly influenced by Bruner, with whom he worked with early on in his career, and is best known for his book *Frames of Mind* (1993), which details his multiple intelligence theory. Gardner challenged the theory that intelligence was something that could be measured or represented as an IQ score. He wanted to discover how people are intelligent rather than how much intelligence they have. Initially he listed seven intelligences, but later added one to make a total of eight intelligences, as follows:

- linguistic;
- musical;
- mathematical-logical;
- spatial-intelligence;
- bodily-kinaesthetic;
- interpersonal;
- intrapersonal;
- naturalistic.

Children may display more than one of these intelligences and it is important that practitioners are aware of this concept and aim to develop all types in children with whom they work.

Thinking Actively in a Social Context (TASC)

Thinking Actively in a Social Context (**TASC**) (see www.tascwheel.com for more information) is a well-researched universal thinking skills framework developed by Belle Wallace, President of the National Association for Able Children (NACE). TASC was developed from extensive research into:

- how expert thinkers solve problems;
- the latest findings from neuro-science about how the brain works; and
- action-research in classrooms in different cultures around the world.

The TASC Framework lays the foundations for successful learning and is being implemented in thousands of schools nationally, as well as developing inter-nationally. TASC provides teachers with a framework for:

- lesson planning that systematically develops pupils' thinking;
- effective planning for differentiation and extension;
- a holistic approach to incorporating the multiple intelligences; and
- assessing the processes of pupils' learning.

Access the following link online to adapt the mind map about characteristics of effective classroom practice: www.bloomsbury.com/an-introduction-to-the-foundation-phase-9781474264273.

Conclusion

This chapter has only briefly discussed some topics linked to developing effective classroom practice; there are so many more ideas that could have been explored. For example, when interviewing a head teacher in west Wales for this book, the authors became aware of the Leonardo approach for Key Stage 2 learners (an interdisciplinary approach via science and art) – more information can be found using the link at the end of this chapter. It is important for all stakeholders to consider the evidence base of interventions such as SEAL, since they can take some time to implement and may not result in the returns that have any effect on current trends. However, promoting partnership with parents does have a consistently positive impact on children's outcomes. Children's rights and the UNCRC and some of its Articles were considered at length in this chapter to help support the argument that children should always be at the centre of effective classroom practice. Children have a right to play outdoors as well as indoors and they should be given appropriate opportunities to think in context. But this needs to be enacted by well-trained, knowledgeable practitioners who adopt a child-centred, participatory, co-construction approach.

Chapter summary

- SEAL was discussed at some length to highlight the importance of promoting both social and emotional aspects of children's development *and* cognitive and academic achievement.
- Working in partnership with parents can be challenging and practitioners should be aware of the fact that 'parental engagement' as opposed to 'parental involvement' has more of an impact on improving children's outcomes.
- Participation and pupil voice is now more commonly featured in practice and better understood but there is still some work to be done around authentic child participation.
- Children have the right to play outdoors, and practitioners should develop and use the outdoor environment on a *daily* basis.
- Developing children's thinking skills is now more frequently put into practice, yet sustained shared thinking is something that is not often easily understood or implemented.

Thought-provoking questions

- How do you support children's social and emotional aspects of learning?
- In what ways do you promote partnership with parents?
- What do you understand by the term 'participation'?
- How effectively do you use the outdoor environment?
- In your setting, how do you rate the children's thinking skills?

Further reading and information

Allen, S. and M. Whalley (2010), *Supporting Pedagogy and Practice in Early Years Settings*. Exeter: Learning Matters.

Blake, S., J. Bird and L. Gerlach (2007), *Promoting Emotional & Social Development in Schools*. London: Paul Chapman.

Children's Commissioner School Council: http://www.childcomwales.org.uk/en/school-councils-what-can-you-do-next/.

Claxton, G. (2002), *Building Learning Power*. Bristol: TLO.

Hayes, J. (2002), *Children as Philosophers*. London: RoutledgeFalmer.

Key Stage 2 Leonardo approach: http://www.leonardoeffect.com/resources/Testimonials.pdf.

Pupil voice in Wales: a range of helpful resources: http://www.pupilvoicewales.org.uk/.

The Campaign for the Children and Young People Assembly for Wales (Funky Dragon): http://www.funkydragon.org/en/.

Welsh Government School Council: http://wales.gov.uk/topics/educationandskills/publications/guidance/schoolcouncilsbestpracticeguide/?lang=en.

Part II

Making Sense of Theory into Practice

5

Observational Techniques

Chapter aims

To discuss and evaluate why and how we observe children in Foundation Phase settings.

To reflect upon how observation informs planning and assessment in the Foundation Phase.

To evaluate different observation methods.

To consider and reflect upon the role of the adult in observing children.

Why observe children?

The Welsh Assembly Government's (WAG) guidance on observation states:

> By observing children carefully to note their progress, involvement and enjoyment, as well as focusing on the attainment of predetermined outcomes, practitioners should be able to plan a more appropriate curriculum that supports children's development according to individual needs.
>
> (WAG, 2008c, p. 4)

Observation is at the centre of the Foundation Phase curriculum in Wales and there is a statutory requirement on practitioners working with children to carry out regular observations. By observing children on a regular basis, practitioners are able to plan activities that cater for children's individual learning needs. Observations of children should prioritize a child's development and learning and allow for further development to occur. It formalizes the link between theory and practice. Systematic recording of observations will enable practitioners to identify behaviour patterns and to note any behavioural changes in a child, both positive and negative.

Observations of the immediate learning environment can also make you aware of any potential hazards or how to adapt or improve the learning resources you provide.

Observing children on a regular basis enables practitioners to plan an appropriate curriculum, which provides for the full range of individual learning needs within the setting.

The role of observation in other Early Years curricula

The importance of observing children is recognized worldwide as evidenced in Early Years curricula from Italy to New Zealand. In the Italian 'Reggio Emilia' approach (founded in 1963), the practitioners collect evidence about what the children are involved in. This evidence is documented through observing the children, using photographs as evidence, and is collated in an individual child portfolio. These portfolios are used to plan the next steps in the individual child's learning journey.

In the 'Te Whāriki' curriculum in New Zealand, assessment and observation are linked and are viewed as a continuous process (Carr, 2001). By this process of observation, practitioners can assess the whole child and note the developing relationship with adults and peers within the setting. From continual assessments and observations the practitioners have the freedom to create a learning programme suitable for the child's individual learning needs. Thus observations inform practitioner's practice and pedagogy and activities, and are a valid tool to communicate with children and their families. In England, observations are a central part of the Early Years Foundation Stage framework (EYFS), which states:

> Ongoing assessment (also known as formative assessment) is an integral part of the learning and development process. It involves practitioners observing children to understand their level of achievement, interests and learning styles, and then shape learning experiences for each child reflecting on those observations.
>
> (DfE, 2012, p. 10)

Therefore observations, planning and assessments are all central to a child's development throughout Early Years settings both locally, nationally and internationally. Chapter 3 has discussed international approaches to education in more detail.

Observation in the Foundation Phase

Within the Foundation Phase, observations are an integral part of the daily routine of practitioners. Observations should form part of the school's overall assessment procedures and not stand alone. Closely observing children can allow early years professionals an in-depth look at children. The Welsh Assembly Government (2008c, p. 4) has stated that observation and assessment enables practitioners to:

- know the individual child and highlight his/her strengths, interests and needs;
- identify the plan for the child's progress;
- highlight children's development, strengths and abilities across all Areas of Learning;
- provide a graduated response and specific help to children whose progress is not adequate and who may be on the continuum of special educational needs (SEN Code of Practice for Wales);
- inform children of their achievements and next steps for their learning;
- inform staff, parents/carers of children's achievements and next steps for their learning;
- identify, monitor and evaluate the effectiveness of the curriculum provided;
- inform transition during the Foundation Phase and between the Foundation Phase and Key Stage 2.

Therefore it can be argued that observations are a tool for understanding child development. By observing where a child is on the learning continuum, practitioners can plan for the next step in the child's learning journey. This will allow practitioners to provide balanced and flexible daily routines that meet children's needs and helps children to reach their full potential.

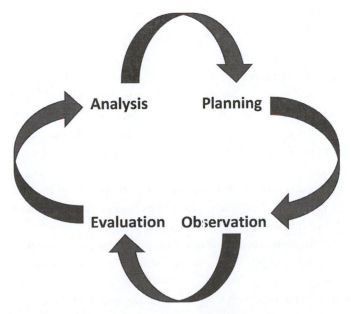

Figure 5.1 The Observation Cycle

Through systematic observations, practitioners can make the crucial links between a child's actual stages of development and the theoretical stages of development. Observations also encourage reflection on the part of the practitioner and empower an evaluation of practice in the setting. It is important to note that observations focus on what a child can do as opposed to what they cannot do (Palaiologou, 2012).

In addition, observations offer an in-depth look at a child and are a means of valuing and listening to children. This takes into account the rights of children within the Children Act (2004) and the UNCRC (1989) (Palaiologou, 2012).

Classroom observations offer opportunities for children's voices to be heard. Clark and Moss (2001) developed the mosaic approach as a way of empowering children's voices and state that observing children achieves this. This is also supported by Luff (2007, p. 189), who states that 'Observing and documenting learning can be a way of valuing and listening to children.' Evidence gathered through observations helps professionals to consider children's voices, their needs and experiences. Practitioners can cater for a child's interests and help to create safe, enjoyable and applicable learning environments.

Observations should be carried out within all seven areas of learning within the Foundation Phase:

- Personal and Social Development, Well-Being and Cultural Diversity
- Language, Literacy and Communication Skills
- Mathematical Development
- Welsh Language Development
- Knowledge and Understanding of the World
- Physical Development
- Creative Development

(WAG 2008c)

Children should be observed in a variety of contexts, including playing alone, in small groups and working alongside and with practitioners. Interaction with parents, practitioners and peers should also be observed. Observations should take place both indoors and outdoors and during structured and unstructured activities. Children need to be observed at different times during the day and on different days of the week.

Through the many varied observations carried out on the children, practitioners should gain a clear picture on how the children are progressing across the Foundation Phase curriculum.

Children's needs, concentration levels, interests, stages of development, patterns of behaviour and relationships in the setting will all be noted through the observations carried out.

Practitioners need to reflect on their own practice and the following key questions can be asked following observations:

- Are the activities too easy or too difficult?
- How are the children using the resources?
- Is there anything missing that the children need?
- Is sufficient time/space provided for the experience and consolidation?
- Are the children fully involved in the activity – if not, why not?
- How independent are the children in their learning? Are the children able to work/play alongside/in cooperation with other children?
- Do the children need practitioners' intervention?
- Has there been opportunity for sustained thinking?
- What needs to be done to move the learning on?
- Is there a balance of activities over time (indoor/outdoor, individual/group, etc.)?

(WAG, 2008c, p. 8)

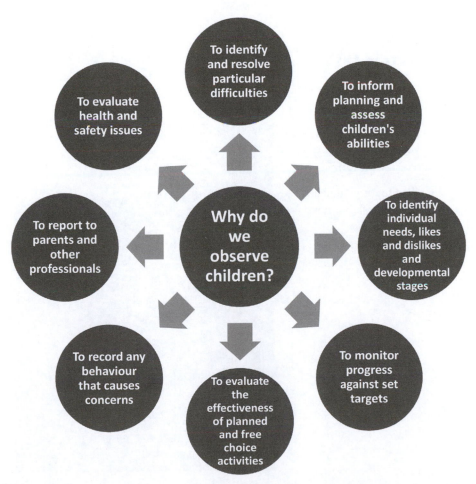

Figure 5.2 Reasons for Observing Children

Observation skills

Planning for observations is essential before an actual observation is carried out (unless they are snapshot observations). There should be clear aims and objectives and there needs to be consideration of parental, team and child involvement in the observational process. The next step is to decide on the chosen observational method as discussed further along in this chapter. Finally there needs to be evidence of how you will record and document the observation and findings (Palaiologou, 2012).

During the actual observation process, one of the key skills practitioners need to develop is that of objectivity. This means the need to record what actually happens during an observation and *not* what is perceived to be happening. In practice this means using a plethora of observation techniques to base evidence on. As practitioners it may be necessary to step out of the role of educator and become an observer on the side lines.

Reflective task

If you are a practitioner, look at the picture below and write one sentence to state what is happening.

Did you record the **facts** about what you have seen, or did you record your **opinion**?

- **The facts:** The child is sitting with her hands over her eyes.
- **Your opinion:** She is crying, hiding, sulking, etc.

Activity 1

Consider the following statements and decide if they are facts or opinions:

- Jo is a very pretty girl.
- Zoe can count to ten.
- Paul is very bright.
- Robert can stand on one leg for five seconds.
- Ali had a tantrum.
- Ellie lay on the floor and kicked her legs while she was screaming.

(Beith et al., 2005)

These are examples of one of the main challenges we face when we observe children. We need to leave behind our personal values, beliefs and cultural stereotypes and remain objective throughout. As Hobart and Frankel (2009, p. 8) attest, 'You need to be careful when you observe children that you are entirely objective and unbiased.' The Foundation Phase practitioner needs to keep an open mind, remain focused and record information in a systematic and logical way.

Confidentiality is a major part of observing children. All settings will have policies and guidance on confidentiality and how to carry out observations. All practitioners working within the setting will need to follow these guidelines. Observations will need to be stored safely, either on a computer which is password protected or in individual portfolios which are kept in a safe place. Access to observations should only be given to the practitioners in the setting, other professionals if required and parents when requested (unless there is a legal restriction preventing it).

In settings, parents are made aware that their child will be assessed throughout their time in the Foundation Phase. In this way informed consent has been given for practitioners to carry out observations on a continual basis. Any other people such as students on placements will also be able to observe the children with the teacher's permission. All staff working in the setting are aware of the importance of maintaining the confidentiality of any observational findings outside of the setting.

Observers can either be participant or **non-participant observers. Participant observations** will involve the observer sitting alongside the child and taking part in the activity or talking to the child as they carry out a given task. Non-participant observations will involve the observer sitting away from the child being observed and taking no part in the actual activity. If the observation is to be the non-participant type then there needs to be an agreement that the observer will not be disturbed and not expected to be involved with any activities while the observation is ongoing.

As mentioned previously, it is essential that all team members are involved in the observational process. More experienced team members can mentor less experienced members in the observation process and guide them through the process. In addition, team involvement in observation planning can become an opportunity to communicate information and to discuss any potential problems. Palaiologou (2008, p. 48) writes that 'The process of becoming a skilled observer is complex and challenging. It requires constant self-development, self-assessment, an addressing of individual needs, and the overcoming of personal emotional boundaries.'

Observations can also be used as a communication tool between children's families and practitioners. Involving parents in the observational process allows practitioners to gain valuable insights into other aspects of children's behaviour and into their stage of development.

Observational methods and techniques

There are many different types of observation that practitioners can use to support their judgements. Observations can be both planned and spontaneous; participant or non-participant. The table gives examples of the most commonly used observation techniques.

Technique	Description
Snap shot	A one-off observation that is not planned
Longitudinal	Taken over a specified length of time (on a specific child/group)
Time sampling/Tracking	Observation repeated at regular intervals throughout the day/session
Event sample	Records when specific behaviour occurs
Free description/Written record	A description of an event as it unfolds – written in the present tense
Sociogram	Used to indicate a child's social relationships within a group
Target child	Focuses on one child and the activities that child does over a set period of time
Checklist	Compares a child against set milestones of development

In the Foundation Phase, children will be observed continually by all practitioners working in the setting. In this way a portfolio of the individual child can be built up and used to plan to meet individual needs. Observations play an important part in understanding individual patterns of behaviour and the reasons why certain behaviours occur.

By observing children within the setting, the practitioner can recognize stages of child development and link these to relevant milestones of development and note any potential problems. It will allow the setting to assess the child and plan for progress, catering for individual needs. This fits in with the Foundation Phase ethos of a child's readiness to learn.

According to Benjamin (1994, p. 14), 'observations play an important role in assessment, either by replacing or by supplementing standardized evaluation instruments'. As stated previously, observers can be both participant and non-participant. Participant observations occur when you are working with the child or children. These observations usually take the form of quickly written notes at the time of the event or notes written straight after the event. The comments are usually brief and the advantages of this is that daily events are recorded that can provide a useful insight into a child or activity. This type of observation is unstructured. However, there are limitations to this method, as it will not give a complete picture of an event. It can also be difficult to manage and needs to be filed in the child's portfolio straight away as otherwise it can get lost.

Non-participant observations require the professional to step outside the role of the practitioner and not be involved or interacting with the children. Preparation and organization is required for non-participant observations. The observer needs to be seated away from the observed child but near enough to be able to see and hear them properly. Try to avoid making eye contact with the child being observed, as some children will alter their behaviour if they are aware you are observing them. The observer will need to be given time to write up the observation and will need to not be disturbed whilst doing this.

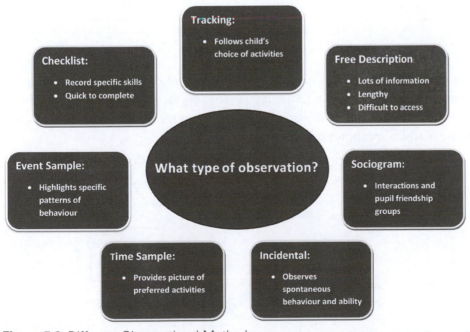

Figure 5.3 Different Observational Methods

As well as participant and non-participant observations there are a variety of other observational techniques which can be used. The diagram below recaps the different methods of observation in more detail.

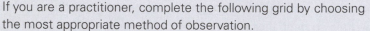

Reflective task

If you are a practitioner, complete the following grid by choosing the most appropriate method of observation.

Scenario	Method
Keira is 2 years old and is attending playgroup three sessions a week. She has bitten four other children in the last two weeks.	
Mohamed has recently joined pre-school and appears to have limited concentration skills.	
Tim settled very well in the first few weeks at the after school club, but has now started to become distressed at snack time.	
Sam always takes a long time to eat his packed lunch.	

(Tassoni, Bulman and Beith, 2005)

All observational methods have their advantages and disadvantages and these are summarized in Palaiologou (2012, pp. 58–60) and the full reference can be found in further reading. In addition, observations can be recorded in a number of ways, some of which are shown below.

Figure 5.4 Methods of Recording Observations

Preparing to observe children – the role of the adult

> Watching children as they learn and understanding their learning moments is complex and difficult work and places the highest of demands upon educators.
>
> (Nutbrown and Carter, 2010, p. 120)

The aims and objectives for each observation need to be clear from the start (unless it is a snapshot or incidental observation). The objectives will determine the nature of the information to be gathered. Aims are about what you intend to observe and what you want to achieve; they need to be focused, precise and unambiguous. Aims focus on an area of development such as physical or creative, and so on.

Objectives need to be underpinned by developmental milestones or norms, or linked to theory and theoretical perspectives. They are about specific skills or abilities being observed. In the Foundation Phase there is a child development profile document which supports observations and assessments. In this document there are milestones of development for different areas of learning in the Foundation Phase ranging from eighteen months to seven years of age. The document can be downloaded from: http://gov.wales/docs/dcells/publications/090624foundationpha seguidanceen.pdf.

However, it should be noted that all children are individuals and that the age each child will reach individual milestones will vary, which is perfectly normal. As Sharman et al. have pointed out, 'All children follow the same sequence of growth and development but the rate varies from child to child' (2004, p. 125).

Every aspect of a child's development is affected by their environment and the experiences they encounter. All children are unique and will progress at their own individual rate. Knowing the milestones of development allows the practitioner to know what to broadly expect at each stage of development and to provide opportunities and an environment to encourage this. In this way a child can be allowed to reach their full potential. According to the *Foundation Phase Child Development Profile Guidance* (WAG, 2009b, p. 5), children need practitioners and environments (indoors and outdoors) that:

- support and challenge their widening interests and encourage them to develop their thinking;
- practitioners who observe, assess and plan carefully for their developmental needs;
- practitioners who encourage and extend conversations;
- practitioners who provide good role models.

The following is regarded as good practice when observing children:

- Be clear regarding the purpose.
- Decide the best method.
- Ensure that you have the necessary equipment.
- Merge into the background (obvious activity will have an effect on the situation).
- Avoid eye contact with the observed child – this can alter behaviour.
- Do not attempt to interpret the results during the observation.
- Do not cause embarrassment to the child.
- Be objective; do not make assumptions regarding the feelings of the child – **SAY WHAT YOU SEE**.
- Ensure that information from observations remains confidential and that results are kept in a safe place.

Observations help practitioners to understand the reasons behind children's behaviour and provide a link between theoretical stages of development and practice (Sharman et al., 2004). Observational records must be kept for the 'safe and efficient management of the settings and to meet the needs of the children' (DCSF, 2008, p. 38). All data collected is regulated under the Data Protection Act of 1998 and the Freedom of Information Act of 2000. Structured observations need a front sheet with information on it regarding the child, the context of the observation and who is present. An example is shown below:

Observation Record:	
Name of child: **Age:**	
Date:	**Start time:** **Finish time:**
Context:	
Observation:	

Figure 5.5 Observation Record

Remember, if you are carrying out a 'free description' type of observation, it must be written in the present tense. It is a written event as it occurs and this type of observation only requires a pen and paper. If you are carrying out a 'time-sample', 'sociogram', 'check-list' or an 'event sample' then you need to prepare a table or chart before you begin the observation. Settings will have their own format for doing these and different settings will have different ways of recording the results. Sometimes children's names will be changed for confidentiality, especially if it is a student carrying out the observation as part of their studies. The observer should also be aware that different factors can affect observations, as shown below.

Figure 5.6 Observation Factors

After the observation has been carried out then the findings need to be analysed and evaluated. Here all the Foundation Phase team need to meet to discuss findings and discuss ways forward for individual children. Different team members bring different expertise and experiences and by working together can enrich the observation process and inform planning. Observations need collaboration between all stakeholders in a setting in order to get a true reflection of each child's development.

Analysis requires objectivity and consideration and interpretation of observed findings. In this way the setting can plan for the individual child and decided on the next step. Observations can provide highly accurate, detailed and verifiable information (Moore, 2001). Judgement about an individual child's progress or behaviour would not be based on just one observation. As stated previously, in the Foundation Phase a child will be observed continuously and a portfolio of observations be built up to give a holistic view of the child.

Children's involvement

The UN Convention on the Rights of the Child (UN, 1989) set the standards for listening to children's voices and promoting children's involvement in any decision-making that is relevant to them. Since the UN Convention there has been an emphasis on children having an increased control over the policies, services and curricula that concern them.

If children are old enough they need to be informed and the process of observation explained to them. This can aid practitioners in providing learning environments that are enjoyable and exciting. However, even at a young age children still need to be treated with sensitivity and respect. Practitioners need to be aware of when children do not want to take part.

Ethical considerations should not be separated from the observation process but an integral part of it. Ethical considerations should underpin the whole of the observation process. There needs to be consideration of what information will be collected. The aims and objectives of the observations need to be clear and under-stood by all the team members and a joint decision made on the observations methods to be used.

Remember that all observations are confidential to the setting, but a child's parents or legal guardian has a right to see any observations written about their child. The whole observational process should be explained to parents and how observations of their child will be beneficial. The involvement of parents in the observational planning can help break down any potential barriers between profes-sionals and parents.

Observational records must be kept for the 'safe and efficient management of the settings and to meet the needs of the children' (DCSF, 2008, p. 38). All data collected is regulated under the Data Protection Act of 1998 and the Freedom of Information Act of 2000.

Limitations of observations

Whilst the usefulness of observations has been discussed throughout this chapter, it is important to remember that observations capture what is actually happening at the time without giving a history of what happened before. Observations need to be used alongside other assessment tools to gain a holistic picture of the child in question. Meetings with other practitioners in the setting, with parents and profes-sionals can offer information and evidence not captured by observations. As Gillham (2008, p. 1) concludes, 'Observations cannot tell the whole story; and even when extended over time, it [sic] can only incorporate a narrow section of evolution of a group, a culture or an individual.'

Conclusion

Observations are used as a tool for practitioners in the Foundation Phase to assess children's learning needs. They allow practitioners to plan effectively and to reflect on their own practice. Children's rights need to be considered and the appropriate observational method chosen depending on the aims of the observation. Observations need to be carried out regularly by trained practitioners and shared with parents when required. It is important to use observations alongside other methods of assessment to get an overall picture of a child's development and to remember that all children are different. In Wales the Foundation Phase should embrace an individual's readiness to learn, and observations are one way to assess this readiness.

Chapter summary

- Observations offer us information and evidence for understanding and extending our knowledge of children's development and learning. Both planned (structured) and natural (unstructured) observations allow the practitioner to identify a child's individual learning needs and to plan accordingly. Observations can be participant and non-participant.
- All observations are confidential and should only be shared with the appropriate person. Practitioners should use observations to reflect on their own practice and provision provided. All stakeholders in the setting should be involved in carrying out observations.
- Observations should be part of daily practice in the Foundation Phase and are a requirement of the Welsh Government for all practitioners working in the Foundation Phase. Different observational methods should be used depending on what is required. There are various ways to record observations and again the focus of the observation will determine the best method of recording.
- Factors that could affect the results of an observation need to be taken into consideration. Children's rights need to be considered and respected when carrying out observations. Practitioners need to remain objective and only record what they see.

Access the following link online to take part in a word search about this chapter:

www.bloomsbury.com/an-introduction-to-the-foundation-phase-9781474264273

Thought-provoking questions

- How does your setting ensure children's rights are met during observations?
- How does your setting use observations to ensure the learning provision is suitable?
- How often do you share the information gained from observing children with other stakeholders to inform the planning process?
- How often do you stop and just watch children play in the setting?

Further reading and information

Carr, M. (2011), *Assessment in Early Childhood Settings.* London: Sage.

Forman, G. and E. Hall (2009), *Wondering with Children: The Importance of Observation in Early Education*: http://ecrp.uiuc.edu/v7n2/forman.html.

Hobart, C and J. Frankel (2004), *A Practical Guide to Child Observation and Assessments*, 3rd edn. Cheltenham: Stanley Thornes.

Ridell-Leech, S. (2008), *How to Observe Children*, 2nd edn. Oxford: Heinemann Educational. Publishers

6

Methods of Assessment

Chapter aims

To discuss different methods of assessment in the Foundation Phase.
To recognize what is meant by 'Assessment for Learning' (AFL).
To illustrate the different approaches to AFL in the Foundation Phase.

What do we mean by assessment?

According to the Welsh Government (2011, p. 2), assessment of children within the continuous, enhanced and **focused provision** of the Foundation Phase curriculum will allow the practitioner to:

- inform children of their achievements and next steps for their learning and development;
- inform colleagues, parents/carers of children's achievements and next steps for their learning and development; and
- inform transition throughout the Foundation Phase and between the Foundation Phase and Key Stage 2.

Assessment must have a purpose and in the Foundation Phase observation is the most reliable way to build up an accurate and informative picture of what a child can or cannot do. Assessment can be both formative and summative and this chapter will examine both.

Getting started

The cycle of planning, teaching and assessment starts with assessing the learners' needs and can be presented in the following way:

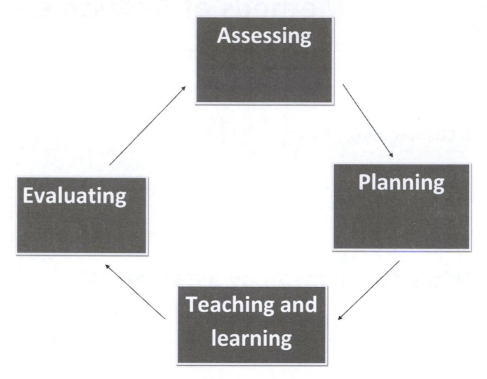

Figure 6.1 Cycle of Assessment, Planning and Pedagogy

As well as ongoing formative assessment through observation, children throughout the Foundation Phase will be assessed using statutory standardized tests.

Previous on-entry assessment (baseline assessment) in the Foundation Phase

In September 2011 the Welsh Government introduced a new 'all Wales baseline assessment' called the 'Child Development Assessment Profile' (CDAP). This assessment was statutory and covered six Developmental Areas which made up the 'Foundation Phase child development assessment profile' (WG, 2011). A written report was given to parents/carers on the child's achievement in each of the six Developmental Areas during the term in which the on-entry assessment was completed. The on-entry assessment addressed each of the following Developmental Areas which make up the profile:

- Personal, Social and Emotional.
- Speaking and Listening.
- Reading and Writing.
- Sort, Order and Number.
- Approach to Learning, Thinking and Reasoning.
- Physical.

(Please note these are different to the seven Areas of Learning within the Foundation Phase framework.)

The assessment of each area was undertaken in the language of the setting. (Consider the implications of this for a child entering Welsh-medium education from an English-speaking background.) The purpose of the profile was to provide a 'baseline' of where the child is and the next steps for their development. For the majority of children that was around the age of three; in other words, the term following their third birthday ('rising threes').

CDAP was made statutory for the first time in settings in September 2011, and practitioners quickly raised concerns about the length of time it took to complete and that there was little or no correlation between the CDAP areas of development and the seven areas of learning in the Foundation Phase. These concerns – and others – were reported back to Welsh Government and as a result a 'rapid response' report by Iram Siraj-Blatchford was commissioned in December 2011 to look at the concerns raised. She reported her initial findings to the then Education Minister, Leighton Andrews, on 5 February 2012 and her final findings on 25 March 2012.

The final report, entitled *An Independent (Unfunded) Rapid Review of the Child Development Assessment Profile (CDAP) on entry to the Foundation Phase in Wales*, was published on 23 April 2012 and identified a significant number of problems with CDAP. In the report, Professor Iram Siraj-Blatchford – an expert at the London Institute of Education – said a 'lack of clarity of core purpose' made CDAP difficult to judge. The full report can be accessed at: http://wales.gov.uk/docs/dcells/publications/120430cdapreviewen.pdf.

In light of these initial findings, Leighton Andrews announced on 21 February 2012 that there were 'significant problems with CDAP' and withdrew it as a statutory assessment tool in all education settings. In fact the authors have interviewed a variety of stakeholders about their feelings and opinions of CDAP and the following are some examples of the responses received:

'Complete waste of money.'
'Confusion for staff and parents.'
'No idea what to do with the data.'
'Totally bizarre.'
'Some statements ridiculous.'
'Time consuming/Workload ridiculous.'
'Shocking and shameful.'

It was made clear to the authors from the stakeholder interviews that there were major concerns raised by settings who had initially piloted CDAP prior to its introduction in September 2011. On querying this with one policymaker, they stated that those concerns had been noted and CDAP was changed to reflect these points. However, this was not the opinion of those interviewed by the authors, with one stakeholder reporting that 'Trialling and piloting was a complete mockery.' The training given on implementing CDAP was also brought into question, with the same stakeholder commenting that on attending a CDAP training session people were split into three groups and that each of the three groups were 'told something different so there was no consistency with WG training'.

The stakeholder went on to say that people were raising real concerns at this training session, but the person chairing it '[h]eld up his hands and said "I'm not an educationalist", and that he '[d]id not feel sufficiently qualified to respond'. In addition, one of the people actually running the training session admitted that 'the first time she had seen the material [CDAP] was that morning'!

Perhaps the frustrations and confusion around CDAP can be summed up best by the following comment from this stakeholder:

> There were so many inconsistencies and we were constantly phoning WG and asking for clarification and there were inconsistencies in the messages coming back. Yes it was frustrating and it caused anxiety.

Up to September 2015, schools did not have anything in place to replace CDAP. On talking to various practitioners and head teachers, it seemed that some schools were using a 'watered down' version of CDAP or had purchased an alternative assessment tool. The implications of this is that there has not be an 'all Wales baseline' in use since 2011 and no consentient means or method of assessing children on entry to the Foundation Phase. In a meeting in the summer of 2012 with the Welsh Education Minister, Leighton Andrews, the authors asked the following questions regarding CDAP: 'What was the cost of implementing the now defunct CDAP and when will a new all Wales baseline be ready for practitioners to use?' The response was as follows: 'The total cost of piloting and publication was £226,173.64 million – the new tool will utilise those elements of the CDAP that worked well … The current timescale is to have a new tool in place for use, possibly on a pilot basis, from September 2013. Exact timescales cannot be confirmed until a suitable contractor is appointed.' The minister went on to say that they 'want to ensure that the new tool is fit for purpose and provides practitioners with the robust information they need to monitor pupils' progress as they move through the education system' (July, 2012).

Another policy advisor to the Welsh Government indicated that there would be a developmental tool to replace CDAP that will cover the age ranges 0 to 7 years. This was confirmed by the following statement issued by the Welsh Government on 13 June 2012:

> The Minister for Education and Skills, the Minister for Health and Social Services and the Deputy Minister for Children and Social Services have agreed that co-operation is needed in drawing up a detailed specification and development plan for a suitable developmental assessment tool to meet the specific needs of health visitors, Foundation Phase, and Flying Start.
>
> (WG, 2012)

On 8 October 2012 the Welsh Government sent out its eNewsletter to all settings asking stakeholders to complete an online questionnaire regarding child development assessment tools. The purpose was to find out which assessment tools settings had used for an on-entry baseline in September 2012 and how continuous assessment was being carried out throughout the Foundation Phase. The Welsh Government wanted to review what was happening in Wales and to take on board practitioners' views and opinions before the introduction of a new Early Years Assessment Tool (EYAT) for 0- to 7-year-olds. This report highlighted that settings were using a variety of assessment tools. The full report can be accessed at: http://learning.wales.gov.uk/resources/review-of-early-years-child-assessment-tools-used-in-wales/?lang=en.

At the time of writing, a new Foundation Phase Profile (FPP) has been piloted in primary schools ready for statutory implementation in September 2015. This will be a baseline and an end-of-phase assessment tool. This is discussed in more detail in Chapter 12, and the current information available from the Welsh Government can be found at: http://gov.wales/topics/educationandskills/earlyyearshome/foundation-phase/foundation-phase-profile/?lang=en.

Ongoing assessment in nursery, reception and Year 1

Practitioners will gather evidence through observations on each child's progress in all seven Areas of Learning and parents will continue to receive written reports on their children's progress in all of these areas. Since May 2013, children in Wales aged between seven and fourteen years have been required to sit statutory numeracy and reading tests. The results from these tests are reported to parents at the end of the summer term and the national data received from every school is published in the autumn of that year on the Welsh Government website. Pupils aged five to fourteen years (Year 2 to Year 9) are also taught and assessed through a statutory National Literacy and Numeracy Framework (LNF) which started in September 2013. Teachers assess pupils against the expectations set out in the framework and give a 'best fit' at the end of each year. The next section will discuss the tests and framework in more detail.

The all Wales literacy and numeracy tests

Since May 2013, children in Wales aged between seven and fourteen have been required to sit national tests in literacy and numeracy. The numeracy test consisted of procedural numeracy from May 2013 and numerical reasoning from May 2014, and the literacy test consisted of a reading and comprehension task. These tests were introduced to help raise the standards of literacy and numeracy amongst children in Wales, driven in part by the poor Programme for International Student Assessment (PISA) results from the 2009 and 2012 tests, where Wales came bottom out of all the home nations in literacy and mathematics. The tests give each child across Wales a standardized score indicating how well a child has done compared with other children of the same age (in years and months). For these tests, the age standardized score is set at 100 and it is expected that approximately two-thirds of children sitting the test will have a standardized score of between 85 and 115. The tests also give a progress measure and this shows how well a child has done compared with all other learners taking the test in the same year group. This will allow children's progress to be measured over time, and if similar results are evidenced from year to year, then this would suggest a child is making steady progress. The Welsh Government has produced information for parents in relation to the tests, and further information can be found at: http://learning.gov.wales/resources/browse-all/reading-and-numeracy-tests-information-for-parents-carers/?lang=en.

In addition, there are sample tests available on the Learning Wales website: http://learning.gov.wales/resources/improvementareas/assessment-and-target-setting/national-reading-and-numeracy-tests/?lang=en.

These tests have had an impact on the delivery of the Foundation Phase in Year 2, with some practitioners feeling under pressure to teach to the test at the expense of a play-based pedagogy. Additionally, there have been reports of children becoming stressed and upset at having to sit these tests. This is discussed in more detail in Chapter 11.

The Literacy and Numeracy Framework (LNF)

As well as the introduction of the tests, the Welsh Government introduced the Literacy and Numeracy Framework (LNF) on a statutory basis in September 2013. Again, the purpose of this was and is to raise standards in literacy and numeracy in schools across the whole of Wales. This replaced the communication and number element of the non-statutory skills framework introduced in 2008. As Estyn reported in July 2012, the skills framework had not been effective and schools were not using it in their teaching and planning for learners (Estyn, 2012c).

The LNF was developed in partnership with an advisory panel of Local Authority literacy and numeracy advisors, and the Welsh Government undertook a consultation exercise on the LNF between the 11 June and the 12 October 2012. The LNF is intended to be a curriculum-planning tool for schools with expected annual outcomes in literacy and numeracy for all learners aged five to fourteen (Year 2 to Year 9). The LNF allows teachers to embed literacy and numeracy in their teaching across the curriculum in all areas of learning (Foundation Phase) and in all subjects (KS2 and KS3).

The LNF is split into components for literacy and numeracy, which in turn are split into strands. The literacy strands are oracy, reading and writing across the curriculum. The numeracy strands are developing numerical reasoning, using number skills and using measuring and data skills. The literacy component is available in both Welsh and English, with some distinctive element in the Welsh literacy component reflecting the unique requirements of the Welsh language. As well as being used as a curriculum-planning tool, the LNF is to be used as a method of formative assessment, and teachers will report on learners' literacy and numeracy skills annually to parents from September 2104 onwards. In developing the LNF, the Welsh Government has realigned learner expectations at the end of Key Stage 2 and Key Stage 3, with learners expected to work at level 5 and level 6 respectively. Learners are expected to acquire and apply the literacy and numeracy skills and concepts they have learned across all areas of the curriculum. By providing year-upon-year expectations, there is a clear understanding of what the children are expected to achieve and what they will learn in future years. The LNF also supports the more able and talented learners and provides support to those who are struggling with the *Routes for Learning* expectations.

There will be no national data collection in relation to assessments made against the LNF. Instead, the LNF should be used alongside other methods of assessment (including the literacy and numeracy tests) to highlight learner strengths and identify areas for development. The assessment made against the LNF will be used to generate information to support whole-school improvement.

In light of the introduction of the LNF, the Welsh Government engaged in consultation in 2014 on proposals to introduce new Areas of Learning for language, literacy and communication skills and mathematical development, as well as new programmes of study in maths and English and Welsh (first language) for Key Stages 2 and 3; there were also revisions to the Routes for Learning. The aim of this consultation was to strengthen literacy and numeracy pedagogy in these Areas of Learning and programmes of study by complementing and aligning them with the LNF. The revisions to the literacy and numeracy Areas of Learning and programmes of study for maths, English and Welsh (first language) are statutory from September 2015.

The revisions made to the literacy and numeracy Areas of Learning and programme of study for maths and English have led to changes in the content and presentation of the guidance documentation for these subjects. In addition, there has been an extension to the LNF for nursery children and a comprehensive independent review of the National Curriculum and assessment arrangements in Wales by Professor Graham Donaldson (this is reviewed in Chapter 12). These changes include year-on-year expectation statements for literacy and numeracy and an alignment of the former Areas of Learning and programmes of study and LNF skills in one document. The Areas of Learning and programmes of study are designed as a continuum of learning to allow practitioners to assess where a learner currently is and what the next step in their learning should be.

The Welsh Government has made it clear that in the Foundation Phase the emphasis is still on the stage, not age, approach to learning. There should not be a return to the old approach of whole class teaching and the literacy and numeracy hour, but still a balance of child-led and adult-led active learning. This is reinforced at the beginning of the Areas of Learning for literacy and numeracy through a Foundation Phase pedagogy of statements. This is followed by a range of experiences that provides the context for the development of skills in literacy and numeracy. Practitioners should plan these experiences through the focused, continuous and **enhanced provision** across the Foundation Phase.

The revised literacy and numeracy Areas of Learning have increased expectations and standards compared to the existing curriculum. The new Foundation Phase Profile (FPP, discussed previously) has revised Foundation Phase outcome descriptions (see below) which will reflect the raised expectations in the LNF and the revised Areas of Learning for literacy and numeracy. These will become statutory in September 2015. Information on the revised areas of learning and the revised Foundation Phase outcomes can be found at: http://gov.wales/docs/dcells/publications/150803-fp-framework-en.pdf.

Foundation Phase outcomes

Each of the seven Areas of Learning has Foundation Phase outcomes from 1 through to 6, and these describe the skills and range of performance that children working within a particular outcome should characteristically demonstrate. Based on ongoing observations throughout the Foundation Phase, practitioners should, when deciding on a child's level of attainment in that phase, judge which outcome best fits the child's performance. Each Foundation Phase outcome should be checked against adjacent outcomes to ensure that the outcome awarded is the best fit to the child's performance (WG, 2011).

To arrive at a rounded judgement of a child's performance, practitioners should use a range of evidence over time. At the end of the Foundation Phase, assessment should be based securely on practitioners' collective understanding of the outcomes set out in the Foundation Phase framework (WG, 2011). The Foundation Phase outcomes originally cross-referenced to the old Key Stage 1 National Curriculum (NC) levels as follows:

- Foundation Phase Outcome 4 links with NC level 1.
- Foundation Phase Outcome 5 links with NC level 2.
- Foundation Phase Outcome 6 links with NC level 3.

However, since introduction of the Literacy and Numeracy framework and the revised Areas of Learning for literacy and numeracy (statutory in September 2015), Foundation Phase outcome 5 now links with NC level 3, and Foundation Phase outcome 6 with NC level 4. As discussed previously, the new Foundation Phase Profile (FPP) will have revised Foundation Phase outcomes which reflects the raised expectation of the LNF.

End of Foundation Phase assessment (Year 2)

Currently, and not later than twenty days before the end of summer term, there must be an assessment of the child's attainment in Personal and Social Development, Well-Being and Cultural Diversity; Language, Literacy and Communication Skills in English or Welsh; and Mathematical Development. These attainments are based on the Foundation Phase Outcomes and are teacher assessed, with the results are reported to the Welsh Government. Children are expected to be awarded Foundation Phase outcomes in the range of outcomes 4 to 6 in Year 2.

Guidance issued by the Welsh Government in 2013a stated that leaders and head teachers are responsible for ensuring that Foundation Phase staff gather and record evidence about each child from the seven Areas of Learning as they progress and move through the Foundation Phase. The guidance document can be accessed at: http://wales.gov.uk/topics/educationandskills/schoolshome/curriculuminwales/statutoryassessment/;jsessionid=6DAD9A895FD4F984F49DF57F0CE4D0B7?lang=en.

The child's attendance is also included and parents are invited into settings to discuss the report. There is a commentary on the individual child's areas of strength and areas for development – an example of summative assessment. Schools also need to provide comparative information. This provides the percentage of children in the school at each Foundation Phase outcome for:

- Personal and Social Development, Well-Being and Cultural Diversity;
- Language, Literacy and Communication Skills;
- Mathematical Development.

If appropriate, this information should also include children who have been disapplied, those working towards Foundation Phase Outcome 1 and those not awarded a level for reasons other than disapplication (WG, 2011).

National comparative information

Since 2012, schools have been required to provide national comparative data for inclusion in reports. The information includes the percentage of children in Wales at Foundation Phase outcome 5 and above for:

- Personal and Social Development, Well-Being and Cultural Diversity;
- Language, Literacy and Communication Skills;
- Mathematical Development.

This data is available on the Welsh Government website in August of each year and can be accessed at: http://wales.gov.uk/topics/statistics/headlines/schools2012/1208141/?lang=en.

Reporting to parents/carers

When a child enters Foundation Phase in the autumn, spring or summer term, a written on-entry assessment report must be provided to the parents/carers. This report must be given to parents during the term that the on-entry assessment was completed. Parents are also given the opportunity to discuss the report with staff in the setting.

All children in nursery, reception and Year 1 and Year 2 should receive a final end of year written report. The only exception to this is if a child has entered the Foundation Phase in the summer term and the parents have received an on-entry report.

Assessment for learning (AFL) in the Foundation Phase

All forms of assessment help to shape students' learning (Brown and Knight, 1994), and formative assessment is one of the most powerful forms of assessment that motivates and boosts achievement and empowers the learner (Weeden, et al., 2002; Cauley and McMillan, 2009).

Assessment for learning (AFL) is the continuous formative assessment that goes on throughout the Foundation Phase. This is done through many different methods and is both practitioner- and child-led. Assessment and observation are linked, as shown in the figure below:

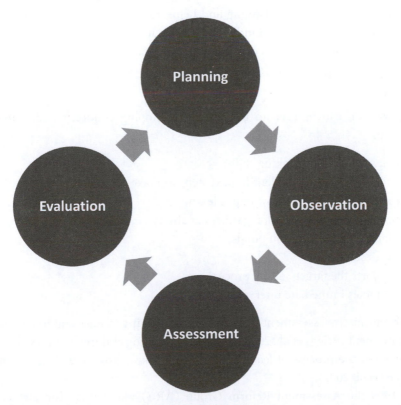

Figure 6.2 Link between Assessment and Observation

Practitioners use observations to assess children against learning objectives and targets set by the staff or by the children themselves. Throughout the Foundation Phase, assessments and observations of the children will be recorded in individual child portfolios that will be added to as the child progresses through the Foundation Phase. It can help to identify children's achievements and their learning needs and strategies. Worthwhile curriculum content can be matched to children's learning needs once those needs have been identified (Nutbrown, 2006).

However, 'assessment for learning is probably the most neglected topic in the whole of the educational world, whether this is educational policy making, educational research or educational practice itself' (Weeden, et al., 2002, p. 150). Black et al. (2003) agree and state that formative assessment is currently one of the weaker elements of educational practice, yet it is something that raises standards (Black and Wiliam, 1998). Furthermore, Black et al. (2003) claim that the most important debate of all is that about improving the learning of all students and developing lifelong learners.

So what is formative assessment? It can be summed up as follows:

- Ongoing cumulative information about a child's progress.
- Provision of weekly/daily information about what children know and can do.
- Helps informs future planning and helps adults to make decisions about the current learning needs of individual children.
- Provision of narrative records of what children do and say.
- Creation of opportunities for you as practitioners to provide recommendations for future sessions.

Therefore AFL can be seen to be vital in developing children's ability to 'learn' because it:

- helps to develop thinking skills;
- encourages pupils to identify next steps to make progress;
- provides insight into how pupils learn;
- promotes success for all, regardless of ability;
- increases self-esteem in pupils;
- raises standards;
- supports the target-setting process;
- promotes immediate intervention.

Effective formative assessment is a key factor in helping to raise children's standards of achievement (Briggs et al., 2008). In addition, getting children to think about their learning and the process of learning is vital in linking assessment and learning in practice (Hall, 2007).

In 1999 the Assessment Reform Group (ARG) wrote that 'The awareness of learning and ability of learners to direct it for themselves is of increasing importance in the context of encouraging lifelong learning' (1999, p. 7). Central to assessment for learning or formative assessment is that it is:

- embedded in the teaching and learning process;
- involves sharing learning objectives with pupils;
- involves pupils in self assessment;
- provides feedback which leads pupils to identify what they should do next to improve;
- involves both the teacher and the pupils reviewing and reflecting on pupils' performance and progress.

It is suggested that 'the use of assessment to help pupils learn is one of the weakest aspects of practice in classrooms across the UK' (Assessment Reform Group, 1999, p. 5). Therefore It could be argued that for students to get the most out of the assessment process they need to be involved in it (Harris and Bell, 1986). One needs to consider whether assessment is something done to students, with students or for students (Brown and Knight, 1994). However if done properly, 'Assessment for learning is assessment which extends children's learning because it enhances teaching' (Nutbrown, 2006 p. 126).

Implementing AFL in the classroom

One of the main issues around assessment for learning, according to Boyle and Charles (2010), is that it has been dominated by gimmicks rather than focusing on helping teachers fully understand its principles. They found that summative assessment, rather than formative assessment, was viewed as integral to teaching and learning. There were also many definitions of formative assessment (between schools) and many ways in which it was being implemented; and it was widely misunderstood. Harris and Muijs (2005) make the point that resources (in this case, AFL gimmicks) are often marketed with the view that they can be implemented in any school, when in reality 'it shows that the variability in implementation is often due to local contextual demands, constraints or differences' (Harris and Muijs, 2005, p. 130). Today, in the Foundation Phase curriculum, assessment for learning is implemented in a number of different ways and each setting will have their own methods in place.

Examples of AFL in the Foundation Phase classroom

- Through interactive displays.
- Visual displays highlight key topics, key words, and key concepts.

- Target walls.
- Evidence of learning objectives/outcomes.
- Evidence of success criteria.

Examples of AFL in the whole school environment

- Celebrating effort and achievement – 'star of the week' etc.
- Creating a learning environment throughout the school (inside and out).
- School council – contribute ideas on developing environment.
- Sharing successes with the wider community.

Examples of AFL implemented by the class teacher

- Clear learning outcomes.
- Success criteria that provides pupils with a template for success.
- Effective questioning.
- Good classroom management that involves all learners.
- Providing opportunities for reflection.
- Pupils involved in personal target setting.

Examples of AFL as a tool for reflection

Children are encouraged to continually reflect upon their understanding and label their work using the traffic light system.

RED – I do not understand this work and can see that I need help to improve my work.

AMBER – There are parts that I don't really understand and can see that I need to go over it to help me improve my work.

GREEN – Work understood. I am happy with the quality of my work.

Pupils use the 'traffic light icons' to label their work, green, amber or red according to whether they think they have good, partial or little understanding. These labels serve as a simple means of communication of pupils' self-assessments.

(Black et al., 2002, p. 11)

Another form of self-assessment is to ask pupils to traffic light a piece of work in the first place and then indicate by using the thumbs-up/thumbs-down method whether they have put green, amber or red. The teacher can then pair up the greens and ambers to deal with problems between them, whilst the red pupils can be helped as a group. Before peer-group work takes place, pupils will need training and guidance on how to work together, listening to one another and taking turns (Black et al., 2002).

Peer assessment

Piaget emphasized the role of peer interaction in a child's cognitive development. He believed that children value activities preferred by their peers and peers can role model new ideas. More able learners can explain activities to less able learners in simpler terms; this also allows the more able learner to learn through verbalizing the problem. Finally both the more and less able learner gains a greater insight into the problem through a shared learning experience (Gray and Macblain, 2012).

According to Race (2001), there are many benefits for the students and significant reasons for conducting peer and self-assessment, including deepening the learning experience; understanding and appreciating the role of the tutor in marking work and experiencing how a teacher thinks; and developing autonomous learners who have the ability to reflect on their work and that of others in a constructive way (Race, 2001).

Furthermore, productive formative assessment should consist of self-assessment strategies that empower students to take control of their learning (Black et al., 2003). Harlen (2006) suggests that teachers should aim to improve self-efficacy (how students feel on approaching a task) through assessment, and Brown and Knight (1994) argue that assessment should be a shared, collaborative process of teaching and learning. This embraces the Foundation Phase principle of teamwork and shared thinking between learners. When teachers take a constructivist view of learning they encourage students to take part in self- and peer assessment and view them as integral co-partners in the teaching and learning process (Harlen, 2006). In addition, 'self-assessment fosters a different, more powerful view of the student than does traditional assessment' (Brown and Knight, 1994, p. 54).

For pupils, one of the reasons peer assessment works is that they may accept criticism from one another more readily than from their teacher. Also the language employed when peer assessing is more user friendly as it is the language the pupils will use themselves.

Before peer assessment can take place there does need to be some guidance given to the pupils involved.

Guidance

- Tends to work more effectively if there is not a wide gap between abilities.
- Pupil needs time to reflect on own work before response partner sees it.
- Always start with a positive comment.
- Partner should be given time to take in work to be assessed.
- Pupils need to be trained in success and improvement process.
- Pupils must agree on part to be changed.
- Response partner should ask for clarification rather than jump to conclusions.

Questionnaires can also be a method for peer and self-assessment. This helps the child to identify how they think they have done with a given activity. Whilst peer assessment is going on, the teacher can be free to observe and reflect on what is happening and frame helpful interventions (Black et al., 2002).

Activities to promote self- and peer assessment

- Tickled pink and green for growth – here pupils are given positive feedback (tickled pink) and targets for improvement (green for growth).
- Group responses (work as a team on activities).
- Phone a friend (ask other pupils to help them).
- Whiteboards (write down answers to questions on mini white boards and show each other).
- Marking an exemplar (mark a model answer to gain practice).

In order to assess each other's work children need to be familiar with the learning outcomes and the success criteria. One way of doing this in the Foundation Phase setting is to use the 'Learning Ladybird' and 'Successful Spider' method.

I am Successful Spider.
I am going to tell you how you will know if you understand what you are learning.

I am Learning Ladybird.
I will tell you what you are going to learn

Practitioners share the learning outcomes with the children at the start of the lesson and they are displayed throughout the lesson for the children to refer to.

Reflective task

If you are a practitioner, consider for the following activities a 'Learning Ladybird' outcome and 'Successful Spider' criteria:

a) Sequencing pictures from a well-known story.
b) Understanding 'full' and 'empty'.
c) Matching animals to their habitats.
d) Being able to write their own name.

Figure 6.3 Learning Ladybird and Successful Spider. Images courtesy of www. sparklebox.co.uk. Used with permission.

The learning outcome and the success criteria are shared with the class and are on display for the children to refer to when completing their work.

Why are success criteria important?

- Improve understanding.
- Empower pupils.
- Encourage independent learning.
- Enable accurate feedback.

Effective success criteria ...

- are linked to the learning intention;
- are specific to an activity;
- are discussed and agreed with pupils prior to undertaking the activity;
- provide a scaffold and focus for pupils while engaged in the activity;
- are used as the basis for feedback and peer/self-assessment.

As Manning (2012) argues, a student needs to understand the aim of an activity and how to achieve that aim in order to succeed. Pupils can then mark their own work or each other's work using a range of formative assessment tools. One way that is regularly used in Foundation Phase settings is the two stars and a wish method (positive feedback: 2 stars; and the way forward: a wish).

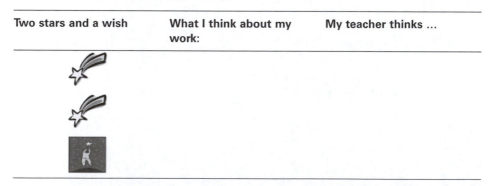

Two stars and a wish	What I think about my work:	My teacher thinks ...

Pupils then refer back to this when they undertake their next piece of work, and work on their 'wish' criteria. 'Peer and self assessment make a unique contribution to the development of pupils' learning – they secure aims that cannot be achieved in any other way' (Black et al., 2002, p. 12).

Think-pair-share

Pupils are paired with a partner to work on a given learning task/outcome. The pupils will think of how they are going to meet the learning outcome; they will pair up and share ideas with each other and work together to achieve the success criteria. This can extend a child's thinking and reflects Vygotsky's theory of social interaction aiding the learning process. This type of interaction between peers introduces relevant vocabulary, challenges the learner and encourages reflection. However, the role of the practitioner is vital here to encourage children throughout the think-pair-share process.

Questioning

Most teachers waste their time by asking questions that are intended to discover what a pupil does not know, whereas the true art of questioning has for its purpose to discover what the pupil knows or is capable of knowing (Einstein, 1920). Questioning pupils is a key teaching strategy because it can:

- assess children's understanding;
- assess errors and misconceptions;
- understand the thinking behind children's methods;
- focus discussions by using children's ideas;
- elicit concrete examples or principles or concepts;
- explore language and vocabulary;
- encourage reflection.

There are two mains types of questions: closed and open. Closed questions require one-word or very brief responses, whereas open questions require more extensive responses. Both types are used in teaching: closed when you want brisk, quick answers, and open when you want to stimulate discussion. The disadvantages of closed questions are that only the children that are confident of providing the answers will participate. To engage more learners and higher-order thinking skills, open questions need to be asked. Clarke (2001) states that starting questions with *Do you think …?* is important as it shows the teacher is not asking for certainty.

It is common for practitioners to begin a new topic through assessing what the children know through questioning the class. However, according to research carried out, many practitioners do not leave enough time after asking a question for pupils to answer (Rowe, 1974). The key to changing this is to allow a longer waiting time, but this is hard to do, especially when no answer is forthcoming. Increasing the waiting time can lead to more pupils being involved in question-and-answer discussions and an increase in the length of their replies. This allows everyone to think of an answer and to contribute to the discussion. All answers, right or wrong, can be used to assess understanding. Effective questioning should be used whilst pupils are engaged in an activity. This allows pupils to extend their thinking through immediate feedback on their work.

Target setting

Pupils are involved in setting their own targets throughout the Foundation Phase. Teachers will work alongside pupils and discuss their work with them and set targets for improvement. Once set, the child brings home the targets to share with the parents. Targets are usually reviewed every half-term or once a term. If the child has met the targets then new ones are set. Sadler (1989) argues that it is the role of the teacher to enable the student to develop the ability to do their own assessment of their learning and to develop the skills to plan their future learning experiences. Some settings will set realistic and challenging targets for pupils.

Gathering evidence

A rich range of different types of evidence needs to be gathered to build up a complete picture of each child. Examples can include:

- *products* – end results such as a piece of written work or a creative model;
- *observation* – carried out during a lesson in order to see if a child understands a process;
- *questioning* – used during lessons, in plenaries and can be formal or informal;
- *other methods* – videos, photos, audio recordings;
- *children's self- and peer assessment* – ask the children to provide own evidence
(Manning, 2012).

Providing effective feedback

The quality of feedback and the way in which we provide it can have a huge impact on learning. Simply giving a 'house point' or awarding a 'smiley face' and writing 'Good work' has no educational benefit to the pupil apart from promoting their self-esteem. In contrast, returning work to a child covered in red ink will lower their self-esteem and again is not helpful educationally with too much information to absorb.

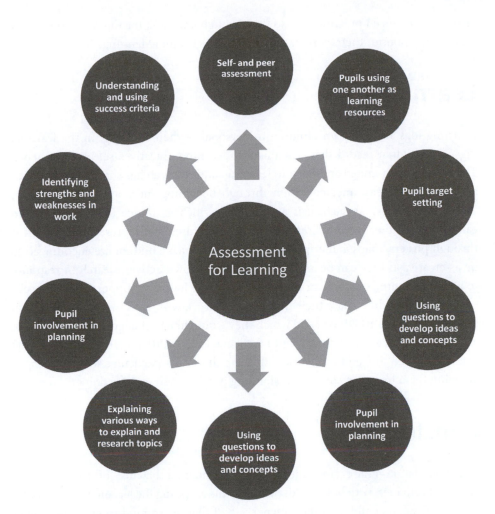

Figure 6.4 Assessment for Learning

Effective feedback needs to focus on the learning intentions/outcomes and the success criteria. Children can review their final work against a checklist to reduce careless errors. Both oral and written feedback needs to be given to either individual children or to groups of learners and time given for the children to reflect on this. Assessment for learning can be summed up in Figure 6.4.

In the Foundation Phase, practitioners should acknowledge prior learning and attainment, offer choices, challenge children and encourage them to move their learning along. Through appropriate planning, observations, assessments and structured experiences in all the Areas of Learning, children should grow, develop and progress in their development (WAG, 2008b).

Another form of assessment can be *dynamic assessment* – the immediate assessment made of a learner's progress and difficulties as they may arise during a lesson. Experienced practitioners do this through assessing the questions pupils ask and observations of their work or play during the lesson (Manning, 2012).

Learning logs

Learning logs are a way for children to personalize their learning. In the learning logs, the children record their responses to learning objectives set by the teacher. They are an open-ended approach to learning, and research has shown that children are likely to increase metacognition through becoming more aware of their own thought processes. As such, it is a document which is unique to the learner and cannot be 'right' or 'wrong'. Some of the ways children can represent their work is through posters, maps, bullet-points and power points. Children are encouraged to be as creative as they can be and to carry out their own active research in response to a given learning outcome or challenge. Learning logs also support peer and self-assessment. Children share their thoughts and work with each other, noting which aspects they are satisfied with and which they would like to change. Practitioners can also use the logs to assess and receive feedback on a child's understanding. Parents can be involved too, and can work with their child on a particular subject or topic, allowing them to have a clear understanding of what their child is doing.

Conclusion

The Foundation Phase curriculum should contain a balance of adult-led and child-led activities, with both children and adults assessing the learning that is taking place. AFL allows children to take ownership of their learning through a mixture of self- and peer assessment. Settings can use a range of methods for assessment for learning, but collaboration between all stakeholders is essential. AFL is an example of formative assessment and along with summative assessment allows practitioners to build up a detailed picture of a child's individual learning needs. Children are encouraged to set their own targets for learning and these are shared and reviewed on a regular basis. Some proponents agree that when children are set targets it gives focus to the learning. However, from the authors' classroom experiences this can be viewed as suggesting that children have to reach the same goals regardless of individuality. This reinforces the point made by Gerver (2010) in Chapter 1 about all children being the same.

Chapter summary

- Children are assessed on entry to the Foundation Phase using the new new Foundation Phase Profile (FPP). For the academic years 2012–15, schools used different methods to assess children on entry. This has meant no consistency between schools on the assessment used.
- A written report is given to parents at the end of each year of the Foundation Phase and children are assessed using Foundation Phase outcomes. Children at the end of the Foundation Phase will be awarded a Foundation Phase outcome in three Areas of Learning, which is reported to the Local Authority and the Welsh Government. The results for those children achieving Foundation Phase outcome 5 and above in each of the three areas can be found on the Welsh Government website for all Local Authorities in Wales. This is an example of summative assessment.
- The new National Literacy and Numeracy framework (NLNF) will become statutory in settings from September 2013. From September 2014, children aged between five and fourteen years will also be assessed against expectations in the LNF. Children aged seven to fourteen years will be tested in numeracy and literacy commencing in May 2013. The National Foundation for Educational Research (NFER) is designing the tests, which are paper-based assessments.
- Assessment for Learning (AFL) is a tool that allows both the practitioner and the child to assess their work. AFL is formative assessment and allows children to take ownership of their learning. There are many different methods to assess AFL as detailed earlier in this chapter. Questions should be used to assess learning and should be a mixture of both open-ended and closed types of questions.
- Schools set targets for their learners and these are agreed with the children and reassessed regularly. The authors feel that setting targets is a 'one size fits all' approach to learning and children should not be 'labelled' with targets in the Foundation Phase.

Access the following link online to take part in a word search about this chapter:

www.bloomsbury.com/an-introduction-to-the-foundation-phase-
9781474264273

Further reading and information

Cockburn, A. and G. Handscombe (eds) (2012), *Teaching Children 3–11*. London: Sage.

Estyn and Assessment for Learning: http://www.estyn.gov.uk/english/search/?keywords=assessment+for+learning&gobut.x=16&gobut.y=15.

Gray, C. and S. Macblain (2012), *Learning Theories in Childhood*. London: Sage.

Hobart, C. and J. Frankel (2009), *A Practical Guide to Child Observation and Assessment*. 4th edn, Cheltenham: Nelson Thornes.

Learning logs: http://www.learninglogs.co.uk/learningjournals.htm.

7

Planning for Purposeful Play in the Foundation Phase

Chapter aims

To explore how practitioners plan effectively in the Foundation Phase.

To discuss the importance of a play-based approach to teaching and learning.

To examine barriers to a play-based approach to teaching and learning.

Planning in the Foundation Phase

Practitioners need to plan across the seven Areas of Learning, promoting balance, appropriateness and progression in teaching and learning. Personal and social development should be at the heart of the curriculum and there needs to be parity between structured learning through child-initiated activities and those directed by adults.

> It is important that children are not introduced to formal methods of learning too soon as this can have a detrimental effect on their future learning and development.
>
> (WAG, 2008d, p. 8)

Everyone working with children *should* have good knowledge of child development, the milestones children are working towards appropriate to their age and how to use this knowledge to plan appropriate learning activities. Practitioners need to be reflective in order to ensure that their practice is continually evolving and that their knowledge is up to date. Gray and Macblain (2012, p. 12) write:

> It is essential that all of us who work with children, and who study their development, maintain a strong sense of critical reflection and openness in how we view child development and education as well as our own professional practice.

Foundation Phase planning needs to be flexible to allow practitioners to plan and provide an experiential curriculum based on the developmental stage of the child. There are many different structures and formats for planning but usually practitioners use long-term, medium-term and short-term planning which are discussed in more detail in this chapter.

Effective planning

Good curriculum planning is essential to promote balance, appropriateness and progression in teaching and learning. There needs to be a balance of child-led and adult-led activities. According to Ellis (2011, p. 29), 'in planning the curriculum we need to focus on what we want children to *learn*, rather than what we want them to *do*'. Moyles (2011) argues that it is the job of the teacher to translate the curriculum into learning activities for the children. As noted above, there are many different structures and formats for planning, but they usually include long-term plans, medium-term plans and short-term plans.

Long-term planning usually indicates what will be taught over the year and identifies the learning opportunities offered by each area of provision. It links to the continuous provision in the 'bottom up' model of delivery. Medium-term plans are usually for half a term or a term and identify a specific topic and links to the enhanced provision in the model of delivery. Medium-term planning also includes calendar events and visits and visitors. This planning *should* reflect the existing interests and needs of the children. It should include planning for all seven Areas of Learning inside and out. Teachers usually plan with three things in mind:

- Existing knowledge and interests.
- Curriculum guidelines.
- Teacher's own interests, strengths and motivation

(Moyles, 2011).

Short-term planning can be daily or weekly but needs to be flexible enough to adapt to learning needs and interests. This will be informed by the medium-term plans, observations and assessments of the children, individual targets and evaluations of earlier plans and from team discussions. Short-term planning should contain the intended learning outcomes and success criteria along with details of the activities, the adult responsible and differentiation (i.e. catering for different abilities within any given activity).

All types of planning need to be meaningful to others and should make links to the framework. There needs to be a balance between adult-initiated tasks and child-initiated learning. There should be evidence of differentiation, opportunities for planned observations, key questions and pertinent language. There should also be opportunities for choice and flexibility a consideration of the skills development and links made to the skills framework.

Themes and topics need to be imaginative, creative and fun, both for the children and the practitioners. Many settings start off a theme with a 'wow' day which may involve a trip somewhere such as a supermarket if the topic is 'food'. Or sometimes visitors will come in to work with the children, such as the local policeman if the topic is 'people who help us'.

Children's ideas are also encouraged during 'wow' days through mind mapping. This allows them to take ownership over the activities to be pursued and is a good opportunity for the practitioner to find out what they already know about a topic. Parents are informed about the topics being studied through 'termly curriculum maps' issued at the start of each term. Foundation Phase settings will differ in the way they set out their long-term, medium-term and short-term planning, but the key concepts will remain the same.

Access the following link online to view an example of a termly topic planner: www.bloomsbury.com/an-introduction-to-the-foundation-phase-9781474264273.

Building the Foundation Phase model of delivery

The Foundation Phase model is a 'bottom up' model which builds on what children can do and this means the *child* is at the centre of learning, not the *curriculum*.

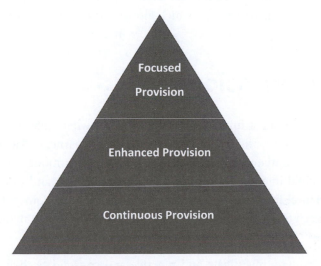

Figure 7.1 The Foundation Phase Triangle

If you are a practitioner, how would the triangle look in your setting?

Continuous provision

Long-term planning is the continuous provision from the model of delivery. Continuous provision encompasses the Areas of Learning that are always available for the children to access. Examples include:

- Construction (small and large)   ICT
- Sand (wet and dry)   Role-play
- Water   Reading Corner
- Clay/dough   Painting
- Mark-making   Creative Area
- Outdoor classroom   Music Table

When practitioners are planning for the long-term continuous provision, it is crucial that they are aware of the progression of skills needed to be developed throughout all areas of the curriculum. The skills for each Area of Learning can be found in the Foundation Phase framework documentation and the non-statutory skills framework (see further reading).

Enhanced provision

Medium-term planning is the enhanced provision from the model of delivery and is usually half-termly or termly. Enhanced provision is what we add to the continuous provision to create additional, enhanced and enriched learning opportunities. This can be based on a topic or a theme which also incorporates some of the long-term plan objectives.

Focused provision

This is how practitioners initiate, direct and model what children need to learn in order to become confident, independent lifelong learners. These are specific activities that are initiated and modelled/led by the practitioner, involving high-quality adult–child interaction. This is short-term planning and can be weekly or even daily. All three levels of delivery have quality learning outcomes. The key points to note from each type of provision are that the continuous and enhanced provision gives children:

- time to explore, investigate and practice and consolidate their learning and understanding;
- an opportunity to follow and develop their ideas and interests;

- a way to take risks and problem-solve in a supervised environment;
- an opportunity to revisit skills and concepts until they are comfortable with them;
- time and opportunity to make connections necessary for understanding.

Focused provision allows practitioners the opportunity to introduce new skills and concepts and model what we want the children to do independently.

This model of delivery allows a balance between practitioner-led and child-initiated activities, teaching and learning, planned and spontaneous play, independent and directed learning and free choice and directed activities. Foundation Phase settings have the freedom to interpret how they are going to achieve this balance. An example of how the three areas of provision can link together is shown below.

Area: water tray
Continuous provision: water, water tray and aprons
Enhanced provision: containers of different sizes, funnels and scoops, tubing
Focused provision: work 1:1 with the children on understanding capacity

---

Copies of the enhanced and medium-term planning sheets can be sent home to parents to promote home–school links. When practitioners and parents work together there is a positive impact on the child's development (QCA, 2000).

Focused tasks

These are specific planned activities, usually initiated and modelled by the practitioner and involving high-quality adult–child interaction. The features of focused tasks are as follows:

- Direct teaching of skills/concepts/knowledge – the adult is leading the learning.
- Focused tasks can be whole group or individual and will vary according to the nature of the task.
- Learning is measured and the assessment of the learning links back to the learning intention.
- Next steps in the children's learning are identified and planned for.

Focused tasks should not stand alone; children need opportunities to practice skills/concepts/knowledge during play and in a relevant context. Focused tasks must be reflected in the environment, as **enhancements** to the **continuous** provision. An example of focused planning is shown below.

Foundation Phase Focus Plan:

Date_____

Class_____

Learning Intention	Activities	Resources/Key Vocabulary	Assessment of Learning	Assessment for Learning (Next Steps)
Knowledge and understanding of the world				
Creative development				
Welsh language development				
Physical development				
Personal and social development, well-being and cultural diversity				
Language, literacy and communication				
Mathematical development				

Key skills: LNF links, thinking skills and ICT skills should be identified under each Area of Learning.

It is important to note that these are **examples** – individual schools will have their own versions of planning for the three types of provision. An example of focused planning for a reception class studying the topic 'The supermarket' is shown below.

Area of Learning: Literacy, Language and Communication skills

Learning Objective	Activity	Key Skills	Success Criteria	Vocabulary
To write a simple shopping list	Children to look at a range of different food items and to choose their favourites to make a simple shopping list.	Communicating, listening, questioning, thinking skills, ICT	Are the children able to write a simple shopping list? Are the children able to choose which food items they want on their list independently?	Like Dislike Names of food

Individual settings will have their own format for planning and their own planning sheets; the above is just **one example**.

Organizing the classroom and learning environment

Practitioners need to set up an environment that allows skills to constantly develop (**continuous provision**). Some areas should be permanent to enable children to build on previous experiences (reading area, maths area, writing area, etc.). Topics/themes are opportunities to enhance the skills the children are developing to reflect their interests and take the learning forward (**enhanced provision**). What is planned for in **focused tasks** should then be reflected in the learning environment to allow consolidation. **Adult involvement in play** is crucial in order to model, extend and promote learning in different areas. Take time to **observe** the children in their play, to identify where they are in their learning, their needs and interests.

Experiential learning is the central focus throughout the day. It is the **stage not age** of the child that is of paramount importance. Time should be given for observation and interaction. Foundation Phase settings need to consider the organization of their areas of provision. For example:

- Would it more suitable to have the continuous provision such as sand and water in the same area?
- Would it be a sensible idea to have the writing area near to the role play if the children are going to be doing emergent writing in their role play?

- Where are the resources for outdoor learning and play going to be kept? Are the resources clearly labelled and can children access them easily?
- Is there a set timetable as to which resources children have available to them at specific times or on certain days of the week?

All of the above will depend on the size of the setting, the layout of the building and the needs of the children. However, all settings will need to ensure that children are given choice and opportunities to develop their independence.

Foundation Phase practitioners need to create an environment:

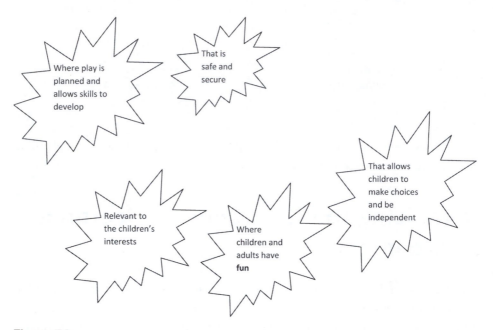

Figure 7.2

Foundation Phase practitioners need to consider the whole environment, both indoors and outdoors, and the impact on children's sense of well-being. Planning needs to be equally effective for both the outdoor and indoor environment. The learning environment should provide a wealth of learning possibilities and opportunities across all seven Areas of Learning. Teaching and learning experiences should be complementary both inside and outside.

In the Foundation Phase there needs to be a balance between free, child-led spontaneous activities and structured, focused and adult-led activities. In contrast to the belief of Maria Montessori, most Foundation Phase settings are rich and stimulating, with colourful wall displays and interactive Areas of Learning, and are enriching and fun. There should be free-flow access between the outdoors and indoors and between Foundation Phase classrooms (although this will depend on the building structure and layout of classrooms). The setting should be language rich in both Welsh and English and offer opportunities for the children to be independent, be loud and quiet, mark make and explore, read and investigate. Resources should provide for equal opportunities and meet individual needs. Activities should be stage and age appropriate and enable children to consolidate existing learning and acquire new skills. Children need to be able to make choices and engage in experiences that interest them. Remember, visitors are an excellent resource as they can provide first-hand experiences for the children. Most settings will have the following learning/play areas:

- Home corner
- Sand/water area
- Writing, mark making area
- Maths area
- ICT area
- Book corner/listening station
- Music table
- Construction area
- Craft table/painting area
- KUW/discovery area
- Outdoor area with equipment to enhance physical development.

All adults in the setting need to be involved in planning, doing, observing, assessing, evaluating and reviewing. This collaboration can be summarized as follows.

- **Continuous Provision:** Adults ensure children get the most out of their play. This is not about children completing tasks, but having fun.
- **Enhanced Provision:** Here the adult extends and enriches the learning by providing additional resources and introducing new ideas.
- **Focused Tasks:** The adult's role is to lead and develop the children's ideas, listen and respond to the children's theories and suggestions, teach skills, knowledge and concepts.

Adults need to be good role models, show empathy, be consistent, encourage and guide the children. They need to talk with the children, question them and share expertise with each other and use observations to improve practice. The learning environment needs to build upon the biological processes of child development and learning, the context in which development and learning takes place and the area of knowledge to which the child is introduced. In a quality learning environment these come together in an integrated way (Bruce, 2005).

Planning for play

The Welsh Assembly Government (2008d, p. 5) argues that 'Play is an essential ingredient in the curriculum which should be fun and stimulating.' The Plowden Report in 1967 acknowledged the importance of play and Chapter 2 discussed how both past and present pioneers of education recognized play as a crucial part of a child's learning and development.

Piaget saw play as a vital ingredient in the development of cognition. Children who engage in play are learning together by sharing, negotiating, problem-solving and communicating thoughts and ideas. He identified five types of play:

- Functional play
- Physical activity play
- Constructive play
- Symbolic play
- Formal games

Across the UK and internationally the importance of play has been recognized and it has an established place in the Early Years Foundation Stage (EYFS) curriculum in England and in the Foundation Phase curriculum in Wales (ATL, 2012). Play is viewed as vital for a child's natural growth and development – play is seen as just as appropriate in a child's world as work is in an adult's world. However, it is worth pointing out here that sometimes parents may not share this view of learning through play as worthwhile for their child. This is where open, honest communication between the setting and parents is needed to alleviate parental concerns and fears. Many settings have open days where parents can come in and observe their child at 'play' and where practitioners are on hand to explain the value and purpose of a play-based approach to teaching and learning. Through planning a play-based curriculum, practitioners can allow children to:

- have learning experiences that help them to make sense of the world;
- practice and consolidate ideas, concepts and skills;
- understand the need for rules;
- play alone, alongside and with others;
- communicate ideas and thoughts;
- take supervised risks;
- problem solve;
- think in creative way;
- re-enact fears in a controlled and safe environment

(QCA, 2000).

Practitioners planning for young children in the Foundation Phase need to offer opportunities for open ended learning and cater for individual needs. Learning is a process and not a product; it should be a journey of discovery with endless possibilities and outcomes (Drake, 2005). Isaacs (1929; as cited in Drake, 2005, p. xi), argues that 'play is a child's work' and should not be seen by adults as a separate activity. Children are motivated to learn through play and play needs to be carefully planned. Children need to be able to choose whether to play indoors or outdoors and they need to be given time and space to become deeply involved in their learning. They need to be able to return to play equipment and play experiences to ensure knowledge and understanding becomes deeply embedded.

When planning for play in the Foundation Phase, staff must take into account the different ways children learn and play. Children need to explore and investigate using their senses. They need to use their emotions and feelings to express themselves. Alongside this, there must be structured activities and experiences with planned learning outcomes to extend children's learning and development. Planning for play should consider the three types of provision previously discussed. It needs to consider the children's individual needs, the seven Areas of Learning, the setting, the children's input into the planning process and the learning environment.

The aim of the Foundation Phase practitioner is to provide a broad and balanced curriculum that allows learning to take place in a meaningful context. The environment needs to be accessible, well resourced and well planned. Therefore the value of play/active learning cannot be emphasized enough as, according to the Welsh Assembly Government, 'when children are involved in their learning they take ownership'. Play and active learning can motivate children, support and develop skills and concepts, enhance language development and consolidate learning (WAG, 2008d, p. 7). A play-based approach supports learning across all seven areas of the Foundation Phase curriculum.

Stages and types of play

Foundation Phase practitioners need to be aware that there are different stages of play and that children move through these stages at their own pace. By having knowledge of these different stages, practitioners are able to plan for progression. The different stages of play are outlined below.

- **Solitary**: Children play alone with little or no interaction with others.
- **Spectator:** Children observe their peers, watching but not joining in.
- **Parallel:** Children play alongside each other, each playing separately.
- **Associative:** Children begin to play together; interaction is developing and they enjoy the same activities and playing with the same equipment.
- **Cooperative:** Children play in group situations and share outcomes from their play; play is intricate and detailed.

Although children progress through these stages they often choose to return to an earlier stage, so they may play cooperatively but still return to solitary play.

Case study

Rhys arrived in nursery and went straight to play in the sand tray; he then went to the painting areas and painted a 'blue dog'. Rhys then went outside to ride on the bikes and to play with the tool box.

Throughout these activities Rhys made no effort to interact with other children but was quite content to have fun on his own. This is an example of solitary play.

Activity

Consider the following scenarios and decide if they are examples of **spectator play**, **parallel play**, **associative play** or **cooperative play**.

Scenario 1

Ellie is watching two other girls make cakes out of playdoh. After they have left the craft area she sits down and copies what she has seen the other girls do.

Scenario 2

Daniel and Gareth were working on the carpet with the construction kit. Gareth spent a long time making a car with four wheels and then ran this car up and down the carpet. Daniel built a house out of blocks and placed several toy figures in the house which he said were his family.

Scenario 3

Several children were in the outdoor area. They decided to play a game of hide and seek and decided who would be the seeker and which children would hide. They continued playing for nearly half an hour, taking it in turns to hide and seek.

Scenario 4

The children built an obstacle course from the outdoor equipment. They helped each other over the course and discussed different ways to adapt the course as their play progressed.

Types of play

In addition to different stages of play there are also different types of play. Practitioners need to take in to account resources, space, time and organization within the setting when planning for all types of play. Activities need to be exciting, challenging and differentiated for the children (WAG, 2008d). Some examples of the different types of play are as follows, though they are often not used in isolation but in conjunction with each other.

Pretend/imaginary play

All Foundation Phase settings will have a role-play area where children are encouraged to act out different situations and roles. Here the children can develop communication skills, social skills, confidence and solve problems. Physical development can be improved with the use of both **fine motor** and gross motor skills. Children learn to cooperate and to extend their vocabulary and practise their reading and writing skills. Examples of pretend play resources are:

- Home corner
- Café
- Farm shop
- Post office
- Travel agents
- Seaside café
- Cave

Small world play

Here children can re-enact experiences using small world resources. Examples are sets of figures, animals (zoo and farm), vehicles, dolls houses, farm houses and castles. Small worlds play allows children to problem solve, cooperate with others, share and take turns, develop knowledge and understanding about different jobs people do and to extend their vocabulary. Manipulative and hand–eye coordination are also developed.

Construction

Through construction play, children are given opportunities to develop an understanding of materials and their properties. Children build with blocks of different sizes and make and take apart things. Children are given opportunities to work with different types of wood and tools including recycled materials. They are encouraged to design their own creations and to reflect upon and evaluate their finished products.

Construction play allows children to take care of equipment and tidy up resources after use; share and work with and alongside others; value their own work and that of others; and communicate their ideas in a variety of ways, including using ICT packages. Children will develop their manipulative skills and develop an understanding of area and spatial awareness. Problem-solving and investigative skills will develop alongside creativity. It is important that children are given opportunities to work with natural materials as much as possible in the Foundation Phase. This will give them tactile experiences and allow them to investigate the properties of the materials such as what happens to water when it is heated or cooled.

Creative play

Creative play celebrates a child's individuality. It allows them to express their feelings and emotions imaginatively through various forms of self-expression. Ways include through drawing, painting, craft work, role play, dance, poetry, drama and writing. Creativity needs to include both the indoor and outdoor environment, with resources that stimulate imagination and thinking. Creative play activities allow children to handle new materials, play different roles, make new pictures and models and create sounds and movements. Children will develop observational skills, have opportunities to explore and investigate, listen and respond, reflect and problem solve, and persevere and collaborate. There is no right or wrong in creative play and children's uniqueness and diversity should be celebrated.

Physical play

Physical play can involve the development of gross motor skills and fine motor skills. It involves spatial awareness and balance and is also concerned with a healthy lifestyle and physical well-being. Children need space to move about in both indoors and outdoors and have access to both large and small equipment. Gross motor skills include walking, running, stopping, pedalling, pushing and pulling, balancing and throwing and catching. Fine motor skills include building a tower of bricks, holding a pencil, completing a jigsaw puzzle and tying shoe laces.

Role of the practitioner in children's play

Before the role of the practitioner can be discussed it is necessary to look at the most typical lenses through which early childhood practitioners have viewed and continue to view the child.

The empiricist lens

The child is seen as an empty vessel that needs to be filled or something that needs to be moulded by the adult into a desired shape. This derives from John Locke's philosophy (1632–1704).

The nativist lens

This is the opposite view to the empiricist view. Here the nativist practitioner sees the child as biologically pre-programmed to unfold in certain directions. This stems from the philosophy of Jean-Jacque Rousseau (1712–78).

The interactionist view

> This view sees children being partly empty vessels and partly pre-programmed. There is an interaction within and between the two. Immanuel Kant (1724–1804) originated this approach.
>
> (Bruce, 2005)

So the role of a practitioner adopting an empiricist approach would be to identify missing experiences, skills and concepts and to select experiences for the child to fill in these gaps. Learning is broken down into meaningful sequences and children are taught step by step. Prior to the introduction of the Foundation Stage in England and the Foundation Phase in Wales, many four-year-olds were taught through a numeracy and literacy hour in adult-led groups. In contrast, the **nativist approach** would mean that the adult should not interfere in the child's learning, but can offer help when needed. Children are thought to need to play and develop creatively, with imagination and without interruption. The **interactionist approach** believes that biological structures of the child's brain interact with each other but will also adapt and alter in light of the experiences of the child. This view contends that the role of the adult is critical. Here, children are supported by adults who help them to make maximum use of the environment and cultural experiences within the setting.

Reflective task

If you are a practitioner, what lens do you view a child through? Which view of the child supports the Foundation Phase approach to learning? What about other practitioners in your setting?

Dockett and Fleer (1999) suggest three roles for adults in play-based learning environments. The adult needs to manage resources, time and space. As a facilitator the adult mediates and interprets children's play whilst promoting equality. Foundation Phase practitioners need to be aware of when to intervene in children's play and when to extend their learning and challenge their thinking skills and when to allow children to come to conclusions on their own. Practitioners need to scaffold and support children's learning when necessary and withdraw support when the child has succeeded with an activity.

When planning for different play/active learning activities, practitioners need to consider their role, what questioning skills to use, how to organize the learning environment and how the activities will be differentiated to accommodate all learning needs. In the Foundation Phase the development of the whole child is seen as paramount and this reasserts the view of the early childhood pioneers Froebel and Steiner who considered 'the development of the whole child to be of enormous importance' (Bruce, 2005, p. 15).

These pioneers believed in starting where the child is at, focusing on what the child can do rather than on what they cannot do. For Froebel, play allows the practitioner to see what the child can do and what is needed to support and extend learning at that stage (Bruce, 2005). In addition, Foundation Phase practitioners need to plan time to observe, monitor and assess children as well as evaluate the provision provided. Perhaps, however, the value of learning from play can be summed up best by Vygotsky (1978, p. 102):

> In play a child always behaves beyond his average age above his daily behaviour; in play it is as though he were a head taller than himself. As in the focus of a magnifying glass, play contains all developmental tendencies in a condensed form and is itself a major source of development.

Barriers to a play-based approach

As with any initiative, concept or idea, there will be opposition, and the notion of children 'playing' whilst learning has divided opinion for centuries. Perhaps the very first difficulty is in deciding what is 'play' and what is a non-play activity? The classic definition of play would be self-determination, autonomy, freedom to choose and independence. However, there is no clear and commonly understood definition of play (Andrews, 2012). Hughes (2010) argues that we cannot understand a child's development without a complete understanding of play.

Prior to the introduction of the National Curriculum in 1988, play was given a high status in settings. The United Nations states the right of all children to play, but with the introduction of the National Curriculum and Desirable Outcomes for

Early Years there seemed to be an increasing emphasis on childcare and education provision in the place of play. Policymakers are almost afraid to advocate the notion of children playing unless there is a purpose or a set number of learning criteria being met. Even the Foundation Phase documentation considers play to be a 'learning vehicle' and that play 'consolidates their learning' (WAG, 2008b, p. 4). Practitioners may consider that they are offering child-led play activities whilst in practice they are putting boundaries on the play being offered to ensure it meets the intended learning outcome.

Consider the following scenario in a setting.

The practitioner presents activities that address the seven Areas of Learning in the Foundation Phase. The children are allowed to choose which activity they want to access but the practitioner tells the children what she wants them to do with each activity.

1 Is this child-led or practitioner-led?
2 Who has ownership of the play?
3 Who has the power in this scenario?

The children begin to play with the activities as directed, but gradually start to take over the activities and begin to mix them up.

1 Is this now child-led or adult-led?
2 Who now has ownership of the play?
3 Has the power shifted?

Else (2009) observes that something may not start out as play but as children engage, becomes more playful. The EPPE project (2003) indicated that the most effective learning approach was a combination of adult-led and child-led activities (Andrews, 2012). However, as long as we have an education system that is target driven, linked to learning outcomes and advocates testing children, can we ever have a play-based curriculum in the truest sense? Even now, Foundation Phase children in nursery classes are labelled with realistic and challenging targets!

Practitioners can also find it difficult to describe what approaches they take when supporting play, how their setting supports child-led play and the true benefits of a play-based curriculum. Is this because we still see play as the opposite to work and therefore not an instrument of learning? There will always be people who do not see the purpose or value of play and will consider it to be a 'reward' after children have finished their work.

The Foundation Phase curriculum has gone some way in embedding the ethos of 'play' and its benefits. The *Learning and Teaching Pedagogy* document (WAG, 2008a) discusses the importance of practitioners and children as partners on a learning journey and that children should have ownership of that environment. Nevertheless the introduction of literacy and numeracy tests in 2013 for all learners in Wales between the ages of seven and fourteen will have an impact on curriculum delivery. The difficulty facing many Foundation Phase practitioners in Year 2 will be how to prepare children to sit tests in a play-based, child-centred curriculum. Will it still be an equal partnership and learning journey or will it revert to being an adult-led didactic curriculum approach? This is explored in more detail in Part III of this book.

Conclusion

The Foundation Phase is a play-based curriculum with an emphasis on balance between child-led and adult-led activities. This could be challenging for practitioners as there are barriers to a play-based approach to learning and not everyone is supportive. Numeracy and literacy tests were introduced in May 2013 and the Literacy and Numeracy Framework (LNF) in September 2013. The impact of testing on a child's ability to learn may lead to a 'test readiness' culture in the Foundation Phase. This could lead to practitioners having to revert to an 'age not stage' approach to learning.

Chapter summary

- The Foundation Phase is a 'bottom up' model which builds on what the child can do through three types of provision: continuous, enhanced and focused. Practitioners need to plan across the seven Areas of Learning, promoting balance, appropriateness and progression in teaching and learning.
- The role of the practitioner is to facilitate play if needed, whilst observing children, and to use these observations to inform future planning. There needs to be a balance between adult-led and child-led activities. At times practitioners need to stand back and allow children to play freely.
- Children can be viewed through different lenses. Practitioners need to be aware of which lens they view children through as this will have an impact on their practice. Children need to have ownership of their play and learning. Children go through different stages of play and will revisit earlier stages at times.

- There are barriers to a play-based approach – such as testing – with some opposition to the idea of the value of play. The introduction of 'testing' children in the Foundation Phase will have an impact on curriculum approaches and delivery. Children and adults can see play and learning as two separate things. Play should be regarded as a child's work.

Thought-provoking questions

- As a practitioner what do you consider are the benefits of a play-based curriculum?
- Can you think of any disadvantages to learning through play?
- Which lens do you view a child through?
- Consider your setting in terms of provision. What do you provide in terms of continuous, enhanced and focused provision?
- How does your classroom environment provide opportunities for learning through play?

Further reading and information

Bruce, T. (2011), *Early Childhood Education*, 4th edn. Oxon: Hodder Education.

Children's rights and research on play: http://playengland.org.uk/about-us/about-play-england.aspx.

Moyles, J. (1989), *Just Playing?* Milton Keynes: Open University Press.

Pioneers of play information: http://www.infed.org/index.htm.

Play resources and publications in Wales: http://playwales.org.uk.

Pound, L. (2009), *How Children Learn 3: Contemporary Thinking and Theorists*. London: Practical Pre-School Publications.

Woods, A. (ed.) (2013), *Child–Initiated Play And Learning*. Oxon: Routledge.

8

Being Reflective: Skills and Techniques

Chapter aims

To explain the importance of reflecting on practice in the early years.

To identify the skills and characteristics needed to be a reflective practitioner.

To discuss a range of reflective models/cycles.

Chapter 1 highlighted the curriculum changes that have taken place within Welsh Early Years practice and strongly advocated the following quote, that, if policy change and curriculum reform are going to be successful, 'the Foundation Phase proposals in Wales require a way of thinking, acting and being within the Early Years classroom that is substantially different from the requirements of previous statutory curricula' (Aasen and Waters, 2006, p. 128). Reflective practice theory could be a catalyst for Foundation Phase practitioners to begin to think and act differently in the best interests of the child. It should also be noted that reflective practice should be an aspect of practice that senior stakeholders understand and consider and not a concept that only applies to practitioners in the classroom.

Activity

Below, there are four sets of footprints and you will notice that they are different sizes. Who could they represent?

You might also notice that the footprints of different sizes are positioned in four different ways. Discuss the reason for this.

Do you think the larger footprint should be in front of the smaller one, behind it, parallel or in an opposite direction? If you are a practitioner, consider how you would achieve a balance between adult-led and child-initiated provision.

Consider ownership of the footprints with regard to all stakeholders and positions of power:

larger footprint = teacher/teaching assistant/senior stakeholder

smaller footprint = child

What is reflective practice?

As with play, there is not one single universal definition of reflective practice, but many agree that being reflective is an important concept for practitioners to grasp, particularly when there are many initiatives, developments and curriculum changes to cope with (Reed and Canning, 2010). Reflective practice has been defined by some as the ability to take a critical stance on something, and analyse a situation. Being reflective can often involve reacting emotionally to a situation and showing intuition and insight. Briefly, 'reflection can be described as a means of helping those most closely involved to think about what they already know and consider ways they might want to improve or refine a situation' (Reed and Canning, 2010, p. 2). According to Neaum (2010, p. 126), 'reflection is a way of learning. It is a process of actively considering what we do, and why and how we do it, in order to better understand children's learning.' A professional practitioner can be defined as someone who thinks during (knowing-in-action) and after a situation (reflection-on-action) (Smith, 2012). Gray and Macblain (2012) state that reflective practice is simply about stepping back from a situation and making sense of deeper concepts. Hallet (2013) describes reflective practice as 'a change agent for practitioners to modify, develop, improve or change provision for children' (p. 29). If you are a practitioner, you may be considering listening to children's ideas (more than you already do), or planning for more outdoor play, or you may be considering how to develop a better partnership with the parents in your setting. If you are working in the Local Authority, you may be considering how to support settings in achieving a balance between child-led and adult-directed tasks, or how you might help practitioners include more sustained shared thinking in their daily work with children.

An important question to consider in relation to reflection is why do we do what we do and what evidence is this based on? Too often, practice and policy directives are not always supported by evidence-based theory. For example, where is the substantial evidence to suggest that testing our youngest learners in the Foundation Phase will raise standards?

Benefits of reflective practice

Neaum (2010) argues that reflective practice should not be viewed as a one-off event. It should be understood as an ongoing cyclical process and this is evident in some of the models discussed later on. When professionals learn from their reflections, and the process is effective, then the quality of provision *should* improve (Hallet, 2013). Reflective learning allows practitioners to make links between theory and practice and explore pedagogy in more detail, which (should) in turn enhance their provision. Smith (2012) suggests that reflection provides opportunities for staff to problem solve, but one of the main benefits of reflective practice is 'to provide better quality experiences for children and their families' (Hallet, 2013, p. 25). If you are a practitioner, do you feel this is a feeling shared amongst all practitioners? What is the general feeling shared amongst practitioners?

Reflective practice provides an opportunity for practitioners to develop a professional voice and a professional identity. Part of developing an identity is recognizing a professional change in knowledge and personal understanding (Appleby, 2010; cited in Reed and Canning, 2010).

Reflective task

Reflect on your professional journey so far and consider what you now know before you embarked on your career. What has helped you gain new knowledge? If you are working within an Early Years setting, compare your journey with another colleague? What do you notice?

Characteristics of a reflective practitioner

Effective reflection involves analysing a situation or event to better understand it, and according to Neaum (2010, p. 132) 'the process of analysis requires that you think deeply and systematically about what happened'. To support the analysis, additional reading around the topic needs to be conducted and links should be made between what you know about Early Years and what you have observed or analysed. Early Years students often have to meet criteria that link to their ability to reflect and will use a proforma provided by their college/institution. Practitioners who lead demanding jobs, however, might not always find the time to read or write about what they have analysed or observed. So in this situation it is imperative that staff communicate thoughts, views and findings and act on their reflection via a verbal discussion. Discussions can take place about the interpretation of a situation which may lead to decisions about making changes to the provision. Neaum (2010) suggests that changes can be small but the main priority is being realistic. She also highlights the importance of all staff being committed to the change if it is going to be successfully integrated into the practice. Practitioners in Northern Italy (applying the Reggio Emilia system) regularly reflect on children's learning due to the variety of documentation they collate such as video, drawings, models, written notes, photographs, audio recordings, and so on (Hallet, 2013).

Students and practitioners need to remember that 'acquiring skills and embedding them in practice takes time' (Neaum, 2010, p. 133). This may be the case for many Foundation Phase practitioners, where they have to make sense of a new framework and develop a different skill set, particularly if they are working as a team leader and managing more staff.

Using the table below, reflect on whether you think you have some of the characteristics listed on the left-hand side. If you feel you need to improve or refine a skill, write down a realistic target on the right-hand side.

Characteristic/skill ⇨	➡	Action/target
Creative		
Listener		
Critical observer		
Flexible		
Critical thinker		
Curious		
Open-minded		
Analytical		

The challenges of reflective practice

There can be many interpretations of improving or refining a situation and this can make it challenging for teams to agree on a possible solution to a situation (Reed and Canning, 2010). It is important to remember that 'our actions in the classroom are informed by our beliefs, our understandings and our prejudices' (Smith, 2012, p. 149). Regardless of experience, practitioners will have views about how children learn and it is these views that influence the way they work with the children (MacNaughton, 2003). There will inevitably be a range of different viewpoints in a setting that need to be acknowledged. Smith (2012) suggests that practitioners need to learn to live with uncertainty and be willing to accept that some questions may never be fully answered about their practice (or policy directives) and this can be very frustrating.

It can be difficult at times to know what to reflect on and why, but Neaum (2010) suggests three ways of selecting a situation or event.

1 Develop knowledge in a specific area that enhances your job and then reflect on how the new knowledge has influenced your practice.
2 If an activity or event in the classroom has had a successful outcome, there is scope for reflection; as is equally the case if the activity was not successful.
3 Reflect on critical incidents or moments that have been turning points in your

understanding and your practice. You may like to consider this as a light-bulb moment or a cognitive breakthrough!

Being reflective involves being able to think about your own thinking, which is known as metacognition. Neaum (2010) reminds us that this is a higher order skill which both students and practitioners find challenging when they first embark on a reflective journey. Higher order thinking can take time to develop. Many courses now require students to write reflectively and this is a strong component of a Foundation Degree, but Penn (2008) suggests that returning to book learning and linking theory to practice can be quite challenging. Understanding and accessing academic texts can often be like learning another language and this poses a challenge for some. Penn (2008) makes the point that 'students may be very competent in their everyday dealings with parents and children, but analysing those actions and then writing about them are very different processes' (p. 164). Furthermore, Penn (2008) suggests that the links between theory/research, policy and classroom practice are very complex and not straightforward.

Penn (2008) suggests that there are many traditional ways of doing things in the classroom that practitioners often find difficult to explain or justify because that is the way they have always done things. A study that was conducted by Joseph Tobin in 1995 recorded daily classroom life in China, Japan and America, and encouraged practitioners from the different settings to comment on each other's practice. Tobin (1995; as cited in Penn, 2008, p. 165) reported that staff were shocked at each other's practice and 'basically, each group thought that their own practices were right, and those of the other groups was misinformed'. Penn (2008) writes extensively about her international experiences and strongly argues that 'the way practitioners understand, interpret, and reconstruct early childhood learning and development is intrinsically linked to their beliefs, knowledge and experience as well as to the contextual factors in which they operate' (p. 166). If you are working at Local Authority level you may like to consider Joseph Tobin's research, which captures features of quality practice to show to different settings for evaluation and reflection purposes. It is important to utilize professional expertise across the Early Years sector. Equally, there is a need to work more collaboratively.

Moss (2008; cited in Neaum, 2010) claims that there is a danger that reflective learning can be used as a tool to produce 'excellent technicians', almost robotic in nature, to deliver a prescribed curriculum. It is thought that 'unless we offer ourselves the permission to articulate our own understandings and define how we practise, the power of external forces, outlined in policy and guidance, and embedded in much professional development training, will determine this for us' (Neaum, 2010, p. 137). Put simply, all professionals have the same documentation to hand and should have the confidence to develop a professional voice and identity based on sound judgements and evidence.

Writing reflectively

Smith (2012) claims that writing forces professionals to a) slow their thought processes down and b) analyse a situation in more detail. Making useful notes throughout the day when possible is useful for completing in-depth reflections, and a reflective diary might be something you consider using if you are a practitioner. Practitioners may even notice a pattern to the content in their notes which might help guide a more in-depth analysis of what they have observed. The benefits of writing things down is that it allows students and staff to track any changes in their perceptions and thoughts and enables progress to be tracked. Smith (2012) claims that writing can help 'celebrate success, or see that things are not as bad as you thought they were at the time!' (p. 152). A journal can be 'a place for reflecting, speculating, wondering, worrying, exclaiming, recording, proposing, reminding, reconstructing, questioning, confronting, dreaming, considering and reconsidering' (Smith, 2012, p. 153). Plummer (2001; cited in Hallet, 2013) suggests that when students and practitioners write reflectively they are doing more than capturing reality – they are constructing it.

To help construct reflection, choose a situation from your experience and ask yourself the following questions.

- What was my role in this situation?
- Did I feel comfortable or uncomfortable? Why?
- What actions did I take?
- How did others and I act?
- Was it appropriate?
- How could I have improved the situation for myself, my colleagues?
- What can I change in the near future?
- Do I feel as if I have learnt anything new about myself?
- Did I expect anything different to happen? What and why?
- Has it changed my way of thinking in any way?
- What knowledge from theory and research can I apply to this situation?
- What broader issues, for example ethical, political or social, arise from this situation?
- What do I think about these broader issues?

Reflective cycles/models

Both cyclical (circular) and linear (straight-line) models have been included below and their components briefly explained to help guide reflective practice. These models provide professionals with a structure to write reflectively and some may even like to think of them as a 'writing frame' to guide individual or whole team/ school reflection. The models are also useful for stimulating discussion and debate about a particular aspect of practice, for example how to test young children appropriately from a play-based, children's-rights perspective!

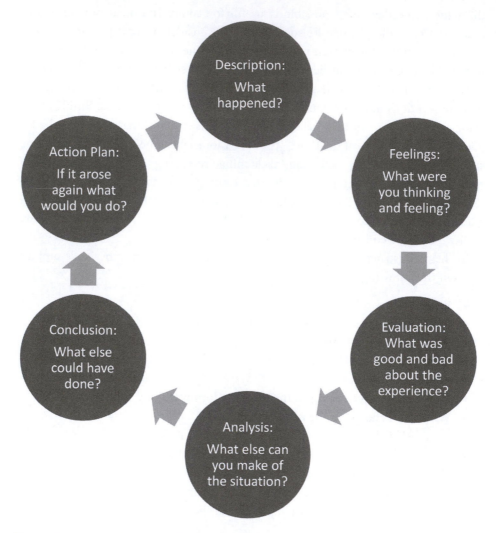

Figure 8.1 Gibbs Reflective Cycle, from Gibbs, G. (1988), *Learning and Doing: A Guide to Teaching and Learning Methods*, FEU

Description = Simply write down what happened in enough detail so that the reader can gain a feel for being there when it happened.

Feelings = These can be positive or negative and considered from different stakeholders' points of view within the situation.

Evaluation = Write about what went well and what was not so successful and consider this from different perspectives. Also consider the children, staff, parents, environment and resources.

Analysis = Try to answer the 'why' question for the analysis. Include evidence of background reading and literature at this point to show that you have learnt from the situation. Identify the concepts and explore them in detail.

Conclusion = Sum up the situation, observation or event and ensure you conclude information from all previous sections. Summarize the key points from the whole situation.

Action plan = Consider what could be done to improve a situation. Consider the action from different perspectives – that of the children, staff, parents, and so on. Consider the action points from a short- and long-term point of view.

Peters (1994)

You can critically reflect by using the following model, known as the DATA process (Peters, 1994):

- D – Describe the problem, task or incident that needs to be looked at and possibly changed.
- A – Analyse the description, looking at assumptions that were made at the time and also any that are now being made about how to respond.
- T – Theorize about a range of ways to respond to the problem, task or incident.
- A – Act using one or more of the theories.

The example below provides you with prompts that may help you reflect on the implementation of the Foundation Phase.

D = Children need to be encouraged to be more independent and autonomous. Too many children are being directed to tasks.

A = Staff assume that children are needy and not very capable of completing tasks and therefore offer a lot of direction and step-by-step instructions for tasks.

T = Investigate and link learning theories such as **behaviourism** and **constructivism** (theoretical models).

A = Understand basic concepts of theoretical models and apply different strategies.

Kolb (1984)

The cyclical model below was devised by Kolb (1984)

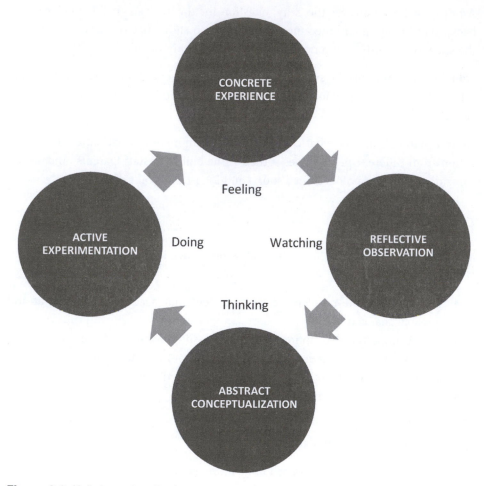

Figure 8.2 Kolb Learning Cycle

Concrete experience = What actually happened?

Reflective observation = What aspects went well for different stakeholders and what did not go so well?

Abstract conceptualizing = What were the key concepts/issues to report and why?

Active experimentation = What is needed next? How successful are your changes to practice?

Boud et al. (1985)

Boud et al. (1985) devised a three-stage model with feelings as the main component.

Stage 1 = Return to the experience and describe what happened; include initial feelings.

Stage 2 = Attend to feelings and acknowledge negative feelings. Consider how you could make them positive.

Stage 3 = Re-evaluate the experience – reflect on the feelings and think about how you could improve a situation or what could have been done differently to alter your feelings.

Schon (1987)

Schon (1987) was significant in this area because it was deemed that he developed the term 'reflective practice'. There are three parts to his model: knowing-in-action; reflection-in-action; and reflection-on-action.

Knowing-in-action = unconscious, intuitive knowing or know-how 'without having to 'think about it'.

Reflection-in-action = 'on the spot' reflection.

Reflection-on-action = done after the event/outcome(s).

Conclusion

Reflection at whatever level is particularly important at the current time in Wales when many curriculum changes and developments are taking place across all sectors. It is important to remember that being reflective is a skill that often needs developing and nurturing to some extent. There are many common features across all of the cycles/models that have been discussed, such as a description of what happened, why it happened, what influenced things to happen and how the situation could be improved – in other words, a description, an analysis and an action. Professionals at all levels should be able to utilize the models as a writing frame to guide their thoughts, views and values or to stimulate discussion and debate. The debates could be around achieving a balance between child-initiated and adult-directed tasks, or ensuring that children are ready for tasks they are being expected to perform!

Chapter summary

- Reflection simply means making an effort to learn from a situation and applying new knowledge and understanding to a situation or issue. Professionals can reflect on positive or negative experiences using the same cycles/models.
- Reflection means different things to different people, but the models discussed in this chapter should help guide reflective writing as well as discussion and debate. The cycles/models vary and professionals should experiment with different cycles for different issues or concerns.
- Reflection is a skill that needs to be developed and nurtured. At this particular time in Wales, with curriculum reform taking place in many sectors, this should become a regular feature of weekly, termly and yearly practice.
- Reflection can be time consuming and may seem like a waste of time to professionals and hence an aspect of practice that may be neglected. This chapter argues that reflection should not be ignored and can be a way of improving situations, making progress and enhancing provision.

Access the following link online to take part in a multiple choice quiz about this chapter:

www.bloomsbury.com/an-introduction-to-the-foundation-phase-9781474264273

Thought-provoking questions

- To what extent do you think the Foundation Phase has been implemented successfully?
- What light-bulb or cognitive breakthrough moments have you encountered with young children and or other staff/professionals and how has this made a difference to your practice?
- What changes have you made in your role in light of curriculum reform and policy changes, and how successful were your changes?
- How regularly do you reflect on your professional role and do you think it is enough?

Further reading and information

Bolton, G. (2010), *Reflective Practice: Writing and Professional Development*, London: Sage.

Bradbury, H., N. Frost, S. Kilminster and M. Zukas (2010), *Beyond Reflective Practice: New Approaches to Professional Lifelong Learning*. London: Routledge.

Paige-Smith, A. and A. Craft (2011), *Developing Reflective Practice*, 2nd edn. Berkshire: Open University Press.

Reflective writing: http://www.tactyc.org.uk/reflections.asp.

Part III

Challenges and Complexities of Policy into Practice

9

Stakeholder Perceptions

Chapter aims

To explore and discuss stakeholder views about the initial introduction of the Foundation Phase.

To explore current perceptions of the Foundation Phase.

Perceptions of the Foundation Phase

This chapter focuses on perceptions of the Foundation Phase from stakeholders interviewed for this book and findings from the recent three-year Welsh Government evaluation of the Foundation Phase conducted by Wales Institute for Social and Economic Research, Data and Methods (WISERD) at Cardiff University (WG, 2015). The authors interviewed a range of stakeholders from parents, classroom practitioners, nursery managers, Early Years advisors and head teachers to Education ministers and Government officials. The authors were interested in finding out initial thoughts about the Foundation Phase and whether these had changed over time. The stakeholders were interviewed during 2012 but more current perceptions are also included here from the evaluation mentioned above.

In 2008, the majority of stakeholders interviewed for this book were enthusiastic and excited about the impending curriculum changes. This was reflected by Jane Davidson, Education Minister for Wales from 2000 to 2007 and responsible for the introduction of the Foundation Phase curriculum in 2004. In a speech given at a conference in 2010, she claimed that 'It was giving the children a fantastic birthday gift' (BESA, 2010).

This positive feeling about the Foundation Phase was also a key finding of the Welsh Government (WG) evaluation in 2014, where it reports:

> The majority of practitioners/key stakeholders interviewed and surveyed initially welcomed the Foundation Phase with a mixture of 'excitement' and 'relief' for offering improved flexibility, freedom, autonomy and developmentally appropriate practice.
>
> (Taylor et al., 2014, p. 1)

However, some stakeholders interviewed for this book expressed some uncertainty and had mixed feelings about the new curriculum when it was first introduced. Four years after its introduction there was far more ambivalence about the subject. Some stakeholders felt that there was room for improvement and that it was difficult to match theory to practice. Possible reasons for this could be lack of guidance, training needs, lack of funding and challenges of matching policy guidance to classroom pedagogy.

One stakeholder interviewed for this book expressed concern about funding. For example, the dilemma faced when piloting the Foundation Phase in 2004 was that the additional practitioners appointed in 2004 are now currently at the top of their pay scale. The implications of this are that a significant proportion of the budget allocated to the schools for the Foundation Phase is being swallowed by salary. This is in comparison to another setting of similar size which may have staff on lower salaries but still receive the same amount of funding. The stakeholder in question feels staffing costs should be taken into consideration when funding is allocated. It appears that having experienced well-trained staff is a disadvantage in relation to funding.

Findings about training, support and guidance are referred to in the three-year Welsh Government evaluation:

> It was generally felt that mixed messages from [the] Welsh Government are leading to Foundation Phase practitioners calling for more frequent, structured and tailored guidance, whilst stakeholders called for better exemplification materials and clearer terminology.
>
> (Rhys et al., 2014a, p. 1)

In summary, when the Foundation Phase was introduced it was welcomed by many; however, at the time of writing there are, as expected, many challenges surrounding the delivery of the Foundation Phase, some of which are discussed below.

Challenges of delivering the Foundation Phase

The focus on a play-based approach, and ownership of learning moving from the adult to the child, caused some stakeholders (who were interviewed for this book) to feel apprehensive. This view is supported by Ainley et al. (2006, p. 23) who argue that 'such a strategy transfers control over what is learned away from the teacher to the pupils themselves. This is unsatisfactory if the teacher has an agenda in which certain specific knowledge should be assimilated.' However, according to the Welsh Government (2008d, p. 39), 'educational practitioners need to understand the importance of play in a child's development and plan an appropriate curriculum'. Despite this, a key finding from the Welsh Government was that:

> Discussions with practitioners suggest that some teachers are 'afraid' to let go of traditional formal pedagogies. This is compounded by the perceived need to ensure children perform well in the recently introduced year 2 reading and numeracy test.
>
> (Waldron et al., 2014a, p. 3)

Some of these challenges were still evident in 2012, with some stakeholders expressing a lack of clarity in relation to the principles of the Foundation Phase and its implementation in practice. There was a great deal of variation in responses regarding how the Foundation Phase was being implemented by settings, with one stakeholder commenting that mixed messages are still being received from Local Authorities and government officials. Another stakeholder reported that 'Nursery children [3- and 4-year-olds] are still sitting on the carpet and not moving; it is still very much whole school.'

Similar findings were produced by Estyn in the 2011 report about Literacy in the Foundation Phase, which found that 'In a minority of schools there is a lack of understanding of the principles and practices of the Foundation Phase and children are not challenged enough to practice their literacy skills' (Estyn, 2011, p. 5). Estyn (2011) also state that too often children do not make *enough* progress in developing their reading and writing skills *across* the curriculum.

This was also a concern raised by a former minister who was dubious as to 'whether or not we could really screw down the literacy and numeracy in the Foundation Phase'. However, it was also strongly felt that 'the challenges are going to be to not retreat to traditional ways of delivering some elements because if you do that the Foundation Phase will lose its chance to work and that is critically important'.

In 2015 one Foundation Phase coordinator strongly asserted that:

> The literacy and numeracy tests [introduced in 2013] put excessive pressure on the children and have no place in the Foundation Phase as far as I am concerned ... They have been imposed to the detriment of the curriculum; the second half of the spring term and the first half of the summer term is disrupted with preparation. Excessive pressure is put on children, even when you attempt to keep them low key, and children who already have low self-esteem and who are aware of their difficulties are made to feel even more inadequate.

The Welsh Government evaluation of the Foundation Phase also reports that:

> Numerous concerns were raised by head teachers about the implementation of the Foundation Phase at the national level, including: ... the perception that the introduction of the literacy and numeracy framework would 'damage' the Foundation Phase ...
>
> (Taylor et al., 2014, p. 2)

According to the Welsh Government evaluation summary report on 'Management and Leadership' (Taylor et al., 2014), the challenges of implementing the Foundation Phase vary amongst different stakeholders. Yet despite these different challenges, there have been a number of successes in the Foundation Phase, as outlined below.

Success of the Foundation Phase

Success in relation to the Foundation Phase can mean different things to different stakeholders. Interpretation of research findings can be problematic and misunderstood and the authors feel it is still too early to assess and discuss the long-term impact of a curriculum such as the Foundation Phase. The following findings have been taken from relevant evaluation reports available on the Foundation Phase.

One of the successes of the Foundation Phase according to the Welsh Government evaluation was that:

> Researcher observations indicated that child choice and physically active, explorative, first hand pedagogies were associated with high involvement *and* wellbeing.
>
> (Waldron et al., 2014b, p. 2)

Another success reported in the same evaluation was that 'There is a positive association between Foundation Phase pedagogies and children's enjoyment and enthusiasm for learning' (Waldron et al., 2014c, p. 1).

In addition, the evaluation reports that children's improved attendance is associated with the Foundation Phase (WG, 2015). Also, children in schools that piloted the Foundation Phase (since 2004) are more inclined to achieve Level 4 or above in Key Stage 2 English. There was also improvement in attainment for children who are in receipt of free school meals.

Estyn (2011) report that the successes of the Foundation Phase include:

- improvements to children's well-being, behaviour and physical development;
- more independent, confident and creative learners;
- a readiness to persevere with activities for longer.

So if the above are deemed to be successes, the question has to be asked why the Welsh Government has found it necessary to introduce a rigid literacy and numeracy framework and have returned to testing the children in Year 2. In the authors' opinion this is a mistake, as surely having happy, confident and independent learners is a far more important measure of success than a score on a test. The appropriateness of testing young children is explored in more detail in Chapter 11.

In order for some of the successes highlighted above to continue into Key Stage 2, then the importance of transition needs to be understood by all stakeholders, as considered below.

Transition to Key Stage 2

In 2012, the authors attended a one-day workshop run by a Local Education Authority (LEA) entitled 'Transition into Key Stage Two', with twenty-three attendees (permission was sought to use responses). The workshop consisted of mainly Key Stage 2 teachers and some Foundation Phase practitioners moving to Year 3 for the first time. There was a general consensus amongst Key Stage 2 teachers that children in the Foundation Phase played a lot, were disruptive and difficult to manage, and that more support staff were needed. In contrast, some participants in the workshop felt that children in the Foundation Phase were more confident and independent with more opportunities for experiential learning and role play.

The authors were concerned about the limited responses given, as there was no mention of any key Foundation Phase principles such as child-led, holistic development, child-centred, child participation and choice, outdoor learning, risk-taking and observation. This could be a reflection on a lack of training and discussion about the implementation of the Foundation Phase or generally a lack of good quality teaching and learning.

Some Key Stage 2 teachers, who had experience of teaching children from the Foundation Phase, raised issues such as the need for more resources, space and support staff. It was felt that children were incapable of doing group work and were too dependent on staff. Also, it was felt it was impossible to follow every child's interests. One teacher said, 'Our head teacher said formalise Year 2 to make it in line with Year 3.'

The transition from Year 2 to Year 3 seems to be a real concern amongst teachers, and one LEA Foundation Phase Advisory teacher (for the workshop) stated that more communication needs to take place between Year 2 and Year 3 staff. The importance of a smooth transition between the Foundation Phase and Key Stage 2 is highlighted by Allen (2013; as cited in Trodd, 2013), who argues that if the transition is not smooth then there could be a detrimental effect on a child's emotions. Allen (2013) also argues that 'an unsupported transition could also result in an achievement plateau or dip' (p. 57).

Findings from the Welsh Government evaluation indicate that 'transition strategies put in place vary considerably' (Waldron, et al., 2014a, p. 1). Siraj (2014) also commented on transition strategies and recommended that this needed addressing in the stocktake report conducted for the Welsh Government on the Foundation Phase (see recommendation 13 of the report). Recommendation 12 in the final Welsh Government evaluation addresses transition and suggests that Key Stage 2 teachers need help and support to ensure an effective transition from Foundation Phase to Key Stage 2 (WG, 2015).

The real concern here is the lack of support for a play-based approach to teaching and learning. If Key Stage 2 practitioners are not supportive, how is the Foundation

Phase ever going to be given the opportunity to be a success? The Foundation Phase needs to be supported throughout the whole school and it could be beneficial for Key Stage 2 teachers to adopt the Foundation Phase pedagogy. If practitioners in both sectors (Early Years and Key Stage 2) reflected on 'quality learning and teaching for children 3–11 years', would it not reflect the principles of the Foundation Phase?

Conclusion

This chapter set out to explore stakeholder perceptions of the Foundation Phase. Perceptions about the initial and current status of the Foundation Phase have been drawn upon from two sources: first, interviews the authors conducted, and second, from the three-year Welsh Government evaluation of the Foundation Phase conducted by WISERD at Cardiff University, led by Professor Chris Taylor.

Initially, there was overwhelming excitement about the principles of the Foundation Phase. However, numerous challenges have been raised by various stakeholders, as discussed in this chapter. Additionally, many different successes of the Foundation Phase have also been highlighted. The transition from the Foundation Phase to Key Stage 2 has also been discussed alongside two recommendations from two significant reports, and links to these can be found in further reading at the end of the chapter.

From the authors' own experience of being classroom practitioners, lecturers and researchers, there was clearly a need for curriculum change and a more play-based experiential framework for our youngest learners. The emphasis on 'stage' or 'age' is also crucial in order to allow children to develop in their own time and without pressure to 'read' and 'write' before they are ready. However, the Foundation Phase will only ever be a success if it is embraced by stakeholders. The next chapter will focus on the implications of a Foundation Phase pedagogy.

Chapter summary

- The majority of stakeholders were very positive and enthusiastic about the introduction of the Foundation Phase.
- Some stakeholders find it difficult to balance child-led and adult-led practice and are unsure about the principles of the Foundation Phase.
- Many practitioners are concerned about delivering the Literacy and Numeracy Framework (LNF) in a play-based, experiential curriculum.
- Foundation Phase pedagogies are associated with higher levels of children's well-being and involvement.
- Key Stage 2 practitioners are not always comfortable with and supportive of Foundation Phase principles.

Thought-provoking questions

- How do you currently feel about the Foundation Phase?
- In your opinion, what are the challenges and successes of the Foundation Phase?
- Are your challenges and successes as a practitioner different to those of other stakeholders (for example the head teacher)?
- What transition strategies are in place in your setting?
- Are the key findings discussed in the reports representative of current practice?
- How will you and others make use of research findings?

Further reading and information

Andrews, M. (2012), *Exploring Play*. London: Sage.

Donaldson, G. (2015), *Successful Futures: Independent Review of Curriculum and Assessment Arrangements in Wales*. Cardiff: Welsh Government.

Morris, M., L. McCrindle, J. Cheung, R. Johnson, A. Pietikainen and R. Smith (2010), *Exploring Education Transitions for Pupils aged 6 to 8 in Wales*. Cardiff: Welsh Government, http://gov.wales/statistics-and-research/exploring-education-transitions-pupils-aged-6-8/?lang=en.

Trodd, L. (2013), *Transitions in the Early Years: Working with Children and Families*. London: Sage.

Welsh Government (2013), *Building a Brighter Future: Early Years and Childcare Plan*. Cardiff: Welsh Government.

10

Practice and Pedagogy

Chapter aims

To explore stakeholder understandings of what constitutes rich learning experiences for young children.

To explore the challenges of delivering a child-centred pedagogy.

The place of play

All stakeholders interviewed for this book indicated that the Foundation Phase offered quality learning experiences for young children in Wales. The Welsh Assembly Government (2008b, p. 4) has stated that 'children learn through first hand experiential activities with the serious business of "play" providing the vehicle'. However, none of the participants referred to 'play' in their responses about quality learning experiences for young children other than for one stakeholder who said, 'I think if we had used experiential learning not play-based learning it would have been a very different story.'

The Welsh Government evaluation of the Foundation Phase found that some stakeholders 'felt that the guidance documentation was too vague, and the wording and exemplar materials were not clear (e.g. the use of the word play), which in turn causes inconsistency in practitioners' understandings of the Foundation Phase' (Rhys, et al., 2014a, p. 3).

Different stakeholders interviewed for this book claimed that there was 'confusion and misunderstanding between child-initiated and adult-directed tasks' and referred to 'attitudes from staff and disagreements about implementing the Foundation Phase' and complained that 'there is no consistency'.

According to Hendricks (1995; cited in Andrews, 2012), practitioners can sometimes feel coerced into turning play into an educational experience to justify it. This is reflected in the Foundation Phase documentation where the word 'play' is always associated with learning. There is no reference to 'pure play' (see Chapter 4) as described on the play continuum as exploratory without adult support (Andrews, 2012). The Foundation Phase framework states that 'there must be a balance between structured learning through child-initiated activities and those directed by practitioners' (WAG, 2008b, p. 6). Therefore, it is understandable that practitioners working within the Foundation Phase are unsure about the place of play. This is supported by Rogers (2011; cited in Andrews, 2012) who expresses concern that play is simply a tool for learning and not the 'freely chosen, transformative, life-enhancing phenomenon in which children are operating at the boundaries of understanding' (Rogers, 2011; cited in Andrews, 2012, p. 155). It could be a valid question, whether we are putting children at a disadvantage by abusing the true meaning of play. According to Andrews (2012), play is restricted when adults demand that children play properly, use play as a reward and link play to outcomes.

The authors feel, having interviewed a number of stakeholders, that play is still misunderstood in an educational context. Also there is still a real concern amongst practitioners that allowing children to 'play to learn' will be slated and not seen as learning. In the authors' opinion, learning through play needs to be celebrated and supported as best practice for our youngest learners.

As stated in Chapter 3, play is very difficult to define and will inevitably mean different things to different people. The tensions that surround play is captured by Wood's (2010) observation that there is a continual struggle for practitioners between their role and the play provision. There appears to be an ongoing conflict between the traditions of early childhood education (formal, adult-led learning) and the unclear messages in relation to translating policy into practice (Wood, 2010). One stakeholder interviewed for this book felt that the Foundation Phase provided 'a balance of traditional approaches and non-traditional approaches'. Wood (2010) explains this by using the terms cultural transmission/directive approach for model one and the emergent/responsive approach as model two. For example, before the introduction of the Foundation Phase, children were more likely to be directed to tasks by the practitioner in a traditional sedentary environment (a cultural trans-missive approach – model one). This is a more behaviourist approach (i.e. adult-led). This is in contrast to an emergent/responsive model where practitioners adopt a more child-centred approach, giving children more ownership of their learning and plan according to their individual learning needs. In this second model, children are viewed as equal partners in the learning process and the exchange of knowledge is shared. This is a more socially co-constructed approach (i.e. child-led).

Findings from the recent Welsh Government evaluation showed that the second model described above was observed more frequently than model one. However, the report also highlighted that the older the children, the less often model two was observed (Waldron et al., 2014a). Recommendation 5 of the final report spotlights the need to improve training for Year 1 and Year 1 classes (Taylor et al., 2015). The report also notes that 'discussions with practitioners suggest that some **teachers are "afraid" to let go of traditional formal pedagogies.** This is compounded by the perceived need to ensure children perform well in the recently introduced Year 2 reading and numeracy tests' (Waldron, et al., 2014a, p. 3). Chapter 11 will explore testing in more detail.

Stakeholders interviewed for this book indicated that quality learning experiences for children would include the following features: being independent, having a positive attitude to learning and a love of school and following children's interests. Fewer stakeholders stated that a quality learning experience would include: risk taking, high levels of involvement, having a sense of achievement and a balance of child-led and adult-directed tasks. Also, a minority of stakeholders interviewed for this book were unable to articulate a quality learning experience for young children, which is somewhat concerning.

There could be a number of reasons why the word 'play' was not specifically mentioned by stakeholders in relation to quality learning experience. These could include an uncertainty about their role in providing play or that it was implicitly understood that they were already providing a play-based curriculum. It could also be the case that 'play' is not associated with learning. Moyles (1989, p. ix) argues that 'it is difficult for anyone to value children's play as anything other than a non-work activity'. The truth of this statement is evident in the following comment from one senior stakeholder: 'There is still a **place for worksheets** in nursery and children can't be allowed to get out what they want.' The authors query how many other nurseries are delivering the Foundation Phase in this way. This further raises the question as to what extent this formal pedagogy for our youngest learners extends across more settings in Wales (with more than the forty-one case study school observations conducted for the Welsh Government evaluation).

The comment above by the senior stakeholder clearly suggests that there are power structures in place, and it is known that when children play, it enables them to challenge power structures and decentralize their position in the learning partnership. The children in question are not freely encouraged to play as this would challenge the power structures in the setting. Wood (2010) argues that when practitioners think of work, such as worksheets, and play as two separate constructs there tends to be more adult-led tasks in practice (Wood, 2010). Furthermore, Bruce (2011a) strongly suggests that 'worksheets seriously constrain the learning of children because adults control what the children do from a distance, but children cannot develop their own thinking' (p. 74).

One stakeholder interviewed for this book also commented that they felt the Foundation Phase was not being implemented properly in some settings, as the children were still doing literacy and numeracy in the mornings and only given opportunities to 'play' in the afternoons. This is particularly frustrating as it indicates that some settings are only paying 'lip service' to the Foundation Phase and not truly embracing it. The return of formal literacy and numeracy teaching could be related to the fact that 'over 70% of head teachers ranked literacy and numeracy as the **most pressing issues** in early years education' (Rhys et al., 2015, p. 2).

Giving children 'play' in the afternoon devalues it, and more so, the children themselves. Play should not be used as a treat or a way to reward children. Put simply, children have a right to play and adults should be well trained in being able to facilitate their play and become play partners with the children.

Empowerment and ownership

Since the introduction of the Foundation Phase, the Welsh Government has advocated the equal use of the indoor and outdoor environment for learning. However, in practice several stakeholders interviewed for this book indicated that free-flow access between both environments can be challenging. Barriers to learning in the outdoors are discussed in more detail in Chapter 3, but the Welsh Assembly stipulates that children should be given opportunities to plan and set up play areas indoors and outdoors (WAG, 2008b). This empowers children to take ownership, make decisions, plan their play choices and become agents of change.

Findings from the Welsh Government evaluation also included research with children. According to Rhys, et al. (2014b, p. 3):

> **Year 1 classroom tours** revealed that children enjoy learning independently, and were more knowledgeable about their learning environment when given more opportunities and choice in a variety of interesting and rich learning zones. [Furthermore] The majority of children who participated in the Year 1 classroom tours said they **rarely did any learning outside**.

This raises an important point about hearing children's voices in research – if the children's views had not been sought, a different perspective on outdoor learning might have been portrayed. Strangely, this seemed to be the case when '75% of **practitioners** reported using the outdoor learning environment *at least* 2/3 times a week with 34% reporting they use it **everyday**' (Rhys et al., 2014b, p. 3).

Edmiston (2008; cited in Broadhead, et al., 2010) suggests that when agency is present in both research and practice, children have the opportunity to make their own choices. However, the concept of agency is much more than children simply making choices (Edmiston, 2008; cited in Broadhead et al., 2010). As Waller (2009) argues, agency encompasses not only making classroom choices but becoming active citizens in everything they do. The term 'agency' is generally associated with the new sociology of childhood and is summed up in the following way by Waller: 'Children as agents can express not only their desires and wishes but they can also negotiate and interact within their environment causing change' (Waller, 2009, p. 8).

Child-centred learning

Child-initiated learning has many definitions and, in reference to Hart's (1992; cited in Andrews, 2012) ladder of participation, can fall into several categories. One stakeholder felt that an advantage of the Foundation Phase was children initiating their own learning. This was also a key finding from the Welsh Government evaluation (Waldron, et al., 2014a).

A significant feature of child-centred learning is the practitioners and how they interact and engage with the children as learners. Goouch 2010 (p. 229) writes that teachers need to be 'co-constructors, co-players and guided participators'. However, none of the stakeholders interviewed for this book referred to themselves as co-players or co-constructors when considering child-centred experiences. This may imply that there is a conflict between the understanding of a play-based, child-centred curriculum and the limited training provided to help staff facilitate the pedagogical principles of the Foundation Phase. The challenge is about moving from knowledge being delivered and discovered to knowledge being constructed jointly between adult and child (Cox, 2012; cited in Cockburn and Handscomb, 2012).

A concept known as Sustained Shared Thinking (SST) is defined in the Welsh Government *Learning and Teaching Pedagogy* document as 'the process where practitioner and child act as co-constructors in learning, both contributing to solving a problem' (WAG, 2008a, p. 35). However, it does not provide a clear example of what this may look like in practice. Chilvers (2012) describes SST as children having the opportunity to:

- explore something *they* are interested in;
- use their imagination *both* indoors and outdoors;
- converse *jointly*;
- develop their thinking *with* others
- have time to absorb *their* ideas and interests;
- re-examine ideas and interests

(Chilvers, 2012).

Adults should focus their attention on the process of thinking rather than the end product and provide a balance of dialogue, questioning and teaching equally through child-initiated and adult-led practice. In relation to SST Chilvers (2012, p. 18) observes that 'sustained shared thinking occurs most often when the child or children have initiated and led an activity'.

In addition, the terms 'co-constructors', 'co-players' and 'guided participators' are rarely used throughout the Welsh Government documentation and according to Broadhead et al. (2010, p. 182), 'the tensions and challenges that practitioners face are influenced by national policy frameworks, because they are not adequately underpinned by theory and research evidence about play, learning and pedagogy'.

Leading and managing pedagogy

Another aspect of Foundation Phase practice is the organization and management of other additional practitioners (e.g. support staff). Some of the challenges relating to leading and managing others were indicated in the following comments by stakeholders interviewed for this book:

'Being a manager and teacher are two different skill sets.'

'Having to get used to working in larger teams in the setting.'

'Learning Support Assistants are not paid enough to stay after school for meetings.'

'I think all teachers were a little bit apprehensive, we were used to being shut in our classrooms and it felt that we were on show the whole time.'

'[T]he teachers were learning alongside the LSAs so it was a learning curve for both.'

It could be argued that there was an assumption that class teachers would easily adopt the role and skills of leading and managing others. Nevertheless, stakeholders felt that this was a difficult transition in their job role. Fullan (1997) argues against leaders who exert power over others. The issue of leadership and management of additional staff in the Foundation Phase is a real concern as one Foundation Phase coordinator commented, '[W]e didn't have any sort of training as such to managing staff.' However, the Welsh Government provided a training module in 2009 called 'Leadership for Learning', but the content simply focused on building effective teams and effective relationships. One could argue this is a much too narrow perspective, on just one aspect of practice. According to Siraj-Blatchford and Manni's (2007) research on Effective Leadership in the Early Years Sector (ELEYS), the role of leadership is essentially that of 'leadership for learning' and can be characterized by:

- Contextual literacy – considering the situation and communicating appropriately within it.
- Commitment to collaboration – understanding the importance of partnerships between multi-agencies.
- Commitment to improvements of outcomes for all children – meeting the needs of all children in the setting.

This appears to demonstrate a much broader understanding of leadership than that documented in the Welsh Government training handbook. This raises an important point about appointing suitable Foundation Phase leaders/coordinators – those who have the necessary knowledge, skills and experience to undertake a vital role. Interviews with different stakeholders by the authors have shown that expectations of the Foundation Phase coordinator are not consistent across settings. Some coordinators are being awarded a Teaching and Learning Responsibility point (TLR) for the role, recognizing it as a senior management position, whereas other settings do not award a TLR point. The authors, therefore, query how there can be consistency in leadership and management of the Foundation Phase throughout Wales if some coordinators are paid extra for this responsibility and others are not. Does this mean that the Foundation Phase and the associated leadership and management of it are deemed more worthwhile by head teachers in some settings than others?

Conclusion

This chapter set out to discuss stakeholder perceptions of what constitutes rich learning experiences for young children. Additionally, it considered the challenges of delivering a child-centred pedagogy. Discussions with stakeholders indicate a misunderstanding about key features of rich learning experiences for young children such as play. Two pedagogical models were discussed and it was highlighted that there was a more adult-led approach being employed with children aged between five and seven.

Another aspect of child-centred practice involves allowing children to take ownership of their learning and environment. However, agency is not commonly used or understood by stakeholders, nor is sustained shared thinking. Both concepts should be at the forefront of Early Years curricula. To achieve this, the Foundation Phase needs innovative thinkers, knowledgeable leaders and effective communicators.

Currently, Foundation Phase practitioners find it challenging to balance child-led and adult-led pedagogy and meet new initiatives imposed by the Welsh Government – such as the recently introduced Literacy and Numeracy Framework (LNF) and testing, which is discussed in more detail in the next chapter.

Chapter summary

- Play and children's agency is largely misunderstood and misinterpreted by practitioners working in the Foundation Phase.
- Some settings deliver the Foundation Phase by formal literacy and numeracy *lessons* in the morning and opportunities to play in the afternoon.
- Children in the Foundation Phase do not always get the opportunity to voice their opinions in relation to where they play.
- Foundation Phase practitioners do not regard themselves as co-players and co-constructors of knowledge.
- Foundation Phase practitioners do not feel that adequate training is provided on leading and managing others.

Thought-provoking questions

- In your opinion, what constitutes a child-centred pedagogy? What does it look like in practice?
- What is the balance between adult-led and child-led tasks in your setting?
- Is there a place for worksheets in a Foundation Phase classroom?
- Are there opportunities for uninterrupted play, and if not, why not?
- How do you deliver literacy and numeracy skills within a play-based pedagogy?

Further reading and information

Aasen, W. and J. Waters (2006), 'The New Curriculum in Wales: A New View of the Child?' *Education 3–13* 34 (2): 123–9.

Alderson, P. (2008), *Young Children's Rights: Exploring Beliefs, Principles and Practice*, 2nd edn. London: Jessica Kingsley Publications.

Andrews, M. (2012), *Exploring Play*. London: Sage.

Covell, K. and R. Howe (1999), 'The Impact of Children's Rights in Education: A Canadian Study', *International Journal of Child's Rights* 7: 171–83.

11

Testing in a Play-based Curriculum

Chapter aims

To explore stakeholder opinions about the appropriateness and impact of testing young children.

To consider the rationale for testing and to discuss other forms of assessing young children's learning in a play-based curriculum.

Perceptions of testing young children

The following quote was made by a former minister on the rationale for testing children as young as seven in the Foundation Phase:

> [U]ltimately I think it is to raise standards but I think what the specific tests should do is give teachers themselves a better understanding of performance, and perhaps narrow the inconsistency between primary and secondary schools.
>
> (Past Minister, 2012a)

The same minister also referred to PISA results in 2009 and Estyn reports in support of raising standards in literacy and numeracy. One of the ambitions of the Welsh Government is that by 2015 Wales will be among the top twenty nations in PISA. The *National Literacy Programme* document notes that the Welsh Government has 'consulted local and international academics and experts specialising in school improvement and have taken account of international research' (WG, 2012d, p. 7).

However, there is no evidence to back up this claim, which is disappointing. This highlights a lack of academic rigour within policy. Conversely, a report (*First Steps*) by the Confederation of British Industry (CBI) (2012) clearly states that by subjecting pupils to exam factory conditions we are not producing the skills needed for the twenty-first-century workforce. The full report can be accessed at: http://www.cbi.org.uk/media/1845483/cbi_education_report_191112.pdf.

The majority of stakeholders interviewed for this book about the appropriateness of testing young children in the Foundation Phase felt that it was inappropriate and a step backwards from Foundation Phase principles. One practitioner said that 'the literacy and numeracy tests put excessive pressure on children and have no place in the Foundation Phase. There have been no benefits to having them and they have been imposed to the detriment of the curriculum.' Other perceptions included that tests add pressure on staff and have the potential to be a limitation. For example, one practitioner felt very strongly that 'Children who already have low self-esteem and who are aware of their difficulties are made to feel even more inadequate.' The authors query whether children's well-being was ever considered by policymakers when they decided to impose testing on some of its youngest learners.

Testing may lead to adopting a highly structured approach in the classroom and raise levels of progress as children are 'hot housed' to reach adult imposed targets and goals. However, this could develop surface level understanding and children will not be confident or competent in making connections to other aspects of learning (REPEY, 2002; cited in Chilvers, 2012). It is this lack of transferable skills that many fifteen-year-olds struggle with when taking the PISA tests.

Testing fails to develop skills such as higher order thinking, ability to adapt, collaborative teamwork and creative thinking (ARG, 1999) – all of which are a necessity for a twenty-first-century workforce. Also, they capture surface level learning rather than deep level learning. Concerns such as these are echoed by the Sutton Trust who warn ministers that:

> … repeated calls for better results in tests such as the Programme for International Students Assessment (PISA) will result in 'teaching to the test' rather than improvements to the system.
>
> (Barker, 2013, p. 12)

Another concern about the impact of testing on seven-year-olds and above is that teachers may feel pressurized to tailor their teaching towards the test. A principle of the Foundation Phase is for children to take ownership of their learning and this same principle can be applied to teachers having ownership of their teaching. However, by imposing testing on both children and teachers this ownership disappears. To some extent testing removes ownership for both children and adults.

In an interview with a former minister it was stated that 'under the old system of Standard Assessment Tests (SATs) at Key Stage 1 what we were seeing were children being marked out to fail from the moment they entered the education system' (Past Minister, 2012b). The authors' query to what extent the introduction of testing in May 2013 is any different to SATs at Key Stage 1 and Key Stage 2. The ethos of the

Foundation Phase is related to **stage** not **age** and individual learning needs, yet testing at seven years of age will mean that all children need to be test ready. Glenda MacNaughton (2005) refers to this as a conforming culture as opposed to a transforming culture. Gerver (2010) states that systems tend to assume 'that all children should be the same, reach the same learning states at the same age, be able to do the same things at the same time in the same way, know the same "stuff" and share the same interests' (p. 65). This is in direct conflict with the principles of the Foundation Phase that support the stage not age of development. Figure 11.1 below shows the mismatch between testing and a play-based curriculum

This diagram deliberately exaggerates the point that formal testing and the principles of the Foundation Phase are poles apart. However, when a former minister was asked about the place of testing in a play-based curriculum, he felt that this was achievable: 'I am not certain about this but some of the best Local Education Authorities are managing to integrate literacy and numeracy within a play-based curriculum' (Past Minister, 2012a). This response still does not clarify how testing fits with a *supposedly* play-based curriculum. The Welsh Government stipulates that the duration of the reading test is one hour and the two numeracy tests are half an hour each. Also, they provide guidance on where the tests can take place, for example stating that 'The National Reading Test and National Numeracy Test (Procedural) may be administered to a whole class in the classroom or to larger groups in larger rooms, e.g. to a year group in the school hall' (WG, 2015, p. 5). In addition to this, the Welsh Government (very kindly) allows young children aged between six and eight to have a short rest break during the tests, but this does not apply to children aged above 8! One participant interviewed for this book stated that guidance issued to parents from one primary school asked the parents for the children to be well rested the night before (the tests) and to ensure that they were on time to sit them.

The three-year evaluation of the Foundation Phase found that 'the majority of Foundation Phase leaders, head teachers and local authority stakeholders **did not agree with the introduction of the Literacy and Numeracy tests**' (Rhys, et al., 2015, p. 2).

Figure 11.1 Mismatch between Testing and Play-based Curricula

Rationale for testing young learners

Testing can be viewed as a method of accountability for teachers in addition to being a means of raising standards (Briggs and Hansen, 2013). Leighton Andrews (the then Education Minister) used Wales's poor results in the PISA rankings (league tables) as justification for introducing the literacy and numeracy tests. However, the Sutton Trust argue that 'league tables exaggerate the importance of raw test scores' (Barker, 2013, p. 12). Black and Wiliam (1998) argue that pupils who do well in tests have been trained for that particular test, which potentially means that children follow a narrow curriculum. One practitioner interviewed for this book expressed concern about limiting children's experiences: '[T]he second half of the spring term and the first half of the summer term is distributed with test preparation … the system places too much emphasis on the three Rs … what about Personal and Social Education and creativity.'

According to Gipps (2002, p. 35), 'a high stake testing programme is often a symbolic solution to a real educational problem. It offers the appearance of a solution, and indeed, as test scores rise over time, because of teaching to the test, policy makers can point to the wisdom of their action.' The concern is that if test scores in literacy and numeracy improve, this may be used to justify testing young children. The authors feel this may be at the expense of well-being, autonomy, curiosity, independence and creativity – all of which are Foundation Phase principles.

Testing may place pressure upon practitioners to limit purposeful play. As one former minister stated, '[Y]ou could whip people into shape by absolutely grounding them in the rhetoric needed for a test, and get better results but you may completely turn off future learning' (Past Minister, 2012b). Findings from the three-year evaluation found that 'incorporating testing practice and preparation into the daily routine as a response to the Literacy and Numeracy tests meant elements of the Foundation Phase were lost' (Rhys et al., 2015, p. 2).

One element that could be jeopardized as a result of testing is children's empowerment. The Welsh Government itself has acknowledged that 'empowerment is seen as a central concept so that children are better equipped to take greater charge of their lives in order to enhance their self-confidence, competence and self-esteem' (Barker, 2013, p. 5). The authors' question how testing can ever be seen as empowering children. In September 2012, one stakeholder interviewed for this book explained that in one Local Authority children at the start of Year 2 (aged six) sat in formal test conditions in a large hall. They got very tearful and upset because they did not know what was going on. The authors feel this is both unacceptable and inappropriate, but fear it could become common practice when getting children test ready.

Although the authors disagree with the place of testing within a child-centred curriculum and were horrified to hear about the incident described above, there will always be arguments for the value of testing. The table below summarizes some of these:

Arguments for testing
Evaluates standards with expected **outcomes** (Hall, 2007).
Provides evidence about school **performance** for a range of stakeholders (Hall, 2007).
Provides objective **data** for individuals and whole schools.
Allows practitioners to gain an accurate picture of where a learner is, which will help to inform future planning (WG, 2012c).
Provides opportunities to **target specific** interventions to children (Bruce, 2011).
Allows progress of learners to be tracked from Foundation Phase through to KS2 and KS3.

The table shows that the vocabulary associated with testing is **data**, **performance**, **outcomes, and target specific**. How is any of this holistic? If personal and social development and well-being is at the heart of the Foundation Phase, are we now ignoring these core elements at the expense of literacy and numeracy? This may also lead to a marginalization of other areas of learning. It is unclear whether children's opinions were sought during the piloting of the literacy testing in 2011–12, as this would have supported the government's agenda on the voice of the child. However, one stakeholder commented that 'I have never seen them in my setting ask the children what they want to learn about.' Although this is just one comment from one setting, it does raise the concern that if children are not being asked their opinions on what they are learning, are they ever going to be asked their opinions of testing?

It is still too early to judge what impact the Foundation Phase will have on educational standards in the future. In fact the Estyn report of September 2011 on *Literacy and the Foundation Phase* states that 'In the majority of schools where leaders and practitioners have implemented the Foundation Phase well, there is a focus on raising standards particularly in literacy' (Estyn, 2011, p. 3). Similarly, the three-year evaluation found improvements in literacy and numeracy skills as a result of the Foundation Phase (Rhys, et al., 2015). Making learners sit a paper-based test seems inappropriate, particularly when evidence shows that the Foundation Phase standalone (i.e. without tests) raises achievement. If we want to create lifelong learners and use education as the route out of poverty then is subjecting seven-year-olds to tests really the way forward?

Alternative assessment methods

The ARG (1999, p. 5) argues that 'the use of assessment to help pupils learn is one of the weakest aspects of practice in classrooms across the UK'. Therefore, in the twenty-first century the Welsh Government should be investing time and resources in forms of assessment other than testing. Testing is a form of summative assessment and is criterion-referenced, which means children are measured against set, fixed criteria. An example of this is the newly developed Foundation Phase Profile (FPP). Another form of summative assessment is norm-referencing. An example of this occurs when the Welsh Government compares children's performance in the literacy and numeracy tests with children of the same age.

A different form of assessment known as ipsative is defined by Blenkin and Kelly (1992) as 'assessment of a pupil not against norms (based on performance of his/her peers) or against criteria (derived from particular conceptions of subjects and/or of education) but against his/her own previous levels of attainment and performance' (p. 12). It is suggested that this form of assessment focuses on children's strengths and capabilities; in other words it focuses on their positive development. Arguably, testing focuses on what children cannot do, which is an example of a deficit model.

The following discussion draws upon assessment practices from various countries, such as New Zealand, Finland and Italy, to highlight alternative forms of assessment. In New Zealand a method of assessing young children utilizes 'learning stories'. These are characterized by narrative practice which tell a story about the child. They can consist of written observations, video recordings and photographs and/or children's work (Carr, 2001). The learning stories represent five learning dispositions, namely (1) taking an interest, (2) being involved, (3) persisting with difficulty or uncertainty, (4) expressing an idea or a feeling, and (5) taking responsibility and taking another point of view. A collaborative aspect of learning stories involves viewing the images with the children and reflecting upon the learning experience. According to Karlsdottir and Garoarsdottir (2010, p. 256), '[T]hrough regular documentation pre-school teachers may become more open towards identifying children's strengths and competencies rather than focusing their "problems" and thus gain better insight into children's capabilities.'

Using multiple types of documentation as a form of assessment is a common feature of Reggio Emilia practice in Northern Italy. The assessment also involves a close relationship between adult and child:

> In Reggio the adults are willing to learn alongside the children. They work together in partnership rather than the adult being 'in charge' and having all the answers … the adults watch and listen carefully to what the children do and say and use their observations to guide and extend each child's learning.
>
> (Thornton and Brunton, 2014, p. 15)

In Reggio settings, documentation may consist of photographs, observations, videos, children's drawings, models, paintings, dance, singing, mime and speaking and play (Maynard and Chicken, 2010). Thornton and Brunton (2014, p. 86) argue that 'in this context observation means not just looking at what children are doing, but listening to what they are saying and tuning in to the many different "languages of expression" which children use'. An important feature of Reggio practice is that teachers and children develop knowledge co-constructively (Thornton and Brunton, 2014). Maynard and Chicken (2010) argue that this 'leads to an emphasis on relationships, collaboration, negotiation, and, ultimately meaning-making' (p. 31).

The New Zealand and Italian approaches to assessment are examples of emphasis being placed on the process of children's learning and development rather than the end product such as a test. Edmiaston (2002) argues that focusing on the end products, which are norm-referenced and criterion-referenced, is inappropriate for young children.

Conclusion

No one working in education in Wales in the twenty-first century would argue with the fact that we need to improve the literacy and numeracy skills of our learners. What is debatable is how this is to be achieved – and testing children at the age of seven seems to be a backward step in the authors' opinion. The Foundation Phase is still in its infancy and has not been given enough time to show if this new approach will improve literacy and numeracy standards. This view is supported by one head teacher, David Pedwell: 'There is a danger here [that] a lot of children will feel that they have underachieved from these tests and that is not going to motivate pupils or teachers for that matter' (BBC Wales Online, 2013).

Alternative forms of assessment such as learning stories, ipsative assessment and individual documentation of children's achievements provide a much more positive way of capturing children's abilities. This is in contrast to a deficit end product model. Arguments for testing young children have been identified, but the authors still feel that this is at odds with the principles of the Foundation Phase.

Chapter summary

- Stakeholders opposed testing young children and felt it was detrimental to children's learning and development.
- The Welsh Government thinks it is appropriate to enforce test conditions for learners as young as six years of age.
- Testing is associated with the raising standards agenda and accountability, but there are alternative methods of assessment.
- Assessment practices from New Zealand and Italy are explored to demonstrate the importance of the process rather than the end product.

Thought-provoking questions

- How do you think children feel about being tested?
- What justifications are there for testing children within a play-based curriculum?
- How do you think standards can be raised in literacy and numeracy without resort to testing?
- Have you ever used alternative forms of assessment in your practice where you *work alongside* children to construct knowledge and understanding?

Further reading and information

Carr, M. and W. Lee (2012), *Learning Stories: Constructing Learner Identities in Early Education*. London: Sage.

Lilly, J., A. Peacock, S. Shoveller and D. Struthers (2014), *Beyond Levels: Alternative Assessment Approaches Developed by Teaching School*. Nottingham: NCTL.

National Foundation for Education Research (2013), *Primary Assessment and Accountability under the New National Curriculum*. UK: NFER.

Welsh Government (2012), *The Review of Early Years Child Assessment Tools used in Wales*. Cardiff: Welsh Government.

12

The Future of Early Years Education in Wales

Chapter aims

To identify and discuss the implications and challenges within Early Years education.

To consider the way forward for future educational policy and practice in Wales.

Transforming pedagogy in Wales

Throughout this book we have seen how Wales has a taken a distinctively different approach to education for 3- to 7-year-olds. In 2010, the then Education Minister for Wales, Jane Davidson, explained at a British Education Studies Association (BESA) conference that breaking away from 125 years of traditional formal learning was 'a major step for a small country like Wales to take' (BESA, 2010). In an interview for this book, Davidson stated that 'education is the route out of poverty' and that 'there was increasing evidence that formal education at an early age is detrimental to the development of the child'. Various government officials interviewed for this book suggested that the curriculum needed transforming because there was huge variation in practice, too many learners sitting behind desks, and learners being switched off from education. Some felt a balance was needed between creativity and formal learning.

As discussed in Chapter 1, in 2003 Wales started to reshape the Early Years curriculum using research gathered from different countries across the world. Jane Davidson has remarked that 'we took on board lessons learned and approaches adopted to review and adapt the provision we deliver in Wales' (BESA, 2010). For curriculum transformation to occur, Davidson suggested that 'all staff need to review their pedagogy and how they empower children to set and achieve high aspirations' (BESA, 2010).

Practitioners may consider the twelve pedagogical elements identified in the three-year evaluation of the Foundation Phase. The report considers these elements to be the embodiment of 'the principles and guidance of the Foundation Phase' (Taylor et al., 2015, p. 22). The 12 elements were mentioned in Chapter 1, but they are listed again here to help practitioners reflect upon a transforming pedagogy.

1   Child choice/participation
2   Exploration
3   First-hand
4   Practical
5   Stage not age
6   Balance of continuous/enhanced/focused activities
7   Open questioning
8   Reflection
9   Physical activity
10 Outdoor learning
11 Observation of children
12 Learning zones

(Taylor et al., 2015, p. 22)

Implementing a transforming pedagogy of this nature may present a challenge for all stakeholders associated with the Foundation Phase. As discussed throughout this book, stakeholders need to adopt a different view of the child as competent and able, as opposed to weak and vulnerable. Stakeholders will need to embrace a more child-centred pedagogy encompassing the child's voice. However, this will take time, as suggested by Michael Fullan in Chapter 1.

If practitioners find it challenging to adopt new approaches from the twenty-first century (the Foundation Phase) then the authors are concerned that in the struggle to do this, practitioners could revert back to what they know best. This could mean that learning approaches and practice from the twentieth century (National Curriculum) will prevail, such as formal didactic teaching (the cultural transmissive approach). This is a concern because practice should reflect what we know about children and what they are capable of – when practitioners reject new ideas, or continue to ignore current research, then children miss out. An opportunity to transform pedagogy is also lost. A recent example of this is reported in the findings of the three-year evaluation:

> Local Authority stakeholders reported that there had been a return towards focussing on a more formal teaching of literacy and numeracy (particularly in the mornings), which they felt was in response to the pressure to raise standards.
>
> (Rhys et al., 2015, p. 1)

One argument for a return to more formal, traditional, sedentary practices could be the Welsh Government's continuous meddling with the original principles of the Foundation Phase, identified above. Numerous aspects of the curriculum, such as the reintroduction of literacy and numeracy tests, target setting, the Literacy and Numeracy Framework (LNF) and a raising standards agenda, are potentially examples of an erosion of a child-centred, experiential curriculum.

Assessment requirements within the Foundation Phase

During the summer of 2013 the Welsh Government started developing the Early Years Development Assessment Framework (EYDAF) project. The intention is to develop 'a single overarching 0–7 assessment framework and a suite of linked assessment tools which can be used to chart children's progress, longitudinally, across the early years' (WG, 2014). The ambitious aim of EYDAF is to provide a coherent approach amongst all Early Years sectors which include health services, Flying Start, Foundation Phase and childcare (WG, 2014).

One of the assessment tools within EYDAF is called the Foundation Phase Profile (FPP), as discussed in Chapter 6. Chapter 11 introduced arguments about product and process type assessment, but the new FPP seems to resemble a product type approach. It highlights the importance of observing children and the use of formative and summative assessment, yet the whole profile is underpinned by outcomes and does not privilege processes. The FPP record forms that practitioners are expected to complete do not appear to be holistic in nature. This is because only four key areas (Personal and Social Development, Well-being and Cultural Diversity, Mathematical Development, Language, Literacy and Communication Skills and Physical Development) are required, which *diminishes* the importance of Creative Development, Welsh Language Development and Knowledge and Understanding of the World.

The authors feel that there is a mismatch between the principles of the Foundation Phase and the statutory assessment requirements. In other words, the Welsh Government espouses a process approach to the curriculum yet expects practitioners to assess product-oriented outcomes.

In order to address the mismatch between a broad, integrated curriculum such as the Foundation Phase and narrow outcomes, Edmiaston (2002) proposes the following seven principles of meaningful assessment:

1 Embed assessment in classroom activities
2 Use multiple sources to collect assessment evidence
3 Set time aside for systematic observation of children

4 View assessment as a process that takes place over time
5 Examine children's reasoning through their actions and words
6 Examine the curriculum through children's actions and words
7 Make assessment a collaborative endeavour

(Edmiaston, 2002, pp. 56–62)

Edmiaston (2002) also makes the point that these principles are not new, and that for practitioners to make accurate judgements about children's learning and development they require a sound understanding of child development. However, the FPP guidance document allocates only one page to child development – and does not explicitly mention the need for practitioners to have a sound understanding of child development.

Training and qualifications

Thirteen out of twenty-three recommendations for the 2014 independent stocktake of the Foundation Phase focus on training. One such recommendation states:

> Ensure that all models/training are underpinned by theory and research making clear the value of effective early education. Links between theory and practice and the important role of the adult need to be explicit.

(Siraj, 2014, p. 8)

The same point was previously raised as a concern in the new FPP. Since the introduction of the Foundation Phase, the number of adults in the classroom has increased. This might be considered a positive outcome in terms of supporting young children, but it is recognized that 'additional practitioners require continued professional development' (Siraj, 2014, p. 10). As discussed in Chapter 1, the recommended ratios in the Foundation Phase were 1:8 in nursery and reception, and 1:15 in Year 1 and Year 2. However, the stocktake report (Siraj, 2014) suggests more children to adults whereas the three-year evaluation recommends more adults to children (Taylor et al., 2015).

In 2014 the Welsh Government launched an education improvement plan called 'Qualified for Life'. Objective one of this strategic plan involves the New Deal for the education workforce. The current Minister for Education and Skills explains that the concept behind the New Deal is to raise learner outcomes by up-skilling the workforce. However, the cost of the New Deal is not explained in detail, which is a concern when it seems to encompass training needs and requirements for all stakeholders from support staff to senior leaders (Lewis, 2015). There is an online presence for up-skilling the workforce in the New Deal, which could be viewed as a blanket approach to training. More information can be found using the links provided at the end of this chapter.

The way forward for Early Years education in Wales

Since the introduction of the Foundation Phase in 2008 there have been a variety of reports that present numerous recommendations. The following table highlights the overwhelming number of implications for policy and practice.

Name of Report	Number of recommendations	Who is responsible?	
An independent stocktake of the Foundation Phase (Siraj, 2014)	23	WG	20
		Setting	2
		Both	1
Successful Futures (Donaldson, 2015)	68	WG	52
		Setting	16
		Both	0
Evaluating the Foundation Phase (Taylor et al., 2015)	29	WG	14
		Setting	2
		Both	13
Teaching Tomorrow's Teacher (Furlong, 2015)	9	WG	9
		Setting	n/a
		Both	n/a
Total number of recommendations	**129**		

Key: WG = Welsh Government, including Local Authorities and Consortia Level

The table highlights the immense task facing policymakers in improving the teaching and learning of children in Wales. The authors argue that:

> Education is littered with examples of innovations that have either failed or only been partially implemented because teachers weren't convinced the change was necessary and result in real improvement. The result has been that they merely modify their practice at the edges and then abandon the change after a while because it didn't work for them.
>
> (Weeden et al., 2002, p. 127)

The authors believe that breaking with traditional educational practices was a step in the right direction for young learners in Wales. Perhaps the focus in the future needs to be on bringing the pedagogy in Key Stage 2 and Key Stage 3 more in line with the principles of the Foundation Phase. This particular view was stated by a policy advisor interviewed for this book: 'I think we need to join up Key Stage two and Key

Stage three and plan the curriculum through skills. We need to take the building blocks from the Foundation Phase and use those to transform Key Stage two and Key Stage three ...'.

However, any major change in policy and practice needs to be developed over time and this can be a very slow process. The Foundation Phase is still in its infancy and its long-term impact unknown. Nevertheless, any curriculum that embraces the principles of child-initiated pedagogy with a readiness for learning and supports collaboration should be commended. The three-year evaluation of the Foundation Phase reports that 'a common theme emerging from practitioner and stakeholder interviews was the **feeling that it's too soon for major changes to the Foundation Phase** as more time is needed to see what effect it might or might not be having' (Waldron, et al., 2015, p. 3).

Conclusion

This chapter discussed the challenges and implications of curriculum change. It summarized the need for curriculum change in Wales and the twelve pedagogical elements that underpin the Foundation Phase. In terms of transforming the curriculum, assessment and training and qualifications were explored. Statutory assessment requirements in the Foundation Phase still focus on end product rather than the processes of learning. Recent Welsh Government plans include the New Deal, which seems to be portrayed as a panacea for raising standards. The chapter includes a useful table highlighting four significant reports on Welsh education policy and practice. The table attempts to demonstrate the number of recommendations associated with each report and also who is responsible for making them happen. The total number of recommendations (129) seems overwhelming for all involved in education in Wales, particularly when the Foundation Phase is still in its infancy.

Chapter summary

- The Foundation Phase was introduced to move away from formal, traditional pedagogies with an opportunity to transform to a child-centred, play-based curriculum.
- The Foundation Phase can be characterized by twelve pedagogical elements.
- The Welsh Government still advocates a product type assessment in the twenty-first century rather than a process type assessment.
- There are conflicting messages about the ratios of adults to children in the Foundation Phase.
- The Welsh Government proposes the New Deal for up-skilling all stakeholders.
- Currently there are 129 recommendations to improve education in Wales.

Thought-provoking questions

- Do you think the introduction of the Foundation Phase has transformed the way in which you work with young children? If yes, in what way?
- Do you think the FPP represents good practice in assessment?
- Do you feel the Welsh Government provides sufficient training in child development?
- Do you feel adequately trained to deliver the Foundation Phase? If not, what training is needed?
- If you could select between five and ten recommendations to improve the Foundation Phase, what would they be and why?

Further reading and information

Cameron, C. and P. Moss (2011), *Social Pedagogy and Working with Children and Young People*. London: Jessica Kingsley Publications.

New Deal: http://learning.gov.wales/news/sitenews/new-deal/?lang=en; http://learning.gov.wales/yourcareer/newdeal/?lang=en.

Papatheodorou, T. and P. Luff (2012), *Child Observation for Learning and Research*. London: Pearson.

Welsh Government (2013), *Building a Brighter Future: Early Years and Childcare Plan*. Cardiff: Welsh Government.

Final Thoughts ...

Even though the Foundation Phase is in its infancy, this book makes an important contribution to understanding and implementing curriculum change for the benefit of young learners. Implementation of the principles of the Foundation Phase needs to be considered from multiple perspectives; this includes the following agents: children, parents, practitioners, advisors and policymakers. Only when the Welsh Government is truly committed to the principles of the Foundation Phase will the policy rhetoric become reality.

To conclude, the authors feel that 'one way of reflecting is in your head as you walk or drive or do household chores. But there comes a point when we need something more. We might want to read something, to talk with others, try our ideas out, or we might wish to write them down' (Smith, 2012, p. 150) – and this is what the authors have tried to achieve in writing this book. The overarching aim is to open up a platform for dialogue about curriculum change, to create discussion and debate and provide opportunities for reflection upon policy and practice. The closing image provides a stimulus for this ...

Figure 13.1 Illustration by Carole Carter

Glossary

Active learning: Children are actively involved within their learning.

Agency: Children having a voice and being accepted as full members of society.

Assessment: Can be formative or summative or holistic and ipsative. It is an evaluation or estimation of the ability of someone or something. In the Foundation Phase there is an on entry baseline assessment, continuous assessment and end of Foundation Phase assessment.

Assessment for learning: Formative assessment that is continuous and ongoing.

Autonomy: Freedom to make own decisions.

Behaviourism: A theory of learning that is based around conditioning human behaviour.

Child-initiated/Child-centred: A curriculum that focuses on a child's interests and development. It starts with the child's interests and individual learning needs.

Co-construction: Shared meanings and communication between adult and child in a learning environment.

Cognitive development: The development of the mind, focusing on thinking and understanding.

Constructivism: A theory of learning that is based around learners linking new knowledge to prior knowledge.

Context: The circumstances that surround an event and allow it to be understood and evaluated.

Continuous provision: Encompasses the areas of learning that are always available to the children. This links to the long-term planning.

Curriculum: The Foundation Phase curriculum has seven Areas of Learning. All areas support the development of children and of skills. All seven areas work together to provide a holistic curriculum.

Curriculum Cymreig: The development of children's cultural awareness of Wales across all seven areas of development.

Devolution: The transfer of central government control (Westminster) to smaller regions (Wales).

Differentiation: A match between children's developmental needs and their ability.

Enhanced provision: An addition to the long-term planning and is linked to the medium-term planning.

Emotional intelligence: Being able to understand oneself and others.

Emotional literacy: The ability to recognize and understand and appropriately express emotions.

Emotional well-being: Development of children's self-esteem, their feelings and awareness of the feelings of others.

Empiricist approach: The child is seen as an empty vessel needing to be filled by the adult.

Empowerment: Enabling children to take ownership of their learning.

EPPE: Effective Provision of Pre-School Education. A project that investigated the effects of pre-school education and care in children aged 3–7 years between the years of 1997 and 2004.

Experiential learning: A hands-on approach to learning.

Fine motor skills: The ability to undertake fine intricate movements, using fingers and hand–eye coordination.

Focused provision: This where adults model what they want the children to know. These are specific activities that are led by the practitioner. This is linked to the short-term planning.

Formative assessment: Ongoing assessment that promotes a learner's attainment.

Gross motor skills: Using whole body movements, coordination and balance.

Hierarchy of needs: A theory proposed by Abraham Maslow. It suggests that people are motivated to fulfil basic needs before moving on to other more advanced needs. Most often displayed as a pyramid.

Holistic development: Concerns the development of the whole child.

Interactionist approach: This approach believes that children are partly empty vessels waiting to be filled, that they are partly pre-programmed and that there is interaction between the two.

Inter-disciplinary: A range of services collaborating with and learning from each other.

Invocation: Developing good practice by asking for support from others.

Learning environment: Should provide a wealth of learning opportunities across all seven Areas of Learning.

Learning styles: Are preferred ways of learning. Styles include visual, auditory and kinaesthetic.

Linear: Arranged or extending models along a straight line.

Nativist approach: The child is seen as being biologically pre-programmed to unfold in certain directions.

Non-participant observations: Involves the observer sitting away from the child and taking no part in the actual activity.

Observations: The act of noticing or paying attention. Ongoing observations of children are at the heart of the Foundation Phase.

Outcomes: The Foundation Phase outcomes include baseline assessment scales and descriptions and National Curriculum level descriptors. There are six Outcomes per Area of Learning. Outcomes 4–6 broadly cross-reference to the National Curriculum levels 1–3.

Paradox: A contradictory idea, viewpoint or concept that seems absurd but in reality when investigated may well be true, for example testing learners and a play-based curriculum.

Participant observations: Involves the observer sitting alongside the child and taking part in the activity or talking to the child as they carry out a given task.

Pedagogy: Refers to the relationship between learning and teaching. The practitioner is a facilitator of learning, meeting individual needs, learning alongside the children and continually reflecting on improving practice.

Philosophy: Underpinning knowledge that informs someone's practice.

Physical development: Divided into gross and fine motor skills. Physical development is closely linked to cognitive development.

Pioneer: One who opens up new areas of thought, research or development.

Play spiral: Free play is followed by directed play, then the child returns to free play using skills gained in the directed play.

Practitioners: Generic term referring to adults who work with children in the classroom in both the maintained and non-maintained sectors.

Problem solving: The ability to assess a problem and then solve it. Children should be given opportunities to draw on previous experience when attempting to solve new problems.

Proponent: One who argues in favour of something (e.g. child-initiated versus adult-led learning).

Researching Effective Pedagogy in the Early Years (REPEY): A report by Iram Siraj-Blatchford et al. which analysed the EPPE project.

Scaffolding: The ongoing support provided to learners by adults or peers.

Schemas: Patterns of repeatable actions.

Spiral curriculum: Children revisit topics and resources as their thinking skills develop.

Summative assessment: Determines/tests what students know at a particular time.

Sustained Shared Thinking: An activity in which two or more individuals work together in an intellectual way to solve a problem.

TASC: Thinking Actively in a Social Context. This is a framework that encourages children to solve problems. It supports the development of independent, creative thinking and personalized learning.

Tokenistic: Paying lip service to a concept, applying minimum effort.

Transition: A process of moving from one class to another.

ZPD: Zone of Proximal Development. This is defined as the distance between the child's actual developmental level and the higher level of potential development as determined through adult guidance and more capable peers. The term ZPD was used by Lev Vygotsky.

Bibliography

Aasen, W. and J. Waters (2006), 'The New Curriculum in Wales: A New View of the Child?', *Education 3–13* 34 (2): 123–9.

Abbott, L. and C. Nutbrown (2001), *Experiencing Reggio Emilia: Implications for Preschool Provision*, Buckingham: Open University Press.

ACCAC (2000), *Desirable Outcomes for Children's Learning Before Compulsory School Age*, Cardiff: ACCAC.

Adams, P. (2006), 'Exploring social constructivism: theories and practicalities', *Education 3–13* 34 (3): 243–57.

Ainley J., D. Pratt and A. Hansen (2006), Connecting Engagement and Focus in Pedagogic Task Design. *British Educational Research Journal*, 32(1), 32–8.

Alderson, P. (2008), *Young Children's Rights: Exploring Beliefs, Principles and Practice*, 2nd edn, London: Jessica Kingsley Publications.

Alexander, G. (1995), 'Children's Rights in their Early Years', in B. Franklin (1995), *The Handbook of Children's Rights: Comparative Policy and Practice*, London: Routledge.

Alexander, G. (2000), *Culture and Pedagogy: International Comparisons in primary Education*. Oxford: Blackwell.

Andrews, L. (2012), *Written Statement – The Child Development Assessment Profile*, http://wales.gov.uk/about/cabinet/cabinetstatements/2012/childdevelopmentprofile/?skip=1&lang=en (accessed 3 March 2012).

Andrews, M. (2012), *Exploring Play*, London: Sage.

Appleby, K. (2010), 'Reflective Thinking: Reflective Practice', in M. Reed and N. Canning (2010), *Reflective Practice in the Early Years*, London: Sage.

Archard, D. (2004), *Children: Rights and Childhood*, 2nd edn, London: Routledge.

Assessment Reform Group (ARG) (1999), *Assessment for Learning: Beyond the Black Box*, Cambridge: University of Cambridge.

Athey, C. (2007), *Extending Thought in Young Children*, London: Paul Chapman.

Association for Teachers and Lecturers (2012), *Playing to Learn*, London: ATL, http://www.dailymail.co.uk/news/article-2008225/Exam-results-plummet-school-league-tables-abolished.html#ixzz2ErmDEoa2 (accessed 11 December 2012).

Ball, C. (1994), *Start Right: The importance of early learning*. Coventry: RSA.

Barker, I. (2013), 'See-sawing rankings are shaky ground to build on', *Times Educational Supplement*, 5 February 2013, p. 12.

BBC Wales Online (2013), 'NUT strike threat over Wales teaching standards plans', http://www.bbc.co.uk/news/uk-wales-21222006 (accessed 28 January 2013).

Beers, H. and C. Trimmer (2004), *Adults First!: An Organisational Training for Adults on Children's Participation*, Bangkok: Save the Children.

Beith, K., P. Tassoni, K. Bulman and M. Robinson (2005), *Children's Care, Learning and Development*. Oxford: Heinemann Educational Publishers.

Benjamin, A. C. (1994), 'Observation in early childhood classroom: advice from the field', *Young Children* 49 (6): 14–20.

Bennett, T. (2001), 'Reactions to Visiting the Infant-Toddle and Pre-school Centers in Reggio Emilia, Italy'. *Early Childhood Research and Practice* 3, no. 1, http://ecrp.uiuc.edu/v3n1/bennett.html (accessed 5 April 2009).

Bennett, N., M. Crawford and C. Riches (1992), *Managing Change in Education: Individual and Organisational Perspectives*, London: Paul Chapman.

Bennett, N., L. Wood and S. Rogers (1997), *Teaching Through Play: Teacher's Thinking and Classroom Practice*, Buckingham: Open University Press.

Bilton, H. (2010), *Outdoor Learning in the Early Years: Management and Innovation*, 3rd edn, London: David Fulton.

Bishop, J. C. and M. Curtis (2001), *Play Today in the Primary School Playground*, London: Open University Press.

Black, P., C. Harrison, C. Lee, B. Marshall and D. Wiliam (2003), *Working inside the Black Box*, London: GL Assessment.

Black, P. and D. Wiliam (1998), *Inside the Black Box*, London: Kings College

Blackwell, S. and L. Pound (2011), 'Forest Schools in the Early Years', in L. Miller and L. Pound (eds), *Theories and Approaches to Learning in the Early Years*, London: Sage, pp. 133–48.

Blenkin, G. and A. Kelly (1992), *Assessment in Early Childhood Education*, London: Paul Chapman.

Booth, T., M. Ainscow and D. Kingston (2006), *Index for Inclusion: Developing Play, Learning & Participation in Early Years & Childcare*, Bristol: Centre for Studies in Inclusive Education.

Bottery, M. (1990), *The Morality of the School*. London: Cassell.

Boud, D., R. Keogh and D. Walker (1985), *Reflection: Turning Experience into Learning*, London: RoutledgeFalmer.

Boyle, W. F. and M. Charles (2010), 'Leading Learning through Assessment for Learning?', *School Leadership and Management* 30 (3): 285–300.

Bradley, M., B. Isaacs, D. N. Livingston, A. True and M. Dillane (2011), 'Maria Montessori in the United Kingdom: 100 Years on', in L. Miller and L. Pound (eds), *Theories and Approaches to Learning in the Early Years*, London, Sage, pp. 71–85.

Briggs, M. and A. Hansen (2013), *Play-based Learning in the Primary School*, London: Sage.

Briggs, M., A. Woodfield, C. Martin and P. Swatton (2008), *Assessment for Learning and Teaching*, 2nd edn, Exeter: Learning Matters.

British Educational Suppliers Association (BESA) (2010), Jane Davidson conference notes.

Broadhead, P., E. Howard and E. Wood (2010), *Play and Learning on the Early Years*, London: Sage.

Broström, S. (2006), 'Children's Perspectives on their Childhood Experiences', in J. Einarsdottir and J. Wagner (2006), *Nordic Childhoods and Early Education*, Greenwich: Information Age.

Brown, F. (2008), 'Services to Children's Play', in P. Jones, D. Moss, P. Tomlinson and S. Welch (2008), *Childhood: Services and Provision for Children*, Harlow: Pearson Educational.

Brown, S. and P. Knight (1994), *Assessing Learners in Higher Education*, London: Kogan Page.

Bruce, T. (1987), *Early Childhood Education*, London: Hodder & Stoughton.

Bruce, T. (2004), *Developing Learning in Early Childhood: 0–8 Years*, London: Paul Chapman.

Bruce, T. (2005), *Early Childhood Education*, 3rd edn, London: Hodder Arnold.

Bruce, T. (2011a), *Early Childhood Education*, 4th edn, Oxon: Hodder Education.

Bruce, T. (2011b), 'Froebel Today', in L. Miller and L. Pound (eds), *Theories and Approaches to Learning in the Early Years*, London: Sage, pp. 55–70.

Bruner, J. S. (1990), *Acts of Meaning*, Cambridge, MA: Harvard University Press.

Brunson Phillips, C. and Bredekamp, S. (1998), *Reconsidering Early Childhood Education in the United States: Reflections from Our Encounters with Reggio Emilia*. In Edwards, C., Gandini, L. and Forman, G. *The Hundred Languages of Children: The Reggio Emilia Approach-Advanced Reflections*. London: Ablex Publishing.

Carr, M. (2001), *Assessment in Early Childhood Settings: Learning Stories*, London: Sage.

Casas, F. (1997), 'Children's Rights and Children's Quality of Life: Conceptual and Practical Issues', *Social Indicators Research* 42: 283–98.

Casey, T. (2007), *Environments for Outdoor Play: A Practical Guide to Making Space for Children*, London: Paul Chapman.

Cauley, K. M. and J. McMillan (2009), 'Formative Techniques to Support Student Motivation and Achievement', *The Clearing House* 83 (1): 1–6.

Children and Young People's Partnership Consortium for Wales and the Partnership Unit (2004), *Save the Children*, leaflet, Cardiff: Welsh Assembly Government, www.savethechildren.org.uk (accessed 14 April 2012).

Children's Commissioner for Wales (2007–8), *Annual Review*, http://www.childcomwales.org.uk (accessed 14 April 2009).

Chilvers, D. (2008), 'Follow me: Planning to follow children's interest', *Nursery World*, 29 October 2008, pp. 18–21.

Chilvers, D. (2012), *Playing to Learn*, London: Association of Teachers and Lecturers.

Clark, A. (2007), 'Views from Inside the Shed: Young Children's Perspectives of the Outdoor Environment', *Education 3–13* 35 (4): 349–63.

Clark, A. and P. Moss (2001), *Listening to Young Children: The Mosaic Approach*, London: National Children's Bureau.

Clark, A., A. Kjorhølt and P. Moss (2005), *Beyond Listening: Children's Perspectives on Early Childhood Services*, Bristol: Policy Press.

Clark, M. and T. Waller (2007), *Early Childhood Education and Care: Policy and Practice*. London: Sage.

Clarke, S. (2001), Unlocking formative assessment: Practical strategies for enhancing pupils' learning in the primary classroom. London: Hodder and Stoughton Educational.

Clements, R. (2004), 'An Investigation of the Status of Outdoor Play', *Contemporary Issues in Early Childhood* 5 (1): 68–80.

Cockburn, A. and G. Handscomb (2012), *Teaching Children 3–11*, London: Sage.

Coffield, F. (2005), 'Learning Styles: Help or Hindrance?', *Research Matters* 26 (Autumn).

Confederation of British Industry (CBI) (2012), *First Steps*, http://www.cbi.org.uk/media/1845483/cbi_education_report_191112.pdf (accessed 24 November 2012).

Corsaro, W. (1997), *The Sociology of Childhood*. London: Pine Forge Press.

Covell, K. and R. Howe (1999), 'The Impact of Children's Rights in Education: A Canadian Study', *International Journal of Child's Rights* 7: 171–83.

Cox, S. (2012), 'Approaches To Learning And Teaching', in A. Cockburn and G. Handscomb (eds), *Teaching Children 3–11*, London: Sage, pp. 33–50.

Craig, C. (2007), *The Potential Dangers of a Systematic, Explicit Approach to Teaching Social and Emotional Skills (SEAL)*, Glasgow: Centre for Confidence and Well-being.

Craig, C. (2009), *Well-being in Schools: The Curious Case of the Tail Wagging the Dog?*, Glasgow: Centre for Confidence and Well-being.

Croke, R. and A. Crowley (2006), *Righting the Wrongs: The Reality of Children's Rights in Wales*, Cardiff: Wales Programme of Save the Children, www.savethechildren.org.uk (accessed 14 April 2012).

Crompton, M. (1980), *Respecting Children: Social Work with Young People*, London: Edward Arnold.

Crowley, K. (2014), *Child Development*, London: Sage.

Curtis, A. (1994), 'Play in Different Cultures and Different Childhoods', in J. Moyles (1994), *The Excellence of Play*, Buckingham: Open University Press.

Dahlberg, G., P. Moss and A. Pence (2007), *Beyond Quality in Early Childhood Education and Care*, 2nd edn, London: Routledge.

Daniels, H. (ed.) (2005), *An Introduction to Vygotsky*, 2nd edn, London: Routeledge Taylor & Francis.

Davies, L. and G. Fitzpatrick (2000), *The Euridem Project, Children's Rights Alliance for England, for Evidence of Democracy in Education in Sweden, Denmark, Germany and Holland*, London: Children's Rights Office.

Davis, E., N. Priest, B. Davies, M. Sims, L. Harrison, H. Herrman, E. Waters, L. Strazdins, B. Marshall and K. Cook (2010), 'Promoting Children's Social and Emotional Wellbeing in Childcare Centres within Low Socioeconomic Areas: Strategies, Facilitators and Challenges', *Australasian Journal of Early Childhood* 35 (3): 77–86.

Department for Children, Education, Lifelong Learning and Skills (DCELLS) (2008), *School Effectiveness Framework*, Cardiff: Welsh Assembly Government.

Department for Children, Schools and Families (DCSF) (2008), *Statutory Framework for the Early Years Foundation Stage*, Nottingham: HMSO.

Department for Education (DfE) (2010), *The Case for Change*, England: DfE

DfE (2012), *Statutory Framework of the Early Years Foundation Stage: Setting the Standards for Learning, Development and Care for Children from Birth to Five*, London: DfE.

DfE, (2014), *Statutory Framework for the Early Yyears Foundation Stage*, London: DfE.

Dickins, M. (2008), *Listening as a Way of Life: Listening to Young Disabled Children*, London: National Children's Bureau.

Dickins, M., S. Emerson and P. Gordon-Smith (2004), *Starting with Choice: Inclusive Strategies for Consulting Young Children*, London: Save the Children.

Dockett, S. and M. Fleer (1999), *Play and Pedagogy in Early Childhood*, Marickville, NSW: Harcourt Brace.

Dowling, M. (2005), *Supporting Young Children's Sustained Shared Thinking*, London: British Association for Early Childhood Education.

Dowling, M. (2010), *Young Children's Personal, Social and Emotional Development*, 3rd edn, London: Sage.

Drake, J. (2005), *Planning Children's Play & Learning in the Foundation Stage*, Oxon: David Fulton.

Durrant, J. and G. Holden (2006), *Teachers Leading Change: Doing Research for School Improvement*, London: Paul Chapman.

Earley, P. and S. Bubb (2004), *Leading and Managing Continuing Professional Development*, London: Paul Chapman.

Edgington, M. (2003), *The Great Outdoors: Developing Children's Learning Through Outdoor Provision*, 2nd edn, London: British Association for Early Childhood Education.

Edmiaston, R. (2002), 'Assessing and Documenting Learning in Constructivist Classrooms', in R. DeVries, et al. (2002), *Developing Constructivist Early Childhood Curriculum*, New York: Teachers College Press.

Edwards, C., L. Gandini and G. Forman (1998), *The Hundred Languages of Children: The Reggio Emilia Approach-Advanced Reflections*, London: Ablex.

Einarsdottir, J. (2006), 'Between Two Continents, Between Two Traditions: Education and Care in Icelandic Preschools', in J. Einarsdottir and J. Wagner (2006), *Nordic Childhoods and Early Education*, Greenwich: Information Age.

Einarsdottir, J. and J. Wagner (2006), *Nordic Childhoods and Early Education*, Greenwich: Information Age.

Einstein, A. (1920), in A. Calaprice (1996), *The Quotable Einstein*, Princeton, NJ: Princeton University Press.

Ellis, N. (2011), 'Foundation Stage-expectations and Vision', in J. Moyles (ed.), *Beginning Teaching; Beginning Learning in Primary Education*, Berkshire: Open University Press.

Else, P. (2009), *Value of Play*, London: Continuum International.

Estyn (2007), *Getting the Balance Right in the Foundation Phase*. Cardiff: Estyn.

Estyn (2010a), *Foundation Phase training and its impact on learning and teaching*. Cardiff: Estyn.

Estyn (2010b), *Annual Report 2010–2011*. Cardiff: Estyn.

Estyn (2011), *Literacy and the Foundation Phase: An Evaluation of the Implementation of the Foundation Phase for Five to Six-Year-Olds in Primary Schools, with Special Reference to Literacy*, Cardiff: Estyn.

Estyn (2012a), *Effective Practice in Tackling Poverty and Disadvantage in Schools*, Cardiff: Estyn.

Estyn (2012b), *The Skills Framework at Key Stage 2: An Evaluation of the Impact of the Non-Statutory Skills Framework for 3–19-Year-Olds in Wales at Key Stage 2*, Cardiff: Estyn.

Estyn (2013), *Annual Report 2011–2012*, Cardiff: Estyn.

Fajerman, L., M. Jarrett and F. Sutton (2000), *Children as Partners in Planning: A Training Resource to Support Consultation with Children*, London: Save the Children.

Fawcett, M. (2009), *Learning Through Child Observation*, 2nd edn, London: Jessica Kingsley.

Fisher, J. (1996), *Starting from the Child: Teaching and Learning in the Foundation Stage*, Maidenhead: Open University Press.

Fisher, S., A. Priestley, J. Allan and J. I'Anson (2005), *Promising Rights: Introducing Children's Rights in School*, London: Save the Children UK, www.savethechildren. org.uk (accessed 14 April 2012).

Fjørtoft, I. (2001), 'The Natural Environment as a Playground for Children: The Impact of Outdoor Play Activities in Pre-Primary School Children', *Early Childhood Education Journal* 29 (2): 111–17.

Fjørtoft, I. (2004), 'Landscape as Playscape: The Effects of Natural Environments on Children's Play and Motor Development', *Children, Youth and Environment* 14 (2): 21–44.

Ford, R. (2004), 'Thinking and Cognitive Development in Young Children', in T. Maynard and N. Thomas (eds) (2004), *An Introduction to Early Childhood Studies*, London: Sage.

Forestry Commission (2001), *Woodlands for Learning and the Learning Country: Education Strategy for Wales*, Aberystwyth: Welsh Assembly Government, p. 3.

Freeman, N. (1998), 'Look to the East – Gain a New Perspective Understand Cultural Differences, Appreciate Cultural Diversity', *Early Childhood Education Journal*, http:// www.pbs.org/kcts/preciouschildren/earlyed/read_east.html (accessed 5 April 2009).

Fromberg, D. and D. Bergen (2006), *Play from Birth to Twelve: Context, Perspectives, and Meanings*, London: Routledge.

Fullan, M. (1991), *The New Meaning of Educational Change*, London: Cassell.

Fullan, M. (1997), 'Planning, Doing and Coping with Change', in M. Preedy (1997), *Organisational Effectiveness and Improvements in Education*, Buckingham: Open University Press.

Funky Dragon (2004), *How Do We Get Effective Participation for 0–10 year olds in Wales: An Open Space Conference – A Summary Report*, Cardiff: Welsh Assembly Government, www.funkydragon.org.uk (accessed 14 April 2012).

Furlong, J. (2015), Teaching Tomorrow's Teachers. Oxford: University of Oxford.

Gardner, H. (1993), *Frames of Mind: The Theory of Multiple Intelligences*, London: Fontana Press.

Garhart Mooney, C. (2013), *Theories of Childhood*, 2nd edn, St Paul, MN: Redleaf Press.

Garrick, R. (2004), *Playing Outdoors in the Early Years*, London: Continuum International.

Gerver, R. (2010), *Creating Tomorrow's School Today*, London: Continuum International.

Gillham,B. (2008), *Observation Techniques: Structured to Unstructured*, London: Continuum.

Gipps, C. (2002), *Beyond Testing: Towards a Theory of Educational Assessment*, London: Falmer Press.

Gleave, J. and I. Cole-Hamilton (2012), A *World without Play: A Literature Rreview*, London: Play England.

Gonzalez-Mena, J. (1993), *Multicultural Issues in Child Care*. California: Mayfield Publishing.

Goouch, K. (2010), *Towards Excellence in Early Years Education: Exploring Narratives of Experience*, London: Routledge.

Gray, C . and S. Macblain (2012), *Learning Theories in Childhood*, London: Sage.

Guskey, T. (2002), 'Professional Development and Teacher Change', *Teachers and Teaching: Theory and Practice* 8 (3/4): 381–91.

Hall, K. (2007), 'Assessing Children's Learning', in J. Moyles (ed.) (2007), *Beginning Teaching Beginning Learning*, 3rd edn, Maidenhead: McGraw Hill, pp. 195–204.

Hallam, S. (2009), 'An Evaluation of the Social and Emotional Aspects of Learning (SEAL) Programme: Promoting Positive Behaviour, Effective Learning and Well-being in Primary School Children', *Oxford Review of Education* 35 (3): 313–30.

Hallet, E. (2013), *The Reflective Practitioner*, London: Sage.

Hammarberg, T. (1994), 'Preface', in B. Franklin (1995), *The Handbook of Children's Rights: Comparative Policy and Practice,* London: Routledge.

Hammond, S. (2007), 'Taking the Inside Out', in R. Austin (2007), *Letting the Outside In: Developing Teaching and Learning Beyond the Early Years Classroom*, London: Trentham Books.

Hanney, M. (2000), *Early Years Provision for Three Year Olds*, Cardiff: National Assembly of Wales.

Harlen, W. (2006), 'The Role of Assessment in Developing Motivation for Learning', in J. Gardner (2006), *Assessment and Learning*, London: Sage.

Harris, A. and J. Goodhall (2007), *Engaging Parents in Raising Achievement – Do Parents Know They Matter?* London: DCSF.

Harris, A. and D. Muijs (2005), *Improving Schools Through Teacher Leadership*. Maidenhead: Open University Press.

Harris, D. and C. Bell (1986), Evaluating and Assessing for learning. Oxon: Routledge.

Hobart, C. and J. Frankel (2009), Child Observation and Assessment. 4th edn. Cheltenham: Nelson Thornes.

Howard, J., G. Miles and A. Gealy (2009), 'Perceptions of Play and Playfulness: Implication of the Implementation of the Foundation Phase in Wales', *Welsh Journal of Education* 14 (2): 104–10.

Hughes, F. P. (2010), *Children, Play and Development*, 4 edn, London: Learning Matters.

Huggins, V. and K. Wickett (2011), 'Crawling and Toddling in the Outdoors: Very Young Children's Learning', in Waite, S. (2011), *Children Learning Outside the Classroom*, London: Sage.

Humphrey, N., A. Kalambouka, M. Wigelsworth, A. Lendrum, C. Lennie and P. Farrell (2010), 'New Beginnings: Evaluation of a Short Social-emotional Intervention for Primary-aged Children', *Educational Psychology* 30 (5): 513–32.

Hyder, T. (2002), 'Making it Happen – Young Children's Rights in Action: The Work of Save the Children's Centre for Young Children's Rights', in B. Franklin (2002), *The New Handbook of Children's Rights: Comparative Policy and Practice*, London: Routledge.

Jenkinson, S. (2001), *The Genius Play: Celebrating the Spirit of Childhood.* Gloucestershire: Hawthorn Press.

Johnson, R. (1999), 'Colonialism and Cargo Cults in Early Childhood Education: Does Reggio Emilia Really Exist?', *Contemporary Issues in Early Childhood* 1 (1): 61–783

Joyce, R. (2012), *Outdoor Learning Past and Present*, Maidenhead: Open University Press.

Kalliala, M. (2004), *Children's Play Culture in a Changing World*, Maidenhead: Open University Press.

Karlsdottir, K. and B. Garoarsdottir (2010), 'Exploring Children's Learning Stories as an Assessment Method for Research and Practice', *Early Years: An International Journal of Research and Development* 30 (3): 255–66.

Katz, L. (1999), 'International Perspectives on Early Childhood: Lessons from My Travels', *Early Childhood Research and Practice* 1 (1), http://ecrp.uiuc.edu/v1n1/katz.html (accessed 5 April 2009).

Knight, S. (2009), *Forest Schools and Outdoor Learning in the Early Years*, London: Sage.

Laevers, F. (2003), 'Experiential Education: Making Care and Education More Effective Through Well-being and Involvement', in. F. Laevers and L. Heylen (2003), *Involvement of Children and Teacher Style: Insights from an International Study on Experiential Education*, Leuven: Leuven University Press, pp. 13–24.

Laevers, F. (2005), 'Deep-level-learning and the Experiential Approach in Early Childhood and Primary Education', *Research Centre for Early Childhood and Primary Education*, http://cego.inform.be/InformCMS/custom/downloads/BO_D&P_Deep-levelLearning.pdf (accessed 2 December 2012).

Lancaster, P. (2003), *Listening to Young Children: Promoting Listening to Young Children.* Maidenhead: Open University Press.

Lansdown, G. (1995), 'The Children's Rights Development Unit', in B. Franklin (1995), *The Handbook of Children's Rights: Comparative Policy and Practice*, London: Routledge.

Lansdown, G. (2001), 'Children's Welfare and Children's Rights', in P. Foley, J. Roche and S. Tucker (2001), *Children in Society: Contemporary Theory, Policy and Practice*, London: Palgrave.

Learning Theories (2007), http://www.learning-theories.com/discovery-learning-bruner.html (accessed 4 April 2013).

Lewis, H. (2015), http://gov.wales/about/cabinet/cabinetstatements/2015/newdealeducation/?lang=en (accessed 28 August 2015).

Louis, S., C. Beswick, L. Magraw, L. Hayes and S. Featherstone (eds) (2008), *Again! Again! Understanding Schemas in Young Children*, London: A&C Black.

Luff, P. (2007), 'Written Observations or Walks in the Park: Documenting Children's Experiences', in J. Moyles (ed.) (2007), *Early Years Foundations: Meeting the Challenge*, Maidenhead: Open University Press.

MacNaughton, G. (2003), *Shaping Early Childhood: Learners, Curriculum and Contexts*, Maidenhead: Open University Press.

MacNaughton, G. (2005), *Doing Foucault in Early Childhood Studies: Applying Poststructural Ideas*, London: Jessica Kingsley.

Manning, R (2012), 'Assessment', in A. Cockburn and G. Hanscomb (eds) (2012), *Teaching Children 3–11*, London: Sage, pp. 161–80.

Martin Korpi, B. (2007), *The Politics of Pre-School-Intentions and Decisions Underlying the Emergence and Growth of the Swedish Pre-school*, Stockholm: Ministry of Education and Research.

Matusov, E. and R. Hayes (2000), 'Sociocultural Critiques of Piaget and Vygotsky', *New Ideas in Psychology* 18: 215–39.

Maynard, T. (2007a), 'Encounters with Forest School and Foucault: A Risky Business?', *Education 3–13* 35 (4): 379–91.

Maynard, T. (2007b), 'Making the Best of What You've Got: Adopting and Adapting a Forest School Approach', in R. Austin (2007), *Letting the Outside In: Developing Teaching and Learning Beyond the Early Years Classroom*, London: Trentham Books.

Maynard, T. and S. Chicken (2010), 'Through a Different Lens: Exploring Reggio Emilia in a Welsh Context', *Early Years* 30 (1): 29–39.

Maynard, T., J. Waters and J. Clement (2013), 'Child-initiated Learning, the Outdoor Environment and the Underachieving Child', *Early Years* 33 (3): 1–14.

Maynard, T., C. Taylor, S. Waldron, M. Rhys, R. Smith, S. Power and J. Clement (2013), *Evaluating the Foundation Phase: Policy, Logic Model and Programme Theory*, Cardiff: Welsh Government.

McConaghy, R. (2008), 'Designing Natural Playspaces: Principles', in S. Elliot (2008), *The Outdoor Play Space Naturally for Children Birth to Five*. Mount Victoria, NSW: Pademelon Press.

McLaughlin, C. (2008), 'Emotional Well-being and its Relationships to Schools and Classroom: A Critical Reflection', *British Journal of Guidance and Counselling* 36 (4): 353–66.

Melhuish, E. and K. Petrogiannis (2006), *Early Childhood Care and Education: International Perspectives*, London: Routledge.

Milchem, K. (2010), 'The Urban Forest: Reconnecting with Nature through Froebelian Pedagogy', *Early Childhood Practice: The Journal for Multi-professional Partnerships* 11 (1–2): 106–18.

Miller, J. (2003), *Never Too Young: How Young Children can take Responsibility and Make Decisions*, London: Save the Children.

Ministry of Education, NZ (1996), *Te Whāriki: Early Childhood Curriculum*, Wellington, NZ: Learning Media.

Moll, I. (1994), 'Reclaiming the Natural Line in Vygotsky's Theory of Cognitive Development', *Human Development* 37: 333–42.

Moore, K. (2001) *Classroom Teaching Skills*, 5th edn, Oxford: Heinemann

Moore, R. C. (1986), *Childhood's Domain: Play and Place in Child Development*, London: Croom Helm.

Morrison Gutman, L., J. Brown, R. Akerman and P. Obolenskaya (2010), *Change in*

Well-being from Childhood to Aadolescence, London: Centre for Research on the Wider Benefits of Learning.

Morrison Gutman, L. and L. Feinstein (2008), *Children's Well-being in Primary School: Pupil and School Eeffects*, London: Centre for Research on the Wider Benefits of Learning.

Moyles, J. (1989), *Just Playing*, Milton Keynes: Open University Press.

Moyles, J. (ed.) (1994), *The Excellence of Play*, Maidenhead: Open University Press.

Moyles, J. (2001), 'Passion, Paradox and Professionalism in Early Years Education', *Early Years* 21 (2): 81–95.

Moyles, J. (2005), The excellence of play. 2nd edn. Berkshire: Open University Press.

Moyles, J. (2011), *Beginning Teaching Beginning Learning*, 4th edn, Maidenhead: Open University Press.

Muñoz, S. (2009), *Children in the Outdoors: A Literature Review*, Forres: Sustainable Development Research Centre.

Musatti, T. (2006), 'Children's and Parents' Needs and Early Education and Care in Italy', in E. Melhuish and K. Petrogiannis (2006), *Early Childhood Care and Education: International Perspectives*, London: Routledge.

National Assembly for Wales (NAfW) (2001), *Everybody's Business*, Cardiff: NAfW.

Neaum, S. (2010), *Child Development for Childhood Studies*, Exeter: Learning Matters.

New, R. (2000), 'Reggio Emilia: Catalyst for Change and Conversation', *Clearinghouse on Elementary and Early Childhood Education* 1–2 (December).

Niikko, A. (2006), 'Finnish Daycare: Caring, Education, and Instruction', in J. Einarsdottir and J. Wagner (2006), *Nordic Childhoods and Early Education*, Greenwich: Information Age.

Northern Ireland Childminding Association (NICMA) (2004), *High Scope in the Family Day Care Setting*, Newtownards: NICMA.

Nutbrown, C. (1999), *Threads of Thinking Schemas and Young Children's Learning*. 2nd edn. London: SAGE.

Nutbrown, C. (2006), *Threads of Thinking: Young Children Learning and the Role of Early Education*, London: Sage.

Nutbrown, C. and C. Carter (2010), 'The Tools of Assessment: Watching and Listening', in G. Pugh and B. Duffy (eds), *Contemporary Issues in the Early Years*, 5th edn, London: Paul Chapman, p. 120.

O'Donoghue, T. and S. Clarke (2010), *Leading Learning: Processes, Themes & Issues in International Contexts*, Oxon: Routledge.

O'Keefe, M. (2001), 'First Impressions of Early Childhood Education in China', *New Horizons for Learning*, www.newhorizons.org/trans/international/okeefe.htm (accessed 8 April 2009).

Organization for Economic Co-operation and Development (OECD) (2006), *Starting Strong II: Early Childhood Education and Care*, London: Children's Society, OECD.

Ouvry, M. (2003), *Exercising Muscles and Minds: Outdoor Play and the Early Years Curriculum*, London: National Children's Bureau.

Overton, J. (2009), 'Early Childhood Teachers in Contexts of Power: Empowerment and a Voice'. *Australian Journal of Early Childhood*, 34/2, 1–10.

Palaiologou, I. (2008), *Childhood Observation*, Exeter: Learning Matters.

Palaiologou, I. (2012), *Childhood Observation*, 2nd edn, Exeter: Learning Matters.

Penn, H. (2008), *Understanding Early Childhood: Issues and Controversies*, 2nd edn, Maidenhead: Open University Press.

Peters, J. M. (1994), *Instructors as Researchers-and-Theorists*. Exeter: CRCE.

Place2Be (2015), *Our Story*, http://website.place2be.org.uk/our-story (accessed 11 August 2015).

Plowden Report, http://www.educationengland.org.uk/documents/plowden/ (accessed 16 June 2012).

Pound, L. (2005), *How Children Learn*, Leamington Spa: Step Forward.

Pound, L. (2009), *How Children Learn 3*, Contemporary Thinking and Theorists, London: Practical Pre-School Books.

Qualifications and Curriculum Authority (QCA) (2000), 'Baseline Assessment', http://www.education.gov.uk/aboutdfe/armslengthbodies/a00200461/qcda (accessed 16 June 2012).

Race, P. (2001), *Assessment Series No 9: A Briefing on Self, Peer & Group Assessment*, York: LTSN Generic Centre.

Reed, M. and N. Canning (2010), *Reflective Practice in the Early Years*, London: Sage.

Rhys, M., S. Waldron and C. Taylor (2014a), *Evaluating the Foundation Phase: Key Findings on Training Support and Guidance*, Cardiff: Welsh Government.

Rhys, M., S. Waldron and C. Taylor (2014b), *Evaluating the Foundation Phase: Key Findings on the Environment (Indoor/Outdoor)*, Cardiff: Welsh Government.

Rhys, M., S. Waldron and C. Taylor (2014c), *Evaluating the Foundation Phase: Key Findings on the Welsh Language*, Cardiff: Welsh Government.

Rhys, M., S. Waldron and C. Taylor (2015), *Evaluating the Foundation Phase: Key Findings on Literacy and Numeracy*, Cardiff: Welsh Government.

Roffey, S. (2012), 'Pupil Wellbeing – Teacher Wellbeing: Two Sides of the Same Coin', *Educational & Child Psychology* 29 (47): 8–17.

Rowe, M. B. (1974), 'Wait Time and Rewards as Instructional Variables, their Influence on Language, Logic and Fate Control', *Journal of Research in Science Teaching* 11: 81–94.

Ryder-Richardson, G. (2006), *Creating a Space to Grow: Developing your Outdoor Learning Environment*, London: David Fulton.

Sadler, D. R. (1989), Formative assessment and the design of instructional systems, *Instructional Science*, 18, 119–44.

Save the Children (2001), *Children's Rights: A Second Chance*, London: International Save the Children Alliance.

Save the Children (2005), *Practice Standards in Children's Participation*, London: Save the Children UK, www.savethechildren.org.uk (accessed 14 April 2012).

Sayeed, Z. and E. Guerin (2000*), Early Years Play: A Happy Medium for Assessment and Intervention*, London: David Fulton.

Schon, D. (1987), *Educating the Reflective Practitioner*, San Francisco: Jossey-Bass.

Schweinhart, L., H. Barnes and P. Weikart (1993), *Significant Benefits: The High/Scope Perry Preschool Study Through Age 27*, Ypsilanti, MI: High/Scope Press.

Shanker, S. and R. Downer (2012), 'Enhancing the Potential in Children (EPIC)', in L. Miller and D. Hevey (2012), *Policy Issues in the Early Years*, London: Sage.

Sharman, C., W. Cross and D. Vennis (2004), *Observing Children: A Practical Guide*, London: Continuum International.

Shenglan, L. (2006), 'Development of Kindergarten Care and Education in the People's Republic of China Since the 1990's'. In Melhuish, E. and Petrogiannis, K. *Early Childhood Care and Education: International Perspectives*. London: Routledge.

Sheridan, S. and I. Pramling Samuelsson (2001), 'Children's Conceptions of Participation and Influence in Pre-School: A Perspective on Pedagogical Quality', *Contemporary Issues in Early Childhood* 2 (2): 169–94.

Silber, K. (1965), *Pestalozzi. The Man and his Work*, 2nd edn, London: Routledge and Kegan Paul.

Siraj, I. (2014), *An Independent Stock Take of the Foundation Phase in Wales: Final Report*, Cardiff: Welsh Government.

Siraj-Blatchford, I. and L. Manni (2007), *Effective Leadership in the Early Years Sector*, London: DfES.

Siraj-Blatchford, I., K. Sylva, J. Laugharne, E. Milton and F. Charles (2006), *Monitoring and Evaluation of the Effective Implementation of the Foundation Phase (MEEIFP) Project Across Wales*, Cardiff: Welsh Assembly Government.

Siraj-Blatchford, I., K. Sylva, S. Muttock, R. Gilden and D. Bell (2002), *Researching Effective Pedagogy in the Early Years*, London: DfES.

Smeets, K. and P. Ponte (2009), 'Action Research and Teacher Leadership', *Professional Development in Education* 35 (2): 175–93.

Smidt, S (2009), *Introducing Vygotsky*, Oxon: Routledge.

Smith, J. (2012), 'Reflective Practice', in A. Cockburn and G. Handscomb (2012), *Teaching Children 3–11*, London: Sage, p. 150.

Smith, M. K. (1997), *Henrich Pestalozzi*, Infed, http://www.infed.org/thinkers/et-pest. htm (accessed 6 June 2013).

Soler, J. and L. Miller (2003), 'The Struggle for Early Childhood Curricula: A Comparison of the English Foundation Stage Curriculum, Te Whāriki and Reggio Emilia', *International Journal of Early Years Education* 11 (1): 57–68.

Sylva, K., E. Melhuish, P. Sammons, I. Siraj-Blatchford and B. Taggart (2004), *The Effective Provision of Pre-School Education (EPPE) Project: Final Report*, Nottingham: DfES.

Taplin, J. (2011), 'Steiner Waldorf Early Childhood Education: Offering A Curriculum For the 21st Century', in L. Miller and L. Pound (eds), *Theories and Approaches to Learning in the Early Years*, London: Sage.

Tarini, R. and L. White (1998), 'Looking in the Mirror: A Reflection of Reggio Practice in Winnetka', in C. Edwards, L. Gandini and G. Forman (1998), *The Hundred Languages of Children: The Reggio Emilia Approach-Advanced Reflections*, London: Ablex.

Tassoni, P., K. Bulman and K. Beith (2005), *Children's Care, Learning and Development*, Oxford: Heinemann Educational Publishers.

Taylor, C., M. Rhys, S. Waldron, R. Davies, S. Power, T. Maynard, L. Moore, D. Blackaby and I. Plewis. (2015), *Evaluating the Foundation Phase: Final Report*, Cardiff: Welsh Government.

Taylor, C., S. Waldron and M. Rhys (2014), *Evaluating the Foundation Phase: Key Findings on Management and Leadership*, Cardiff: Welsh Government.

Teacher Support Network (TSN) and Parentline Plus (PP) (2007), *Beyond the School Gate: How Schools and Families Can Work Better Together*, London: TSW and PP.

Teaching and Learning Research Programme (TLRP) (2007), *Principles into Practice*, London: TLRP.

Thomas, E. and A. Skeels (2006), 'Participation', in R. Croke and A. Crowley (2006), *Righting the Wrongs: The Reality of Children's Rights in Wales*, Cardiff: Wales Programme of Save the Children, www.savethechildren.org.uk (accessed 14 April 2012).

Thomas, N. (2001), 'Listening to Children', in P. Foley, J. Roche and S. Tucker (2001), *Children in Society: Contemporary Theory, Policy and Practice*, London: Palgrave.

Thornton, L. and P. Brunton (2014), *Bringing the Reggio Approach to your Early Years Practice*, Oxon: Routledge.

Tomlinson, P. (2008), 'The Politics of Childhood', in P. Jones, D. Moss, P. Tomlinson and S. Welch (2008), *Childhood: Services and Provision for Children*, Harlow: Pearson Educational.

Tornberg, A. and J. Lindholm (2009), 'The Swedish System', *The Teacher* 3.

Tovey, H. (2007), *Playing Outdoors: Spaces and Place, Risk and Challenge*, Maidenhead, Open University Press.

Trodd, L. (2013), *Transitions in the Early Years*. London: SAGE Publications Ltd.

United Nations (1989), *The Convention on the Rights of the Child*, Geneva: United Nations.

United Nations International Children's Emergency Fund (UNICEF) (2003), *The State of the World's Children*, www.unicef.org (accessed 14 April 2012).

Vygotsky, L. (1978), *Mind in Society*, Cambridge, MA: Harvard University Press.

Waite, S. and N. Pratt (2011), 'Theoretical Perspectives on Learning Outside the Classroom: Relationships between Learning and Place', in S. Waite (2011), *Children Learning Outside the Classroom*, London: Sage.

Waldron, S., M. Rhys and C. Taylor (2014a), *Evaluating the Foundation Phase: Key Findings on Pedagogy and Understanding*, Cardiff: Welsh Government.

Waldron, S., M. Rhys and C. Taylor (2014b), *Evaluating the Foundation Phase: Key Findings on Child Involvement and Wellbeing*, Cardiff: Welsh Government.

Waldron, S., M. Rhys and C. Taylor (2014c), *Evaluating the Foundation Phase: Key Findings on Children and Families*, Cardiff: Welsh Government.

Waldron, S., M. Rhys and C. Taylor (2015), *Evaluating the Foundation Phase: Key Findings on Practitioner and Stakeholder views of the Future of the Foundation Phase*, Cardiff: Welsh Government.

Waller, T. (2009), *An Introduction to Early Childhood*, 2nd edn, London: Sage.

Ward, C. (1990), *The Child in the City*, London: Bedford Square Press.

Watson, D., C. Emery, P. Baylis, M. Boushel and K. McInnes (2012), *Children's Social and Emotional Well-being in School: A Critical Perspective*, Bristol: Policy Press.

Weeden, P., J. Winter and P. Broadfoot (2002), *Assessment: What's in it for Schools?*, London: RoutledgeFalmer.

Welch, S. (2008), 'Childhood: Rights and Realities', in P. Jones, D. Moss, P. Tomlinson and D. Whitebread, *Developmental Psychology & Early Childhood Education*, London: Sage.

Welsh Assembly Government (WAG) (2003), *The Learning Country: The Foundation Phase for 3–7 Years*, Cardiff: WAG.

Welsh Assembly Government (2007), *Out of Classroom Learning: Making the Most of First Hand Experiences of the Natural Environment*, Cardiff: WAG.

Welsh Assembly Government (2008a), *Learning and Teaching Pedagogy*, Cardiff: WAG.

Welsh Assembly Government (2008b), *Framework for Children's Learning for 3- to 7-year-olds in Wales*, Cardiff: WAG.

Welsh Assembly Government (2008c), *Observation Handbook*, Cardiff: WAG.

Welsh Assembly Government (2008d), *Play and Active Learning*, Cardiff: WAG.

Welsh Assembly Government (2009a), *Foundation Phase, Outdoor Learning Handbook*, Cardiff: WAG.

Welsh Assembly Government (2009b), *Foundation Phase Child Development Profile Guidance*. Cardiff: WAG.

Welsh Assembly Government (2012), *LNF*, http://wales.gov.uk/;jsessionid=866844D2C 06B563B67EE7175079C33E9?ssub=true&view=Search+results&lang=en&sort=&sea rchQuery=LNF (accessed 18 December 2012).

Welsh Government (WG) (2010), *Thinking Positively: Emotional Health and Well-being in School and Early Years Settings*, Cardiff: WG.

Welsh Government (2011), *Foundation Phase Child Development Assessment Profile*, Cardiff: WG.

Welsh Government (2012a), *Proposals for the Development of a Single Developmental Assessment Tool for Use Across the Early Years by Health Visitors, including Flying Start Health Visitors and Foundation Phase Practitioners*, http:// wales.gov.uk/publications/accessinfo/drnewhomepage/dr2012/aprjun/cyp/ la1906/?skip=1&lang=en (accessed 3 June 2012).

Welsh Government (2012b), http://wales.gov.uk/topics/educationandskills/ schoolshome/curriculuminwales/arevisedcurriculumforwales/ skillsdevelopment/?lang=en (accessed 29 September 2012).

Welsh Government (2012c), http://wales.gov.uk/topics/educationandskills/ earlyyearshome/foundationphase/?lang=en (accessed 29 September 2012).

Welsh Government (2012d), http://wales.gov.uk/topics/educationandskills/ schoolshome/literacynumeracy/lnframework/?lang=en (accessed 29 September 2012).

Welsh Government (2012e), *National Literacy Programme*, Cardiff: WG.

Welsh Government (2013a), *Statutory Assessment Arrangements for the End of Foundation Phase and Key Stages 2 and 3*, Cardiff: WG.

Welsh Government (2013b), *School Effectiveness Framework*, http://www.sefcymru. org/sef-p2-home/sef-p2-social_justice/sef-p2-social-justice-engaging-families.htm (accessed 30 January 2013).

Welsh Government (2014), http://gov.wales/about/cabinet/cabinetstatements/2014/ earlyyears/?lang=en (accessed 28 August 2015).

Welsh Government (2015), *National Reading and Numeracy Tests: Test Administration Handbook*, Cardiff: WG.

Whitebread, D. (2012), *Developmental Psychology & Early Childhood Education*. London: SAGE.

Williams-Siegfredson, J. (2005), 'Run the Risk', *Nursery World* 4, (8): 26–27.

Wincott, D. (2006), 'Devolution and the Welfare State: Lessons from Early Childhood Education and Care Policy in Wales', *Environment and Planning C: Government and Policy*, 24: 279–95.

Wood, E. (2010), *Play, Learning and the Early Childhood Curriculum*, London: Sage.

Wyn Siencyn, S. and S. Thomas (2007), 'Wales', in M. Clark and T. Waller (2007), *Early Childhood Education & Care: Policy and Practice*, London: Sage.

Index

WITHDRAWAL